THE M & E HANDBOOK SERIES

Public Administration

Michael P. Barber
LLB(Lond), DPA(Lond)
Senior Lecturer at the Brighton Polytechnic

Revised by
Roger Stacey
BSc Econ, Cert Ed
*Lecturer in Public Administration, Plymouth College of Further
Education*

THIRD EDITION

GW00728993

MACDONALD AND EVANS

Macdonald & Evans Ltd.
Estover, Plymouth PL6 7PZ

First published 1972
Reprinted 1974
Reprinted 1975
Second edition 1978
Third edition 1983
Reprinted (with amendments) in this format 1984

© Macdonald & Evans Ltd 1983

0 7121 1754 7 (home edition)
0 7121 0197 7 (export edition)

Filmset in Great Britain by
Northumberland Press Ltd,
Gateshead, Tyne and Wear
and printed by Richard Clay (The Chaucer Press) Ltd,
Bungay, Suffolk

Preface to the First Edition

The object of this HANDBOOK is to provide a guide to the study of British public administration which will not only explain the theoretical and structural aspects of the system, but will also attempt to show the problems facing contemporary public administration. The HANDBOOK attempts to deal with both the theory and practice of public administration, and places emphasis on the current "management" approach to the subject.

The HANDBOOK is intended principally for students studying for the examinations of the Local Government Examinations Board, for the Diploma in Public Administration of the University of London, for the National Certificate examinations in Public Administration and for the BTEC higher level courses. This book is not intended completely to replace textbooks on the subject, but attempts to provide in one work a range of topics which a student would normally only study by having recourse to a wide range of publications. It does not claim, however, to be exhaustive, and it is doubted whether any single book could fill the needs of a student in this vast and constantly changing subject. It is thus confidently expected that students will supplement their studies by experience gained in their employment, especially as regards the day-to-day working of the system, and by reading widely. In particular, useful articles appear regularly in the *Political Quarterly, Public Administration* and *Public Law*. This book deals mainly with central administration, and students are therefore strongly recommended to supplement their study by reference to the HANDBOOK on *Local Government*.

MPB

Preface to the Third Edition

This edition retains essentially the same HANDBOOK format and aims. It has been updated to include changes made by the Conservative Government including for example an analysis of the new investigative select committee system of Parliament. Another important new section is that on the administrative arrangements of the European Communities which exemplify particularly well the problems of public as opposed to private administrative systems.

Greater emphasis has been placed on the importance of wider political forces in society in line with examination trends. It is hoped that the concise HANDBOOK approach will also be useful to students involved with assignment-based courses such as those of BTEC—by providing a means of putting the often specific studies into the wider context.

Some examples of BTEC type assignments have been included in Appendix IV. Space precludes an extensive section and it is not intended that these replace the progress tests which are primarily intended for student self assessment purposes.

1983   RIS

Contents

CHAPTER I

The Nature of Public Administration

INTRODUCTION

1. What is public administration? Public administration has been defined as "... decision-making, planning the work to be done, formulating objectives and goals ... establishing and reviewing organisations, directing and supervising employees ... exercising controls and other functions performed by government executives and supervisors. It is the action part of government; the means by which the purposes and goals of government are realised". (Corson and Harris, *Public Administration in Modern Society*, McGraw-Hill, 1969).

Public administration is basically the administrative side of government, a part of the executive, as opposed to the legislative and judicial powers. Occasionally reference is made to the "administrative power", indicating that power, the ability to influence and make decisions, lies with the administrators as well as the politicians. It is difficult to distinguish accurately the boundaries and responsibilities of the powers of government, particularly in the British system, where there exists a degree of *fusion* of power. It will be seen that the administration effectively exercises what can properly be described as legislative as well as executive functions (*see* V).

2. Framework of study. This Handbook attempts a *critical approach* to the wide subject of public administration. In doing so it runs the risk of understating many virtues of British government in its attempt to isolate the effective issues of efficiency from those of tradition, etc. In an age of reform in all spheres, however, such an approach is justified in order to avoid falling into the approach epitomised by Swift, who commented, "I would hide the frailties and deformities of my political mother, and place her virtues and beauties in the most advantageous light".

The approach to public administration thus involves a study of the principal problem areas in the subject and also illustrates

1

the scope of public administration. This includes the following topics.

(a) The political and constitutional environment of public administration (see II).

(b) Organisational theory and government organisation (see III).

(c) Administrative processes such as planning, decision-making, co-ordination, etc. (see IV, V and X).

(d) Public service – characteristics, personnel, problems, etc. (see VI).

(e) Central and local financial administration (see VIII–IX).

(f) Control of administration (see II, XIV and XV).

(g) The relation of non-central government bodies, e.g. local authorities and public corporations (see XII and XIII).

STUDYING PUBLIC ADMINISTRATION

3. Problems in the study of public administration. Problems associated with the study of public administration may be classified as those of principle, those associated with the overall governmental context, and those of a more particularly administrative nature.

4. Problems of principle. The following points should be noted.

(a) *Efficiency.* "In the science of administration, whether public or private, the basic 'good' is efficiency. The fundamental objective of the science of administration is least expenditure of manpower and materials. Efficiency is thus axiom number one in the value scale of administration" (Luther Gulick, *Papers on the Science of Administration*, Inst. of Public Administration, New York, 1937).

"Efficiency" concentrates attention on the minimisation of costs, and in private enterprise, to the maximisation of profit, which is the aim of the organisation. In the context of public administrative systems the aims are more complex and include, for example, the concept of "public service", public accountability and social responsibility. These differing aims require efficiency in connection with public administration to be redefined.

(b) *Public context.* Decision-making in public administration is unlike that of a private organisation whose customers are usually free to take or leave the organisation's products or services. Public administration decision-making is often not based on commercial forces and the public, who are in a sense the "consumers" of its services, indicate their critical views via their political representatives through the media. All public administration takes place against a background of public criticism.

(c) *Political environment.* As public administration is concerned with the implementation of policies determined politically, and the administrators are accountable and responsible to their political masters, their decisions must therefore reflect this responsibility. Decisions made within the sphere of public administration require delicate political judgment and can be seen as having a "political" element—though it is important that the administrators avoid any discernible partisan political associations.

(d) *Governmental powers.* The constitution gives to the government certain absolute powers of taxation and coercion, for example. While these are primarily political matters, the administration will be involved in the processes of governmental decision-making as to how the powers are to be used. It is in this area of policy determination that the boundary between powers of the executive (the "government" in the narrow sense of the political leaders) and the "administration" (in the narrow sense, the paid officials who are there to serve their political masters) becomes confused. Hence the phrase "the administration" is often used to describe the political leadership and its departments and officials.

5. Problems in the overall government context. The role and functioning of public administration must be set in the context of the problems confronting government, which are as follows.

(a) The reconciliation of liberty with the duty to govern. The government must be strong enough to command obedience and to administer effectively, whilst at the same time being controlled in order to establish responsibility to certain standards, i.e. the conflict between sovereignty and responsibility.

(b) The need to balance achievement of the common good with the demands of vested interests.

(c) The balance of present necessities with future desirabilities.

(d) The need to balance traditional attitudes with scientific curiosity.

6. Administrative problems. On the practical administrative plane particular problems of public administration arise. These were classified by Finer as:

(a) the machinery for co-ordination;

(b) the principles of departmentalisation;

(*c*) the accountability of the executive to the courts and parliament;

(*d*) the provision of expert knowledge;

(*e*) the recruitment and maintenance of qualified personnel in the public services.

These are the traditional areas of study in public administration. Recently the science of administration has developed, and as many of its principles and concepts are applicable to public administration it is necessary to add such areas as organisational theory and behaviour, decision-making and planning (*see* II, X and XVI).

GOVERNMENTAL FUNCTIONS

7. Changes in governmental functions. The role of the state has developed far beyond the basic activities of external defence and internal law and order, to an interventionist and active planning role. The original role can be seen as negative, in that it was primarily concerned with stopping other people doing things that were inconvenient to society; the modern role is more positive— actually providing for society a large range of goods and services in and out of the marketplace. The consequence of the changed role is the growth of large hierarchical professional bureaucracies.

8. Causes of the change. A complex combination of factors has led to the expansion of the role of the state and thus of public administration.

(*a*) *Industrialisation.* The development of a factory system and the associated growth of towns led to various socioeconomic problems such as those relating to housing, health and unemployment. These new problems were not satisfactorily resolved through the marketplace and thus political demands eventually led to state action.

(*b*) *Social cost.* As the scale of commercial activity increased it became apparent that the activities of one organisation or individual could impose extra costs upon society in general, for example environmental damage from pollution, etc. Thus pressure upon the state both to regulate and to take certain responsibilities upon itself was made.

(*c*) *Market inadequacies.* Certain basic facilities for successful economic growth were not being effectively provided by the private sector. Thus, for example, the state, from quite an early stage, took an interest in communications: roads and posts.

(*d*) *Political demands.* As a result of the above factors various groups organised themselves in order to represent their views politically. Amongst the most significant was organised labour, which together with the Fabians and the Co-operative Societies, founded the Labour party which considered active state intervention an integral part of its programme. Industry also has articulated demands for intervention—for assistance and protection against foreign competition.

(*e*) *Increased division of labour.* The realisation that the various units in the economy are interdependent has led to the state intervening in the affairs of private concerns on the grounds that their activities have an impact on society as a whole.

9. Some effects of administrative growth. The growth in size and functions of the government and administrative machine has had certain side results apart from problems directly associated with the growth, e.g. organisational and co-ordination problems. These problems are threefold:

(*a*) the alienation of the individual from the decision-making process (*see* **XV**);

(*b*) difficulties existing in establishing the "public will";

(*c*) problems of general direction or overall nature of the role of the state are accentuated, e.g. between an interventionist or *laissez-faire* approach.

DIRECTION OF GOVERNMENT

10. Factors affecting the direction of government. Before any specific matters of party political controversy arise there are certain factors in existence which affect the general direction of a government.

(*a*) Cultural attitudes both affect the direction of government in a positive sense, and also operate negatively to limit the activities of government. In the former case, for example, it will manifest itself in community attitudes towards the provision of basic services and, in the latter case, values and beliefs held by the community will operate to define boundaries between that which is considered to be in the political sphere and that which is an inappropriate area for anything other than peripheral government involvement.

NOTE: Although cultural attitudes have effects these are naturally general and such matters as the precise limits of government involvement will be a political matter.

(*b*) The general British belief in gradual evolution of government and society as opposed to alterations based solely on pragmatic reasoning, whilst retarding the speed of change, operates to reduce resistance to change when it does take place.

(*c*) The "cultural mix" in British society prevents deep social and class distinctions and produces a general consensus approach to many functions of government.

PUBLIC AND PRIVATE ADMINISTRATION

11. Differences in approach between public and private administration. In III we deal with the difficulties of applying theories of management organisation to public administration where such theories are founded on research in the private sector. However, the following distinguishing factors between public administration and private business must be borne in mind from the outset.

(*a*) *Political environment.* Public administration is concerned with the implementation of decisions made within the political system. In a democratic system the policies of the government duly approved by the legislature should represent the political will of the people, or at least the resultant of the activities of the various competing political interests in the society. In consequence:

(*i*) the government creates individual rights and imposes constraints on individual and group behaviour;

(*ii*) the administrator is in frequent contact with his clients and his major concern is with equity and impartiality;

(*iii*) administrative procedures are built around strict compliance with the law.

On the other hand private industry is essentially guided by the principle of maximisation of profits and does not act as an arbiter between conflicting social interests.

(*b*) *Social costs.* Public administration decision-making varies from that of private business in that where private business is concerned primarily with questions of financial cost and benefit, public administration is intimately concerned with concepts of social costs and benefits in addition to those of a mere financial nature.

(*c*) *Public interest.* Public administration is often evaluated by its ability to operate in a manner so as to maximise and integrate the public interest, whereas private business is evaluated on the basis of profit maximisation. In practice this makes it much more difficult to quantify in financial terms the substantial investment of resources undertaken by the public sector.

(d) *Instability.* As a result of operating in a political environment public administrators are faced with a much greater turnover of political leadership and consequent changes in policy than is encountered in private business.

(e) *Allocation of responsibilities.* The method of allocation of functions in the public sector is often based more on political considerations than on pure tests of efficiency.

(f) *Planning.* Owing to the pressures of political scrutiny public administrators spend a greater proportion of their time on short-term measures than does the equivalent management level in private industry.

(g) *Functions.* Public administration is faced with a much wider variety of functions than those operating in private business, and also deals with matters which are the exclusive province of central administration, e.g. defence, and law and order.

12. Politics and administration. "In the sense that politics has to do with making government generally acceptable through the interplay of multiple interests, ideas and ideals in relation to government courses of action, even very lowly employees of government have at least an indirect part in it. . . . The higher one goes in government, the greater the involvement in politics because of involvement in greater public concerns" (Paul H. Appleby, *Public Administration for a Welfare State*).

Given that political activity is directed at influencing decisions, many of which are made either by the administration or by political leaders on the advice of the administration, the administrator has the opportunity to exercise political power. This is evidenced by the way that interest groups seek to develop contacts within the administration as a part of their political efforts to influence the decision-making process.

The administration must take account of the various interests that interplay over issues and it can be seen to develop its own "line", the "departmental view", on issues and policy generally. It is necessary for the administration to formulate its own view on many questions, particularly of detail, as political leaders will not want to involve themselves in every aspect of the administration's work.

Many politicians in their diaries have praised the political skill and judgment of senior administrators upon whose advice they have to depend. The characteristic of administrative political advice and opinion is based upon practical problems of implementation and an assessment of public feelings on the matter. This inherent conservatism has led to radical politicians occasionally accusing the administrators of attempting to sabotage implementation of their plans.

13. Policy and administration. It is a fallacy that policy and administration can be realistically separated. Political leaders may determine a general policy framework, within which administrators will have to make policy decisions about the way the general principles are to be implemented. This is developed in V.

PROGRESS TEST 1

1. What special problems are involved in the study of public administration? (3–6)
2. Why, and how, has the role of the state changed in the twentieth century? (7–10)
3. Distinguish between public and private administration.   (11)
4. Explain how administrators are able to exert political power. (12)

CHAPTER II

The Constitutional Framework of Public Administration

INTRODUCTION

All constitutions establish a framework within which the government and administrative agencies of a state operate. Analysis of the British constitution in a purely legalistic way is difficult because of its unwritten nature and reliance on conventional practices. Flexibility is often seen as one of the great strengths of the British constitution, allowing adaptation to changing circumstances without loss of the fundamental respect that prevails for the country's institutions.

In a study of public administration it is necessary to examine the constitutional structure and in particular the relationship between the administrative machine and the traditional powers of government: legislative, executive and judicial. Although the administration is attached to the executive branch of government it can be seen as a "fourth power"—the full-time professional civil service, wielding independent power in the field of policy-making.

In the United Kingdom the power of the executive is accepted as having grown at the expense of the legislature especially. All political systems must adapt to circumstances. In the UK the recent developments of new investigative select committees and the National Audit Act (1983), making the Comptroller and Auditor General a servant of Parliament, may be seen as helping to restore the power of the legislature.

1. Some characteristics of the British system. Some of the more important, as opposed to merely more traditional, characteristics of British government may be classified as follows.

(*a*) *Responsible government.* The British governmental system may be regarded as a system of responsible government to the extent that such responsibility is manifested through the doctrine of ministerial responsibility (*see* XV) and collective Cabinet responsibility (*see* **17**). It is through the practical operation of these doctrines that responsibility to Parliament and through Parliament to the electorate is achieved in respect of the administration of government.

(*b*) *Cabinet government*. In so far as Parliament is effectively dominated by the Cabinet (*see* **5–7**) the British system may be treated as having effectively moved from a system of parliamentary to Cabinet government.

> "In the cabinet are found the modern embodiment of a fusion of governmental powers which, more than the eighteenth century separation, has generally characterised British government" (G.C. Moodie, *The Government of Great Britain*, 1967).

(*c*) *Two-party system*. Britain effectively operates under a· two-party system of government. Both the main parties are relatively homogeneous in terms of policy. They effectively organise the House of Commons, provide and sustain governments, and serve as vital links between government and the electorate. They thus arose as organisers and informers after the extension of the franchise.

(*d*) *Conventions*. The absence of exhaustive constitutional law has resulted in a consequent reliance on unwritten conventions (*see* **11–15**) and these conventions serve to regulate the exercise of power to a much greater extent than formal machinery.

2. Basic constitution principles.

(*a*) *The separation of powers*. In the eighteenth century Montesquieu developed the doctrine of the separation of powers as a constitutional device designed to avoid the concentration of legislative, executive and judicial power in the hands of one man or institution. He considered that if the powers were held by separate institutions then each would act as a restraint upon the others. Montesquieu used the British constitution as the basis of his theory and used it to explain the absence of "tyranny". Strictly speaking he was wrong, as in the United Kingdom there are several key institutions and individuals office-holders having executive and legislative power at their disposal. Figure 1 diagrammatically illustrates some of the ways in which the powers are "fused" at the centre of British government.

Although this fusion of power is real enough in a legal sense, the principle of the theory is still significant in the United Kingdom. The Lord Chancellor as head of the judiciary is responsible

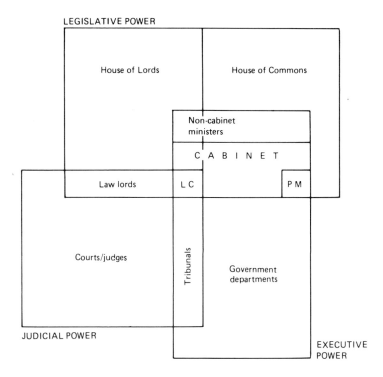

LEGISLATIVE POWER

House of Lords

House of Commons

Non-cabinet ministers

C A B I N E T

Law lords

L C

P M

Courts/judges

Tribunals

Government departments

JUDICIAL POWER

EXECUTIVE POWER

FIG. 1   *Fusion of power at the centre of British government.*

for recommending the appointment of judges; as chairman of the House of Lords he is involved in legislation and as a Cabinet member he is involved in policy-making and control of the administration—in Montesquieu's terms a potential tyrant! However, constitutional practice and convention make it inconceivable that a Lord Chancellor would recommend blatantly political appointees to the judiciary.

Montesquieu's theory is fundamental to the United States constitution, where the latter clearly allocates executive power to the President, legislative power to the Congress and judicial power to the Supreme Court.

(*b*) *The supremacy of parliament*. This doctrine (i.e. that there are no legal constraints upon the will of Parliament), must be regarded as operating through, and to the benefit of, the domination by government of Parliament.

By convention, members of the government must be members

of one or other House of Parliament and invariably, in practice, leading members are members of the House of Commons. Thus the majority party in Parliament not only provides the government but is also effectively required to support the government. Theoretically it may also dismiss a government, though the likelihood of this occurring in anything other than abnormal conditions, e.g. absence of majority governments or wartime conditions, are extremely remote. The government, particularly through the Cabinet which consists of the principal government office-holders and consequently the political leaders of the majority party, is in a position, through reliance on this support, to determine what legislation shall be presented to Parliament, and thus to reduce Parliament to the status of a purely critical body.

(c) *The rule of law.* This principle provides that the law applies equally to everyone, rulers and ruled alike, so citizens may thus do as they like within the law without executive interference. The supplementary *ultra vires* principle provides that government and its administrative agencies must only act within the powers given to them by statute.

3. How is this domination achieved? The factors contributing to Cabinet domination of Parliament, and thus to the effective system of Cabinet rather than parliamentary government, are as follows.

(a) *Party discipline.* The punitive authority of party over individuals is manifested ultimately through "withdrawal of the party ticket" for failure to conform. This disciplinary element tends to be overrated in practice and allegiance may better be regarded from the conformatory aspect.

(b) *Party loyalty.* The adherence of party members to the broad principles and strategies of their party results in the likelihood of their conforming to government programmes even though they may be against certain aspects of these. This response can be illustrated by the fate of revolts against the party whip which reveals that these are generally stage-managed in order to register dissent without defeat, e.g. Conservative back bench dissidence increased in the 1983 Parliament where the larger majority made it a "safe" activity.

(c) *Self-interest.* The fear of MPs that defeat and/or dissolution will endanger their personal constituency majorities and will involve them in unwanted electioneering is a powerful incentive to conform. In addition the increase in the number of government posts provides incentives to regular "party-liners".

(*d*) *The electoral system.* The simple majority electoral system exaggerates the strength of the governing party in terms of seats held in Parliament. For example, the 1983 Conservative government has an overall majority in Parliament having obtained 42.5 per cent of the total votes.

(*e*) *Information.* The government has access and the advice of the administrative machinery—expertise and statistical evidence on all questions—while the average back-bench MP in the UK Parliament has few resources upon which he can draw to question this authority.

4. Effect of domination. The major effects are as follows.

(*a*) The Cabinet has effective control of the parliamentary time-table and private members are in consequence subordinated to the pressures of business chosen by the government.

(*b*) The Cabinet determines the programme of policy to be presented to Parliament in the form of legislation.

(*c*) Parliament takes on the role of approving and amending legislation and thus discussion of its effectiveness must centre on its ability to exercise its critical function (*see* **21** below).

THE CABINET

5. The Cabinet in the British constitution. The report of the Committee on the Machinery of Government (the Haldane Committee), 1918, classified the function of the Cabinet as follows.

(*a*) The final determination of the policy to be submitted to Parliament.

NOTE: The interrelationship of the Cabinet and the bureaurcracy in the exercise of this function is dealt with in V.

(*b*) The supreme control of the national executive in accordance with the policy prescribed by Parliament.

(*c*) The continuous co-ordination and delimitation of the authorities of the several departments of the state.

NOTE: This co-ordinative function and the machinery adopted for its exercise are dealt with in IV.

6. Problems of the Cabinet's legislative role. Three principal organisational problems have confronted the Cabinet in this sphere.

(*a*) Reconciliation of the political ambitions of its members.

(*b*) Organisation of work load and support services.

(*c*) Distillation of actual policy from individual views.

The second problem is facilitated by the development of Cabinet committees and the use of the Cabinet Secretariat, and by the further concentration of power in the hands of the Prime Minister (*see* **10**).

Cabinet committees (*see* IV) operate to discuss in advance matters destined for the full Cabinet, and give interested parties the opportunity to bargain and compromise.

The decisions of the Cabinet and sub-committees, the compilation of agenda, the circulation of memoranda, etc., are in the hands of the Cabinet Secretariat (*see* IV) which, though theoretically a recording agency, has vital co co-ordinative functions.

7. Limitations upon the Cabinet. These are principally the following.

(*a*) The ability of the administrative machine effectively to execute Cabinet policy.

(*b*) The need to justify policies before Parliament, and the consequent need to make concessions.

8. Position of the Prime Minister. It is generally accepted today that the power of the Prime Minister in the system has expanded from that of *primus inter pares* (first among equals) to one of dominance. Personality aside, there are a number of factors behind this development.

(*a*) Growth in size and scope of government, giving the Prime Minister increased patronage power and importance as the overall co-ordinator of policy.

(*b*) The tendency in the United Kingdom for media attention to focus on personalities rather than issues, particularly at election time.

(*c*) Ministers tend to be preoccupied with their own departmental affairs.

(*d*) The Prime Minister's control over the date of dissolution of Parliament.

(*e*) The Prime Minister's personal administrative machinery—both Private Office and the Cabinet Secretariat, both of which give the Prime Minister unique access to the activities and policies of all other government departments (*see* Fig. 2).

CONVENTIONS

9. Nature of conventions. Conventions are at the centre of the

LINKS TO ADMINISTRATION   LINKS TO POLITICAL INSTITUTIONS

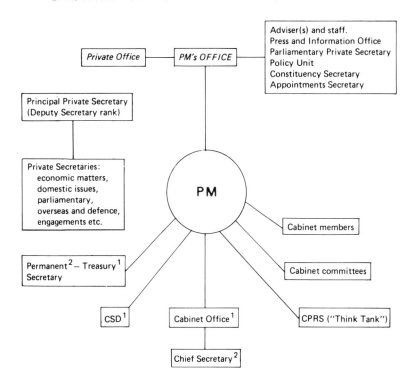

1. Departments for which the Prime Minister has ministerial responsibility as First Lord of the Treasury, Head of the Civil Service and first minister in the Cabinet.

2. Most senior administrative advisers to the Prime Minister.

FIG. 2   *Position of the Prime Minister in relation to the major political and administrative institutions of state.*

adaptability and the representative and responsible character of British government. Their presence, however, is not limited to unwritten constitutions such as the British constitution, and they develop in any constitution in response to political needs, inadequacy of formal rules, etc. Conventions have been formally defined as: "certain rules of constitutional behaviour which are considered to be binding by and upon those who operate the constitution, but which are not enforceable by law courts, nor by the presiding officers in the Houses of Parliament" (G. Marshall, and G. C., Moodie, *Some Problems of the Constitution*, Hutchinson, 1967).

10. Reasons for the existence of conventions. These are as follows.

(*a*) The inability of any rule of law to be self-applying, and the consequent need for informal rules to provide this element of adaptability.

(*b*) The difficulty in changing political and social circumstances, or eradicating doubts as to the interpretation of formal rules by adjudication or legislation.

(*c*) The need to accommodate aspects of political behaviour which are not formally legislatable.

11. Examples of conventions. For detailed consideration of the principal examples, readers are advised to consult a work on constitutional law. Broadly and briefly, however, these may be stated as:

(*a*) the doctrines of ministerial and collective responsibility;

(*b*) conventions regarding the formation and resignation of governments;

(*c*) constitution of committees;

(*d*) accordance of rights to opposition parties, etc.

12. Associated problems. In certain cases conventions may be readily definable, e.g. in the field of Commonwealth relations. In other cases, however, problems of establishing conventions may arise, namely:

(*a*) confusion between what is a prescriptive convention and what is merely a descriptive usage, e.g. the practice of consulting interested parties in the drafting of legislation;

(*b*) determination of the context of a particular convention and its applicability to particular circumstances;

(*c*) the lack of formal adjudicatory machinery for determining the existence of a convention: in particular, the essence of a convention, i.e. its acceptance as binding, may arise as the result of a misunderstanding in a particular case, or may not be regarded as binding by all parties concerned;

(*d*) the relation and necessity of precedents in the establishment of conventions.

13. Obedience to conventions. The absence of formal sanctions for breach of a rule tempts one to think that obedience to the rule is merely permissive. This view does not accord, however, with legal reality; laws are obeyed for reasons other than mere legal sanction, e.g. social pressures, moral attitudes, respect for law, etc. Why, then, are conventions obeyed? The following reasons may be suggested.

(*a*) Dicey's view that breach of a convention would lead to a breach of law is not all-embracing and only applies to certain conventions.

(*b*) Political difficulties might well be the result of a breach of a convention in that such a breach may destroy respect for constitutional practices or could lead to a change in the established balance of political powers.

(*c*) Respect for constitutional practices. A government is by convention required to resign if defeated on a major issue in the Commons. Its resignation may well then be a result of respect for the need to treat such a vote as a manifestation of the public will, as in practice there is no necessary reason to assume that it could not command support for the rest of its policies.

(*d*) Convenience and the desire to be accorded the same privileges, etc., oneself (when, for example, in opposition).

(*e*) Appropriate legislative measures incorporating the conventional practice can easily be introduced in the UK system as there is no special procedure necessary to enact constitutional measures, e.g. the 1911 or 1949 Acts formally curtailing the power of the Lords.

14. Ministerial responsibility. "Ministers are responsible *for* the general conduct of government, including the exercise of many powers legally vested in the monarch; and they are responsible *to* Parliament immediately and ultimately, through Parliament and parties, to the electorate" (G. Marshall and G. C. Moodie, *see* **9**). In practice, ministerial responsibility is not clear-cut and presents problems both as to the definition of its substance and as regards the means by which Parliament is able to secure such responsibility. Responsibility means accountability, but in practice seems to have little punitive effect. In addition, it has certain undesirable side-effects to the extent that it protects individual culpable civil servants. Thus Lord Carrington resigned as Foreign Secretary over his department's failure to interpret correctly Argentinian intentions over the Falkland Islands.

15. Collective responsibility. This is an even looser concept and effectively means that a government must submit its policy as a whole to Parliament and must resign if unable to secure acceptance thereof. Looked at from another aspect it means that a minister who is individually unable to accept government policy must resign, e.g. as did Mr Frank Cousins in 1966 as a result of his disagreement with the government's Prices and Incomes Bill.

16. Safeguards of tradition. The theoretical interdependence of Parliament and the executive in practice gives way to executive primacy. As long as the executive can maintain majority support in Parliament it has the power to force any policy through Parliament. Before dealing with practical safeguards and controls of public administration, it is important to realise the underlying role of tradition in British governmental practice. A basic consensus of political beliefs exists in Britain which effectively prevents complete subjugation of Parliament by the executive. Some of these are the protection of minorities in debates by the Speaker, recognition and accordance of powers to the opposition, methods of constituting committees and activities and institutionalising of pressure groups (*see* XV).

These informal and intangible influences are at the basis of the constitution and their absence has proved disastrous in attempts to export the British constitution to states without these underlying factors, e.g. Nigeria.

The need to match the structure of a country's political institutions to the nature of the political problems found within the country is now recognised. Thus, for example, the Zimbabwe constitution while containing many recognisably "British" elements attempts to take account of contemporary political realities.

THE HOUSE OF COMMONS

17. Criticism. It has been commented that "there is much contemporary evidence to suggest that Britain so lacks effective scrutiny of the executive that a situation is created in which popular esteem for Parliament and government declines and its own effectiveness crumbles" (B. Crick, *The Reform of Parliament*, Weidenfeld and Nicolson, 1972).

18. Basic factors in the relationship between Parliament and government. The major factors to be considered are as follows.

(*a*) Strong government and strong opposition are not incompatible. Executive domination of Parliament is probably necessary to facilitate the pushing through of legislative programmes. However, effective scrutiny and constructive criticism can improve policies and ensure that they represent public opinion.

(b) Parliament remains the most effective scrutinising body, and reliance on both the courts and the press as checks on the administration are inadequate.

(c) Checks and balances do not automatically develop to preserve the traditional relationship of interdependence.

(d) The two-party system does not result in inevitable alternations in governments and thus the sanction of quinquennial elections on its own is an inadequate check.

19. Parliament's role. The House of Commons has changed from a "legislative" body to a "legitimising" body, the old belief in the dichotomy between politics and administration having broken down. However, despite the decline into insignificance of the positive legislative role of the House, it still performs certain vital functions, especially concerning control of the executive, as follows.

(a) *Legitimising.* Parliament is not a mere rubber-stamp for government legislation. It involves publicity, debate, criticism, etc.

NOTE: This function may be curtailed by use of such machinery as the guillotine (as in the Wales Bill and Scotland Bill (1978) and the Telecommunications (privatisation) Bill (1984)). However, the importance of such machinery can be overrated, as it is doubtful whether the true function of the House is discussion of detail (committee stage) anyway, as opposed to criticism of policy (at second reading stage).

(b) *Raising and discussing complaints and grievances.* This is nowadays the crucial traditional function of Parliament. It involves constant examination and criticism of governments. Although a government may confidently expect support from its parliamentary majority, the value of this critical function will be eroded if the government fails to make available sufficient information upon which criticism may be constructively based.

(c) *Control of the executive.* This is principally a matter of politics rather than of law. The ultimate deterrent of the vote is inadequate (*see* **4**). However, governments may be induced to respond to parliamentary criticism where publicity is widely given to such criticisms or where morale of government supporters is undermined. Parliament can thus exercise control by making the government aware of the underlying drifts of public opinion.

NOTE: Control in practice does not mean coercive control but is more indicative of advice, scrutiny, publicity, etc. It is thus important in the control of the executive that Parliament develops machinery which is able to bring about informed criticism and consequent publicity, rather than machinery which will result in inherently weak and unstable government.

THE PARLIAMENTARY COMMITTEE SYSTEM

20. The role of committees. Committees are an inevitable feature of any complex organisation, and their role in the parliamentary context is similar to that in any large organisation—the detailed consideration of issues. It is generally agreed that for committees to be effective the following criteria should be met:

(*a*) they should be as small as possible;

(*b*) their functions should be precisely defined;

(*c*) they must have adequate time for their business;

(*d*) they should contain, or have available, necessary expertise;

(*e*) they should have sufficient power to ensure co-operation and compliance from people and institutions with which they have dealings.

21. Types of parliamentary committee. There are several types of committee—different structures being suited to different functions. The main distinction may be drawn between committees considering legislation and those monitoring the implementation of policy by the executive branch.

22. Committees concerned with legislation. There are various types:

(*a*) *Standing committees.* These are the "work-horse" committees; as many as required are established and they are named A, B, C, etc. They consist of between 16 and 50 members appointed by the Committee of Selection in proportion to party strength in the chamber. They consider public bills clause by clause at the "committee stage" in the legislative process.

(*b*) *Committees of the Whole House.* This is a technical description referring to an arrangement whereby the ordinary House of Commons sits as a committee, with a chairman instead of the Speaker.

(*c*) *Joint committees.* Here Members of Lords and Commons sit as one committee to consider matters relating to both Houses or Private Bills involving key matters of principle.

(*d*) *Private Bills committees*. These are committees which consider *Private Bills*.

NOTE: The distinction between *Public Bills*: which affect the whole country, initiated and/or supported by the government. *Private Bills*: which affect only a specific section of the community, such as in giving powers to a local authority. *Private Members Bills*: which are initiated by backbench MPs and may be Private or Public.

23. Committees monitoring the executive. These are *select committees*; they consider legislative proposals occasionally, but their main role is investigative. They are quite small, membership not exceeding fifteen, and may call witnesses and demand access to government records. There are three basic types:

(*a*) *sessional*—appointed each session to deal with recurring business, for example on the Parliamentary Commissioner for Administration (Ombudsman) and the Public Accounts Committee;

(*b*) *ad hoc*—appointed to carry out specific inquiries and to preconsider complex/important bills prior to consideration by a Whole House committee;

(*c*) *specialist*—a relatively recent development, with the aim that the committee should monitor the performance of a particular area of government responsibility. This form of committee has for many years been advocated by those wanting to restore the balance of power between Parliament and the Executive.

24. Arguments in favour of specialist committees. The main argument in their favour is that though committee work backbench MPs can become more effective in monitoring and criticising the administration. (*see* **18**) Since the mid-1960s a system of committees with investigative powers has been advocated; the arguments in favour may be summarised as follows:

(*a*) expert views can be developed through continuous service on one committee dealing with a single policy area;

(*b*) they develop the knowledge and critical powers of MPs;

(*c*) they provide a training ground for potential ministers;

(*d*) the executive could benefit from criticism from more informed MPs;

(*e*) they represent the logical organisational structure for detailed analysis of the work of a complex administration;

(*f*) they could cut across party lines.

25. Criticisms of specialist committees. The main points of criticism are as follows:

(*a*) they may lead to a narrowness of outlook, MPs only being interested in the areas of policy with which their committee deals;

(*b*) committee investigations and the need to be accountable to them may place additional burdens upon ministers;

(*c*) if they became too closely involved with the work and decisions of the executive, Parliament itself could be weakened;

(*d*) to be effective they require staffing and support services.

26. The specialised committee experiment. The then Labour government set up in 1966–67 three specialised committees. Two were attached to departments (Agriculture, and Education and Science), and one cut across departmental lines (Science and Technology). Two significant powers were given to these committees:

(*a*) they were empowered to examine witnesses in public;

(*b*) the Science and Technology committee had the power to appoint "persons with technical or scientific knowledge for the purpose of public inquiries".

Although the committees were dissolved after only one session various developments took place subsequently and these committees can be seen as the forerunners of the present system.

27. Report of the Williams Committee. This committee, itself a select committee on procedure reported in 1978 in favour of establishing a new select committee system. Its main recommendations were that:

(*a*) there should be a committee to monitor the work of each major department;

(*b*) each committee should be adequately staffed and with reinforced powers to send for persons and papers;

(*c*) membership should be in the hands of a committee of selection rather than the government whips;

(*d*) there should be obligatory consideration of committee reports by the government and subsequent parliamentary debate.

The report was largely the work of Labour radicals and Conservative "hawks" on the committee and was opposed by supporters of the traditional parliamentary procedures. Michael Foot, then Leader of the House of Commons, took no action to implement the proposals of the committee.

28. The new specialised select committee system. Norman St John Stevas, the first Leader of the House in the Conservative government elected in 1979, organised the introduction of a system of fourteen committees covering Agriculture; Defence; Education; Science and the Arts; Employment; Energy; Environment; Foreign Affairs; Home Affairs; Industry and Trade; Social Services; Transport; Treasury and Civil Service; Scotland and Wales.

These committees have the power to question ministers, senior civil servants and interested bodies and to call for papers and records. Some of the committees have the right to establish sub-committees to deal with particular problem areas.

29. Effectiveness of the new committees. At this relatively early stage it is hard to judge their performance; however, the Treasury and Civil Service Committee has secured considerable publicity following its report on the government's management of the economy in December 1980. This committee has amongst its staff Alan Budd from the London Business School (LBS), who is well-placed to criticise the work of the Treasury, and the government's Chief Economic Adviser, Terry Burns, who was a former colleague of Alan Budd at the LBS. Edward du Cann, chairman of the committee considers it is necessary "if you are taking on a government department and ministers, you need an intellectual strength at least equal to their power and knowledge".

A number of factors may be identified that suggest these committees may be failing to achieve a significant change in the balance of power:

(*a*) governments may effectively reject their reports;

(*b*) relatively few reports (less than 5 per cent) are debated;

(*c*) front benchers tend not to sit on them—they may thus be seen to be out of the main power structure to some extent;

(*d*) high turnover of members, and chairmen especially, weakens the establishment of each committee's identity and expertise.

30. Other forms of control.

(*a*) Public opinion and pressure groups (*see* XV).

(*b*) Judicial control (*see* XIV).

(*c*) Treasury control (*see* VIII).

(*d*) Cabinet control (*see* VI).

PROGRESS TEST 2

1. Outline some of the characteristics of the British system of government. (**1**)

2. Consider the meaning and application of the doctrine of the separation of powers. (**2–3**)

3. Why does the government dominate Parliament? (**3–4**)

4. Consider the position of the Cabinet and the Prime Minister in the British system of government. (**5–7**)

5. Examine the reasons for the existence of conventions. To what factors may obedience to conventions be attributed? (**9–12**)

6. Consider the contemporary role of Parliament. (**19**)

7. Explain the need for an investigative system of committees to reinforce the role of Parliament in monitoring the executive. (**23–28**)

8. Outline the operation of the new select committees and consider the implications of their being given powers to demand access to "persons and papers". (**27–29**)

CHAPTER III

Organisational Theory

INTRODUCTION

1. Relevance to public administration. Since the 1920s organisation theory has developed rapidly. Its primary purpose as an academic study is to understand and explain the behaviour and functioning of organisations. However the reason for the diversion of resources towards it lies in the hope that it will lead to the creation of new, more effective organisational forms. The similarity between large private administrative organisations and the bureaucracies (*see* VII) of the state has meant that much of the work of organisational theorists is relevant to public administration.

The relevance is particularly apparent to those public sector organisations that are concerned with the provision of goods and services—for example, the nationalised industries as well as departments such as Health and Social Security, and Employment. The Fulton Committee (*see* VI) with its emphasis on the importance of management principles to the administrative civil service generally may be seen as an acknowledgement of the connection of the theories to the operation of all public sector administration.

In many fields such as organisation and methods, manpower planning, and operational research, developments in the public sector have paralleled similar innovations in the private sector.

2. Constraints. It must always be borne in mind that public administration operates within a political environment, the most obvious effect of which is that its "goals"—aims and objectives—are more widely based and subject to more frequent change. In addition, the following constraints on the application of theory should be borne in mind.

(*a*) The nature of the basic administrative problem which varies substantially from the basic problem in private business. This problem has two basic elements:

(*i*) administration must accord with the social and economic environment;

25

(*ii*) it must provide that environment with services needed by society if it is to function and progress.

(*b*) In particular government disposes of coercive powers which do not arise in the private sector, and, partly for this reason, administrative decision-making is bound by rules of consultation, objection and appeal, which have no parallel in the private sector.

(*c*) Government undertakes or sponsors speculative ventures, e.g. in technology, which have no close equivalents.

(*d*) Whilst businessmen are strongly oriented to market innovation, public administration can be said to be concerned more with market compression, i.e. with the limitation of competing demands not all of which can be met.

(*e*) The greater emphasis in public administration on law and the legal context within which such administration must function.

(*f*) The greater relationship in public administration with public welfare and its consequent organisational and operational ramifications.

(*g*) The responsibility of the public administrator to the public, a situation not matched in private industry.

(*h*) The difficulties of quantifying the goals of public administration in the absence of reliance on a pure profits test.

(*i*) The different considerations in determining goals in public administration, which are much wider than those in private industry.

3. Objectives of public administration theory.

(*a*) Understanding organisational problems as they relate to the structure of public departments, their inter-relationships, co-ordination, and internal functioning.

(*b*) Understanding how people in organisations behave and how organisations function.

4. Problems of administrative functioning. Gaps between administrative functioning and the demands of society may arise for a variety of reasons:

(*a*) the slow reaction of administration to changes in society;

(*b*) the loss of the faculty of initiative by administrators (*see* VII).

(*c*) the absence of coherence in action, which may be due to the overlapping of departmental functions, problems of co-ordination, and team-work;

(*d*) the imprecise and often obscure allocation of decision-making responsibilities, which involves difficulties in adapting to both individual and changing circumstances, as well as raising fundamental questions of competence.

5. Common organisational defects. Deficiencies common to all types of organisation include:

(*a*) unsatisfactory means of pursuit of objectives;

(*b*) failure of departments and sections within organisations to contribute to overall objectives at full cost value;

(*c*) lack of functional co-ordinative machinery;

(*d*) lack of co-ordination of inter-departmental activity;

(*e*) slow and poor quality decisions as a result of:

(*i*) overloading of managers;

(*ii*) inadequate information;

(*iii*) tendency to make decisions at an inappropriate level.

These problems thus necessitate solutions aimed at directing organisational activities and behaviour in the pursuit of organisational objectives, rationalising the intra-organisational structure to achieve full cost-value, providing machinery for co-ordination of functions and departments, and improving decision-making by provision of adequate information systems and satisfactory delegation principles.

ORGANISATION THEORY

6. Warning. In considering management theory and its application it is important to bear the following points in mind.

(*a*) Organisation theory does not exist as a coherent and universally accepted set of concepts.

(*b*) Organisation theory is not traditionally concerned with public administration. It is thus necessary when applying such theory to public administration to bear in mind that whilst organisational features may be similar, public administration operates in a much different institutional setting.

7. Approaches to organisation theory. Three broad approaches to organisation theory may be discerned.

(*a*) *Scientific administration.* This is concerned with the study of activities that have to be undertaken to achieve objectives, and the grouping of such activities to achieve efficient specialisation and co-ordination.

(*b*) *Human relations or behavioural approach.* This involves a study of motives and behaviour and the development of criteria to help design an organisation that stimulates members to co-operate in achieving the organisation's aims.

(c) *Systems approach.* This approach concentrates on decisions that need to be made to achieve objectives, and the organisation is thus designed to facilitate decision-making.

THE CLASSICAL APPROACH

8. Basic principles. The nature of the scientific administration approach was epitomised in the report of the Brownlow Committee on Administrative Management (Washington, 1937) in which it was stated that "the foundations of effective management, in public affairs no less than in private, are well known. They have emerged universally wherever men have worked together for a common purpose ... stated in simple terms, these canons of efficiency require the establishment of a responsible and effective chief executive as the centre of energy, direction and administrative management; the systematic organisation of all activities in the hands of qualified personnel under the direction of the chief executive, and to aid him in this, the establishment of appropriate managerial and staff agencies."

The following are brief statements of the main features of the classical approach to organisations.

9. Determining objectives. The basic purpose of determining organisational objectives is seen as being to:

(a) establish management priorities;

(b) indicate key departments and activities;

(c) to avoid the "decibel" system of management;

(d) provide consistency of human and materials organisation with the objectives.

10. Specialisation and groupings. Classical theory treats specialisation as the basis of efficiency, and consequently places emphasis on the most effective management groupings of specialist functions.

11. Grouping. The approach identifies four relevant factors in grouping.

(a) *Span of control.* The classicists considered that one manager is only capable of controlling a limited number of subordinates. This view may be represented by the general approach of those such as Gulick ("where work is diversified, qualitative and ...

scattered, one man can supervise only a few") or the more specific approaches of those such as Graciunas, who claims specific practical maxima, e.g. three to six being representative.

(b) *Economies of scale.* Grouping should be achieved to produce economies of scale both from the technical and resource aspects, and from the management aspects.

(c) *Co-ordination.* Groupings may be justified and should be operated to achieve advantages of co-ordination. Co-ordination results in integration of individual effort, and weak co-ordination results in lack of "goal" consistency, uneconomical organisation, and poor specification of duties.

(d) *Grouping by nature of activity.* Key activities may be grouped under higher management for direct supervision. Such "key-ness" may result from the long-term nature of an activity, its important qualitative function or the repercussions its failure would have on other aspects of the organisation. The essence of such groupings is thus to place highly interdependent units under a unified head.

12. Delegation. Delegation has been defined as "the institutionalised right to make decisions or give orders on behalf of an organisation" (J. O'Shaughnessy, *Business Organisation*, Allen and Unwin, 1972). In the classical approach it was felt that delegation should be to the point closest to that of operation. Factors relevant to delegation include the following.

(a) Delegation makes possible the achievement of economies of scale and specialisation.

(b) Key activity decision-making is likely to evolve upwards to higher management.

(c) It diffuses the authority to make decisions to lower levels of the organisation thus enhancing initiative and job satisfaction as well as identification with the goals of the organisation.

(d) The view of the classicists was that authority should be delegated to the extent and in the way necessary for the accomplishment of the results expected. Therefore the extent of delegation should be matched by the particular job to be done.

13. Divisionalisation and decentralisation. Divisionalisation consists of dividing the organisation into units based on such factors as product type, geographical operation, etc. Decentralisation consists of the systematic delegation of authority to all organisational units. Centralisation, on the other hand, is the tendency to withhold such authority.

In practice, complete decentralisation is impossible, as central organisation must retain at least a minimum of power necessary to achieve the following:

(*a*) approve divisional objectives and ensure that these are compatible with the overall organisational objectives;

(*b*) approve the divisional organisational structure by indicating key departments.

14. Advantages and disadvantages of decentralisation. The advantages of decentralisation are as follows:

(*a*) it focuses efforts directly on performance and results;

(*b*) poor results do not remain hidden;

(*c*) management by objectives becomes fully effective;

(*d*) managers have the incentive of independent command;

(*e*) economies of scale, co-ordination, etc., are achieved.

The disadvantages are:

(*f*) the danger of over-independence from overall objectives;

(*g*) some delay in decision-making;

(*h*) the possibility of poor co-ordination at local level.

15. Essential conditions for effective decentralisation. The following points should be noted.

(*a*) There must be both strong parts and a strong centre.

(*b*) Decentralised units must be strong enough to support the standards of management required.

(*c*) Each federally decentralised unit should have growth potential.

(*d*) There must be enough scope and challenge in the managerial posts.

(*e*) Federal units should exist side by side.

16. Specifying responsibility. "Authority is not to be conceived of apart from responsibility which goes with the exercise of power. Responsibility is a corollary of authority; it is its natural consequence and essential counterpart, and wheresoever authority is exercised, responsibility arises" (H. Fayol, *General and Industrial Management*, Pitman, 1967). The classical approach thus emphasised the need for clear specification of responsibility for the following reasons.

(*a*) Vague assignment of responsibility results in confusion and jurisdictional conflict.

(*b*) Accountability without specification of responsibility is inequitable.

(*c*) This permits the anticipation of future needs and the making of comparisons.

(*d*) It limits interference by supervisors.

17. Line and staff relations. Classical theory emphasised the establishment of line relationships, i.e. between superior and subordinates, for the following reasons.

(*a*) It establishes official lines of communication throughout the organisation.

(*b*) It establishes to whom each subordinate is accountable.

(*c*) It establishes responsibility for co-ordination of the functions of subordinates.

Line services are thus conceived of as vertical relationships, and staff services as horizontal supporting activities. The former are thus direct contributors to the organisation's objectives, whereas staff units provide the necessary adjectival services to the line functions and thus contribute indirectly to the overall organisational objectives, e.g. personnel, finance, purchasing. In classical theory, line is equated with command and staff with advice.

18. Conflicts in the theory. The following points should be noted.

(*a*) Line members frequently resent control exercised by staff.

(*b*) Staff personnel are generally new additions to an organisation, and therefore uncertain as to their status. This gives rise to relationship difficulties, namely:

(*i*) difficulty in quantifying staff functions;

(*ii*) the indirect nature of staff functions;

(*iii*) the possibility that staff may push line too hard in order to justify their existence;

(*iv*) a tendency to appear superior on the part of the staff;

(*v*) the possibility that staff may adopt an "ivory tower" approach.

19. Improving relations. These difficulties may to some extent be resolved by the following measures.

(*a*) Specify responsibility clearly.

(*b*) Encourage each to become better acquainted with the other's work.

(*c*) Rotate staff and line assignments.

(*d*) Establish an "overall management climate".

20. Major defects in classical theory. In broad terms the approach has been criticised by A. K. Rice (*The Enterprise and Its Environment: A System Theory of Management Organisation*, Tavistock Publications, 1963) as being based on a "closed system with an inherent ability to accommodate changes in the external environment". In particular the following major criticisms may be made.

(*a*) *Underlying assumptions.* The basic classical assumptions have been challenged in that they oversimplify, and fail to take account of the development of small informal groups and sub-groups which may be at odds with the overall organisation goals.

(*b*) *Problem definition.* Problems arise, in public administration, particularly where objectives are difficult to define or where various activities are unquantifiable, e.g. where social criteria are involved. The classical approach presumes both the importance and the ease of defining objectives and fails to recognise that in public administration the definition of such objectives is interwoven with the broad political process.

(*c*) *Means not ends.* The approach concentrates on the means whereby objectives may be achieved, but gives little or no guide to the relevant elements in establishing such ends. Consequently the approach is unrelated to the social and political problems faced by members of an organisation.

THE HUMAN RELATIONS APPROACH

21. Principles. The human relations or behavioural school is primarily concerned with the analysis of the behaviour of groups and individuals within the organisational context. Much of their work is experimentally based and concludes that social satisfaction must be taken into account when explaining behaviour and in planning structures.

According to behaviourist thinking it is important that organisations should devise objectives taking their staff's needs into account as well as those of the organisation as a whole. For example, positive measures to stimulate co-operation and to avoid conflict should be made. Behaviourist criticism of the classical, scientific administration approach is based on the latter, ignoring the impact staff satisfaction and psychology have on the performance of the organisation as a whole.

22. Practice. In practice, the approach is concerned with the following.

(a) *Needs and wants*. The approach involves the study of an individual's wants and needs, factors stimulating these goals which satisfy such needs. Needs have been classified as physical, safety, social, egoistic, and self-actualisation (C. Argyris, *Personality and Organisation*, Harper and Row, 1972). The classical concentration on specialisation, span of control, etc., is rejected as being inconsistent with needs and wants.

(b) *Work groups*. The approach recognises the influence which associates of an individual have on the individual's attitudes and behaviour. It points out that an individual does not operate in isolation and in particular:

(i) he tends to conform to group pressures;

(ii) his attitudes and morale are influenced by group associations;

(iii) problem-solving and leadership are often group functions.

(c) *Supervisory behaviour*. This is treated as a vital factor in influencing work group behaviour, as the supervisor represents the link between the group and the formal organisation.

23. Criticism of group participation. Group participation in decision-making has been criticised for the following reasons:

(a) it increases group domination of its members;

(b) responsibilities become blurred;

(c) group and expert judgments may conflict;

(d) the cost of reorientating supervisory functions may exceed the benefits of group participation;

(e) the process is not automatically effective and depends greatly on supervisory and management attitudes.

NOTE: The approach is also vitally concerned with inter-group behaviour and study of relations between groups rather than between individuals. Such behaviour is an important factor in achieving objectives, and in assessing the degree of co-operation and co-ordination required.

24. Conclusions. The classical and human relations approaches thus vary in the following important respects.

(a) Whereas the human relations school is concerned with the organisation evolving effectively from inter-personal behaviour, the classical approach predetermines the organisation within which individuals are required to function.

(b) The human relations approach results in a comparatively flat organisational structure, whereas the classical approach results in a pyramidal structure as, for example, in the British civil service.

(c) Authority is regarded by the human relations approach as a social factor, by the classicists as organisational.

(d) Interdependence is a key factor in the human relations approach, which considers that the classical definition of responsibility creates competition.

THE SYSTEMS APPROACH

25. Principles. The systems approach treats an organisation as an example of a "system", i.e. a set of interdependent parts forming a whole with the objective of fulfilling some definable function. A business organisation is essentially regarded as a decision-making system, and the organisation is treated as being built up from an analysis of information requirements and communications networks. It thus treats the process of decision-making as basic to the determination of objectives and policies.

26. Scope. The methodology of the systems approach thus consists of the following steps:

(a) specifying objectives;

(b) establishing subsystems (main decision areas);

(c) analysing these decision areas and their information needs;

(d) designing the communication channels to facilitate information flow within the organisation;

(e) grouping decision areas to minimise communication problems. In practice the approach illustrates the importance of organisation of information, the advantages of project rather than functional division and the need to concentrate centrally the information network.

27. A contemporary outlook. The contemporary approach to the theory of organisations is to abandon the idea of treating organisations as mere passive instruments operating in response to external pressures. Organisations are regarded as semi-autonomous systems which develop their own internal goals, e.g. Simon (*see* **45**) refers to their having "performance objectives" and "conservation objectives", the latter relating to the organisation's desire to survive.

Argyris defines an organisation as "an organic inter-relation of parts" which has essentially three activities, namely:

(a) achieving particular objectives;

(*b*) maintaining itself internally;
(*c*) adapting to the internal environment.

28. Relation of theory to practice. The schools of thought on organisation have developed mainly to explain aspects of performance and behaviour that can be observed. From the point of view of the practising administrator each of the schools is likely to offer useful perspectives and be helpful in revealing past weaknesses and enabling the establishment of better structures.

DECISION-MAKING

29. The decision-making process in management. The rational comprehensive approach deals with decision-making as a programme of logical and sequential steps, namely:

(*a*) recognition and diagnosis of problem;
(*b*) determination of alternative solutions;
(*c*) investigation and analysis of facts relating to each alternative;
(*d*) comparison of the consequences of the alternatives;
(*e*) selection of solution.

Decision-making is essentially *complex*. A decision is not the province of any single individual, but the result of contributions of knowledge from both inside and outside the organisation being integrated, even though the final direction might emanate from a single person or group of individuals.

30. Advantages of process.

(*a*) It can be used to clarify the general logic of a problem and to accustom decision-makers to look out for aspects of the problem which are capable of quantification.

(*b*) It can be simulated under laboratory conditions to ascertain the effects of different incentives, working conditions, and social factors on the speed and accuracy of possible solutions.

31. Limitations. The approach is, however, an essentially static process and is subject to the following limitations.

(*a*) Values to be realised are not usually set out clearly and distinctly.

(*b*) Implicit objectives emerge during the decision-making process itself which may conflict with the originally perceived objectives.

(c) It is generally difficult for the individual decision-maker to take a comprehensive view of the whole problem, as the solution is invariably a lengthy and cumulative process.

(d) Most organisations would be paralysed if the process was carried out completely in all cases. Because of the need for speed decisions will often necessarily have to be taken on the basis of incomplete data.

32. Behavioural approach. This attempts to examine how people make decisions under conditions of imperfect information. It seeks to show as a *dynamic* process how decisions are affected by individual differences, social pressures, leadership styles, and communication structures.

It suffers, however, from certain methodological problems, in particular:

(a) confidentiality in decision-making will often necessitate research being carried out under simulated conditions;

(b) there are considerable difficulties in isolating the actual decision under consideration from the stream of consultations, committee deliberations, etc.

However, the approach provides a framework descriptive of the decision-making process.

33. Framework for decision-making. A decision is seen as being reached in the following stages:

(a) *awareness* of the existence of the problem, e.g. through political channels, interest group consultation, internal research and information;

(b) the problem is then *structured*, i.e. it is interpreted and related to other information so that the nature of the problem is clarified;

(c) *exploration*, where possible courses of action or inaction are listed and an estimate of the consequences made;

(d) *evaluation* and provisional decision;

(e) *consultation*;

(f) *authorisation* by higher level authority.

34. Bounded rationality. There is a need with complex problems which are beyond the competence of a single decision-maker to resort to factorisation. This division may be on a horizontal, or, more typically in public administration, on a vertical basis. The vertical approach is a reflection of hierarchical structure, i.e. the typical Weberian Bureaucracy (*see* VII). In such cases the basic structural problem is to bring together the independent factors involved, and in this respect an organisation can be perceived as a system of communication. As such it involves the allocation of duties in such a way as to allow individuals to contribute rationally to the solution of complex problems, but however rational the structure it is *bounded* by the competence of its members.

35. Organisational restraints in decision-making. The internal restraints of an organisation may prevent the following of the ideal process. Research has shown that an organisation contains certain norms which inhibit the open confrontation of certain issues, and which generate a resistance or feeling of resistance to change. These are as follows:

(*a*) social constraints;

(*b*) leadership style;

(*c*) outside pressures, including awareness of public opinion and interest groups;

(*d*) complexity, making deviation from established methods difficult.

36. Common errors in decision-making. The most common errors are as follows.

(*a*) *Cognitive nearsightedness.* This is the tendency to make decisions satisfy immediate needs. This is particularly attractive in intra-government business, with expediency being the key factor, e.g. the overcrowding of Negroes in some cities in the USA was expedient to solve the housing shortage but has unfortunate long-term effects which were not considered.

(*b*) *Over-simplification.* The tendency to deal with symptoms to the exclusion of causes.

(*c*) *Over-reliance on personal experience.*

(*d*) *Preconceived notions.* These lead to ignoring of social science findings if they contradict the ideas of the decision-makers. This has been particularly noticeable in British economic policy-making (*see* VII).

BEHAVIOUR IN ORGANISATIONS

37. Importance of behavioural studies. Public administration studies often tend to concentrate on the machinery of administration, to the exclusion of those factors influencing behaviour in organisations, and consequently influencing an organisation's effectiveness. Any public administration system depends for its effectiveness on both organisational factors and behaviour within that structure.

38. Preliminary factors. As with organisation theory in general, there is a need to consider the special requirements of public administration structures when considering behavioural theory. Peter Self (*Administrative Theories and Politics*, Allen and Unwin, 1972) identifies the following conditions in particular:

(*a*) that the senior administrator works within three interlocking circles—his own agency and its special public, other public agencies, and the organs of political control;

(*b*) that senior staff in large agencies are remote from the consequences of their decisions;

(*c*) and that political control tends to lead to anonymity and a low level of appreciation and recognition of administrative achievement.

Behavioural studies have tended to concentrate on those aspects of administrative performance that are lacking and conflict with the Weberian ideal of a rational bureaucracy (*see* VII); Self describes these aspects as the "dysfunctions of bureaucracy", i.e. "the unwanted byproducts of methods which are in themselves rational". It follows that a major objective of these studies is the reduction of such "dysfunctional" aspects.

39. Value premises. These may be understood as factors influencing behaviour apparent in organisational structures. They principally include the following.

(*a*) *The organisation's objectives.* The organisation's objectives expressed as objects of activities, groups to be served, level or quality of service, etc., enter into every administration system.

(*b*) *Efficiency.* Examined pragmatically public administration is concerned with the efficient utilisation of resources, as are other organisations.

This premise operates towards the adoption of methods of achieving objectives which will involve lower costs or, where appropriate, will provide the greater results.

NOTE: In public administration measurement of efficiency becomes a major problem as pure economic results must often be set against social objectives, etc. This does not, however, invalidate the value premise of efficiency but merely requires different standards of measurement, e.g. management by objectives.

(*c*) *Individual rights.* In organisations involving regular contact with individuals and social problems, an underlying premise of "fair play" may operate. This premise will be devalued in organisations where the structure approaches a pure bureaucratic model (*see* VII), as the members will be trained or the rules framed to minimise personal factors.

(*d*) *Personal values.* These are "non-organisational" values and arise where individuals tend to evaluate the organisation's objectives in terms of their own personal objectives. The success of an organisation may well depend on the degree to which it is able to replace such personal values with the organisation's objectives.

40. Organisation and non-organisation objectives. When personal values conflict with the goals of the organisation it will be necessary for the organisation to offer such incentives as will effectively subjugate the personal values of individuals to those of the organisation. Incentives may be defined as the appeals an organisation makes to the personal values of its employees to induce them to accept organisational values in choice and decision-making. Incentives have been classified by Chester Barnard as follows:

(*a*) material inducement;
(*b*) opportunities for distinction;
(*c*) good physical working conditions;
(*d*) personal confidence and satisfaction in social relationships within the organisation;
(*e*) conformity with habitual practices;
(*f*) feeling of participation.

41. Factual premises. These are difficult to tabulate, but in general terms include those factors resulting in the acquisition of skills and knowledge to deal with information.

42. Organisational influences on behavioural premises. The two principal organisational influences are as follows:

(*a*) influences brought to bear on individuals through the formal organisational process;
(*b*) influences brought to bear by informal organisations, i.e. by informal social structures and relations which develop within a formal organisation.

43. Extra-organisational influences on behavioural premises. These may in general terms be regarded as conditioning that the individual receives before he becomes a member of the organisation, and influences to which he is subjected whilst a member of the organisation but which do not stem from the organisation itself, e.g. personal factors, family and social influences. The principal extra-organisational influences are as follows.

(*a*) *Community mores.* This involves the behavioural attitudes and beliefs held by the community in which the individual lives. They will include established patterns which are enforced throughout society in the form of social customs, obligations, standards, etc., and will affect the individual's attitudes towards such matters as authority, status and efficiency as business and personal concepts.

(*b*) *Personality factors.* Although this is primarily a subject of psychological study it is worth observing that individual differences in personality will exist as a result of varying heredity and environmental factors. In the context of administrative organisations these will manifest themselves in an individual's attitudes to objectivity, sociability, ambition, etc.

(*c*) *Outside organisations.* The behavioural patterns and objectives established by the organisation in which the individual operates may be subject to opposing standards and patterns of behaviour set by organisations to which an individual belongs or is influenced by outside the work context, e.g. church, political organisations, etc.

(*d*) *Prior training.* This may influence attitudes taken by individuals towards various organisation objectives or means of achieving objectives. A particularly good example is the antipathy of the civil service administrative class towards professionalism.

44. The influence of formal and informal organisations. An organisational setting will result in an individual acting differently than he would do in a non-organisational context, or if he was in a different organisational setting. There is thus an assumption of an organisational role, i.e. an organisationally and socially defined standardised pattern of behaviour. In consequence behaviour is affected by the following:

(*a*) assumption of the organisation's objectives;

(*b*) acceptance of the influence of informal organisations within the organisation;

(c) expectations;
(d) organisational morale.

45. "Administrative man." As a result of such influences, an individual becomes what has been described by Simon as "administrative man": "He accepts the organisation's goals as the value premises of his decisions, is particularly sensitive and reactive to the influences upon him by other members of his organisation, forms stable expectations regarding his own role in relation to others and the roles of others in relation to him, and has a high morale in regard to the organisation goals" (H. A. Simon, D. W. Smithburg and V. A. Thomson, *Public Administration*, Alfred Knopf, 1967).

46. Formal and informal differences. In formal organisations patterns of behaviour and relations are deliberately and legitimately planned for members of the organisation; i.e. the division of work and allocation of responsibilities, authority relationships, etc., are established. In informal organisations the actual pattern of behaviour and relations of members of an organisation will depart to differing extents from the formal organisational plan. This difference may arise through the need to supplement an incomplete formal organisation or to reduce conflicts therein. In consequence, an individual's behaviour will be a result of both formal and informal organisational influences.

PROGRESS TEST 3

1. What constraints restrict the use of organisation theory in public administration? **(2, 38)**

2. Outline the main groups of organisation theory. **(7, 8, 21, 25)**

3. Explain the meaning and importance of (a) grouping, and (b) specialisation. **(11, 12)**

4. What are the main defects of classical organisation theory? **(20)**

5. Distinguish the classical and human relations approaches. **(20, 24)**

6. What are the advantages and difficulties in the rational comprehensive method of decision making? **(29–31)**

7. Identify and explain some of the particular influences on behaviour within public administrative agencies. **(38)**

8. How do organisations influence value premises?   (**39, 42, 44**)

9. What are the main extra-organisational influences on behaviour? (**43**)

CHAPTER IV

Central Administration
I: Machinery

FEATURES

1. Introduction. There are few discernible trends underlying the principles upon which British central government departments have been developed. Basic patterns which have emerged, however, include the following.

(*a*) *Functional principle.* In general terms, the basic allocation of responsibilities has developed on a functional basis.

(*b*) *Absence of uninterrupted development.* With the principal exceptions of the Treasury and the Foreign and Home Offices the majority of government departments have incurred functional reorganisation since the nineteenth century, in consequence of which it is impossible to portray an uninterrupted development of the central government machine.

(*c*) *Continual process.* The process of development is best viewed as one of continuous fusion and fission (*see* **4** (*b*) and (*c*)).

(*d*) *Integration.* The trend in the early 1970s in departmental organisation was towards integration as the best means of achieving co-ordination and policy formulation and execution. This was typified by the reorganisation of the Department of the Environment and the Department of Trade and Industry, though the latter was subsequently dismantled by the Labour Government in 1974 into four separate departments, and the Department of Transport was hived off from the Department of the Environment, both due to management difficulties in organising and co-ordinating "super-departments".

2. The continuous process. The continuous and changing pattern and bases of development of the central departments is due to a number of factors, in particular the following:

(*a*) expansion of the scope and nature of government activity;

(*b*) development of new areas of policy, e.g. the social services;

(*c*) fluctuations in the degree of emphasis accorded to different fields of administration;

(*d*) party political factors, i.e. the tendency to create a department for a minister rather than vice versa.

3. The system of departments. Although in the British system the major organisational unit is the Ministry or Department, these vary in a number of important respects.

(*a*) *Policy administration.* Although most departments have some degree of responsibility for subordinate organisations distinctions may be drawn between departments which are responsible for the direct administration of policy, e.g. the Treasury, and those charged with formulating policy as a basis for the control of other agencies, e.g. the Department of the Environment with its overall responsibility for local government. However, certain departments cut across this division, e.g. the Department of Trade and Industry (D.T.I.), which whilst having been responsible for executing policy in relation to commerce and industry was also responsible for administering policy in relation to various public corporations. However, from its inception, the D.T.I. had management problems. It was a huge department and, although its responsibilities had a common basis in being related to trade and industry, it was more like a conglomerate than a really close-knit integrated department. The break-up of the D.T.I. was completed by the Labour Government in March 1974, and its work split between four departments, each headed by a Secretary of State with cabinet status, i.e. Energy, Prices and Consumer Protection, Industry, and Trade.

(*b*) *Executive or service.* The former type of department is primarily concerned with the execution of services authorised by Parliament, whereas the latter is concerned with the provision of common services for the administration itself. With the absorption of the Ministry of Works which was the most important service department, and with the growing tendency of departments to operate their own manpower and accounting functions this distinction is now less valid, but does still include such as the HMSO, which, like the Central Office of Information, is an agency without a political head.

(*c*) *Geographical coverage.* Various departments can be considered in geographical terms, e.g. the Foreign Office and the Board of Customs and Excise.

(*d*) *Centralised and decentralised.* A distinction may be drawn on the basis of contact with members of the public, as opposed to contact with representative interests of the public. Examples in this category may be drawn from the Department of Employment, the Department of Health and Social Security, and the Inland Revenue.

However, the above represents a descriptive approach and as such does not attempt to provide a formula for the allocation of responsibilities (*see* 4), nor guidance as to the major problems of control and co-ordination (*see* 15–26).

ALLOCATION OF FUNCTIONS

4. Theory of allocation. The following means of allocation should be noted.

(*a*) *By function.* The creation of departments to administer particular functions of government is generally regarded as offering the best chance of achieving efficiency despite the frequent difficulty of deciding exact criteria for such allocation. In particular, if operated with reasonable accuracy, it should avoid excessive duplication and overlapping of functions and will encourage the acquisition of special skills and knowledge. Additionally it allows a complex of matters to be studied as a whole, and enables a clarity of decision-making responsibility to emerge to consequent benefit of the public.

However, it cannot entirely eliminate overlapping, it is not always appropriate and in certain cases there is a demonstrable need for a clientele or regional basis.

(*b*) *By clientele.* The creation of departments related not to function but to clientele is only suitable where a group is so special that its problems are incapable of being related to those of the nation as a whole.

"The inevitable outcome of this method of organisation is a tendency to Lilliputian administration. It is impossible that the specialised service which each department has to render to the community can be of as high a standard when its work is at the same time limited to a particular class of persons and extended to every variety of provision for them, as when the Department concentrates itself on the provision of one particular service only by whomsoever required and looks beyond the interests of comparatively small classes" (Haldane Committee, 1918).

(*c*) *By process employed.* Advocates of allocation according to "work process" claim that this results in the highest possible degree of technical specialisation. The main objection to such an allocation is that departments would require a high degree of subsequent co-ordination in order to execute policy, whilst at the same time making such co-ordination difficult. This would result from the impossibility of achieving any one complete administrative process from any department, and would necessitate co-operation to achieve execution of policy from a number of other departments each staffed by probably antagonistic experts.

(*d*) *Regional principle.* Despite its application in certain limited circumstances, e.g. Scottish and Welsh Offices, this method of allocation poses the problem of assimilating regional matters to those of the nation as a whole. This is particularly the case in national economic and physical planning. Regional interests are probably best dealt with by regional decentralisation (*see* XI).

5. Underlying distributional criteria.

(*a*) The location of any governmental service or activity may depend on the policy of the government within a particular field rather than on any theoretical basis of allocation, e.g. defence procurements were transferred from the Ministry of Aviation to the Ministry of Technology in 1967 and then to a sub-group in 1970, viz. the Ministry of Aviation Supply. In 1971 the Ministry of Aviation Supply was abolished and its functions split between the Ministry of Defence and the Department of Trade and Industry. In 1978 the responsibility lay solely with the Ministry of Defence. As has been commented "the great changes in administration have come about through causes partly fortuitous, partly political, but on the whole outside the range of administrative planning" (MacKenzie).

(*b*) Trends towards the development of super-ministries may be explained on the grounds of political desire to keep the size of the Cabinet to manageable levels, and by a preference for co-ordination of different functions within a single ministry rather than face the problem of inter-departmental co-ordination. The Labour Government which took office in 1974 reversed markedly the trend towards super departments, in particular it split the Department of Trade into four Ministries in 1974, and re-established the Department of Transport in 1976.

(*c*) Though this should not be overstated there is consideration of the force of individual political personalities in determining administrative structure.

6. The process of departmental creation. It is now appropriate to relate theories of allocation, etc., to the pattern of development in British central departments. Although the pattern assumed has varied between different services and over different periods, four main concepts have emerged as follows.

(*a*) Separate departments will be developed where individual or grouped functions become sufficiently important or complex, or involve other administrative problems which necessitate the creation of a single department for their resolution.

(*b*) The process of fusion may occur, which involves gathering together related services into a single department, the object being to ensure coherent development and co-ordination of such functions, e.g. the 1970 government reorgansiation (*see* **7–10**).

(*c*) The process of fission involves the division of responsibilities between departments which have previously been concentrated in a single organisation. It will generally occur where the diseconomies of concentration exceed the economies of scale and lead to the growth of unwieldy masses with accompanying administrative inertia, e.g. the division of the old Ministry of Health into Health, Housing and Local Government, and Social Security.

(*d*) Although the transfer of functions is an automatic adjunct to the processes of fusion and fission, the converse is not the case, and may result in the transfer of functions between two or more existing departments. This has been described by Appleby as having "the object of producing coherent missions" (quoted in A. M. Hanson and M. Walles, *Governing Britain*, Fontana, 1973).

NOTE: The interaction of political and administrative factors often accompanies the transfer process, and thus administrative convenience, though being the pragmatic motive for transfer, is not the sole criterion.

WHITE PAPER, 1970

7. Reorganisation of government. The White Paper (Cmnd. 4506, 1970) had the following underlying policies:

(*a*) the improvement of the quality of policy formulation and decision-making;

(*b*) the improvement of the framework in which public policy is formulated by "matching the field of responsibility of government departments to coherent fields of policy and administration" and "ensuring that the government machine responds and adapts to new policies within the broad framework of the main departmental fields of responsibility".

In order to translate these broad aims into organisational principles, changes were necessitated both in the methods of operation between departments and in departmental organisation itself.

8. Functional approach. The White Paper recommended that government departments should be functionally based for the following reasons:

(*a*) the purpose of organisation is to serve policy;

(*b*) related policy issues should be grouped in organisational terms;

(*c*) lines of demarcation are clarified by such groupings and overlapping is minimised;

(*d*) economies of scale are achieved;

(*e*) diffusion of expert knowledge is avoided, and co-ordination difficulties reduced.

NOTE: The White Paper contained the proviso that functional organisation does not always invalidate other allocations, but should provide a basis for allocation within non-functionally organised departments, e.g. the Welsh and Scottish Offices.

9. Unification of functions. The groupings of functions into wide-span departments was considered to provide the best basis for a series of fields of unified policy, and offered the following advantages.

(*a*) *Single strategy.* Such departments would have the capacity to propose and carry through a single strategy for clearly defined and accepted objectives.

(*b*) *Resolving conflicts.* It would provide a basis for the resolution of executive decision and policy-forming conflicts within the line of management, rather than by inter-departmental compromise.

(*c*) *Management.* It enlarges a department's capacity to manage and co-ordinate large resource-consuming projects within departmental boundaries.

(*d*) *Delegation.* A more rational and effective delegation of executive tasks is facilitated.

(*e*) *Identification.* The enlarged comprehensive departments will have a more direct identification with the community.

(*f*) *Contribution to strategy.* A more effective contribution to the government's overall strategy will be possible.

10. Reservations. However, the following disadvantages operated.

(*a*) The advantages would have been reduced if issues which truly necessitate inter-departmental discussion were taken solely in the unified department, without collective ministerial participation and responsibility.

(*b*) Mere aggregation of functions into a series of large departments could have given rise to management problems due to the size and complexity of the top organisational structure. It was therefore necessary to clearly define the boundaries of the functional wings which made up a large department. It would also be necessary to ensure that blocks of executive work would be delegated to accountable units of management, thus lightening the load on top management.

11. The swing from super-departments.

(*a*) *Department of Trade and Industry.* When this was divided in 1974 into four separate departments—Industry, Trade, Prices and Consumer Protection, and Energy—the concept of the super-department was in eclipse.

(*b*) *The Foreign and Commonwealth Office.* The pattern of change in this policy area reflects the rise and fall of the super-department.

(*i*) In 1965 the old Colonial Office and the Commonwealth Relations Office were merged to form the Commonwealth Office.

(*ii*) In 1967 the Foreign Office and the Commonwealth Office were merged into the Foreign and Commonwealth Office.

(*iii*) In 1969 the Foreign and Commonwealth Office (including the Overseas Development Administration) was established and took in the Ministry of Overseas Development (established in 1963 to take over responsibility for technical co-operation).

(*iv*) In 1973 the process reversed and the Foreign and Commonwealth Office was split into the Foreign and Commonwealth Office and the Ministry of Overseas Development.

(*v*) In 1975 the Ministry of Overseas Development was again incorporated into the FCO under a minister of state. In 1979 it was redesignated the Overseas Development Administration.

(*c*) *Department of the Environment.* In 1976 a separate Ministry of Transport Industries was created apart from the Department of the Environment, though the Department retained responsibility for common services. Therefore the functions of the Department of the Environment largely reverted to those of the former Ministry of Housing and Local Government but with the additional responsibility for the construction industry and oversight of the Property Services Agency.

(*d*) *Department of Energy.* In 1976 the responsibility for negotiations with the oil companies regarding North Sea Development was transferred to the Department of Energy from the non-departmental Duchy of Lancaster.

(*e*) *Recent change.* Initially the Conservative administration elected in 1979 made relatively few changes in the organisation of government departments. However the Department of Prices and Consumer Protection was amalgamated with the Department of Trade and in 1982 the Civil Service Department was reabsorbed by the Treasury.

Following a series of "leaks" through ministers at the Defence Department designed to head off expenditure cuts a major change was made. The new structure is intended to ensure government control over service chiefs and defence policy rather than vice versa. The traditional arrangement whereby the three services each had a minister under the Secretary of State for Defence was scrapped and the four defence ministers under the Secretary of State are now responsible for all of the services—two dealing with procurement, the other two with management and operations.

CONCLUSIONS ON DISTRIBUTION

12. Distinguishable principles. The following points should be noted.

(*a*) The Haldane Committee (1918) made a general attempt to define criteria for functional distribution. It considered the choice to lie between functional and clientele bases and concluded strongly in favour of the functional method. The Committee's approach, however, was too general to be of any real value.

(*b*) No consistent pattern has been followed. "They are the product of specific attempts to remedy imbalances and incoherences, to place functions where they may be most effectively performed, to emphasise certain responsibilities of government at the expense of others and to give satisfaction to political demands whether emanating from party politicians or the public" (A. M. Hanson and M. Walles, *Governing Britain*, Fontana, 1973).

(*c*) Because of the incoherence of principles of development, emphasis has been placed on the problems of co-ordination and overall planning, rather than on those of demarcation.

13. Observations on the White Paper. The following points should be noted.

(*a*) It has been suggested that the reorganisation increases the power of the executive arm of government and consequently reduces its effective accountability to Parliament (*see* II).

(*b*) As the government grows stronger, its relative strength is increased by concentration of power in a diminishing number of hands.

(*c*) It is illustrative of the trend to co-ordination through integration.

(*d*) The innovation of the Central Policy Review Staff should be noted (*see* V, **16**).

14. Internal organisation. Before examining general features of such organisation it is important to bear in mind that whilst subscribing to the ideal of an internal organisation which fosters efficiency, such ideals must be seen in the light of other, and possibly conflicting, ideals, which will affect such structures, e.g. accountability to Parliament, Treasury control, and compatability with civil service procedures. Given these constraints it may be stated that a "typical" department will exhibit the following features.

(*a*) It will be headed by a *Secretary of State* in the case of a major department, who may have *Ministers of State* responsible for particular areas of the department's work. They carry the political responsibility to Parliament for the work of the department. Senior ministers may have *Parliamentary Private Secretaries* to assist them.

(*b*) The head of the permanent administrative staff will be a *Permanent Secretary*. He is effectively the accounting officer of the department and the nature of his role effectively results in centralisation and hierarchy in organisational terms.

(*c*) The Minister's *Private Office* will consist of the personal secretariat of the Minister headed by a civil servant of principal rank. The function of the private office is to organise, in conjunction with his parliamentary counterpart, the work for which the Minister is responsible for on a day-to-day basis, e.g. the answering of parliamentary questions.

(*d*) Departments are then typically divided into *divisions* each responsible for the department's major responsibilities. Each division is headed by an *under-secretary* and further divided into *branches* headed by an *assistant secretary*. Branches are again subdivided under the control of *principals*. Finally divisions will normally be grouped under a *deputy-secretary* (*see* Figure 3, VI, **13**).

(*e*) Departments tend structurally to reflect the structural divisions in the civil service ranking hierarchy, thus resulting in a hierarchical structure characterised by an excessive number of levels.

(*f*) *Special advisers.* Since the mid-1960s some ministers have brought with them into Whitehall their own advisers—committed party supporters who are generally either subject experts or political advisers. Their role is to act as a sounding board for ministers to test their views against and to provide support in dealing with the administration.

Their numbers in the United Kingdom have always been small, by contrast, say, with the United States, where senior administrative posts are held by "in and outers" and in France where ministers have their own personal *Cabinet*. The growth of policy units within departments by 1983 was considered sufficient to justify the abolition of the Central Policy Review Staff (CPRS) known as the "Think Tank" (*see* V, **16**).

CO-ORDINATION OF CENTRAL GOVERNMENT

15. The problem of co-ordination. The absence of uniform principles of allocation has led to a relative increase in the study of methods of co-ordination. Such co-ordination may be grouped into the following.

(*a*) *Primary co-ordination.* This deals with the co-ordination of interdependent activities with a department or between departments carrying out related functions. Simon (*see* III, **45**) has defined the need for such co-ordination in the following terms: "group behaviour requires not only the adoption of correct decisions, but also the adoption by all members of a group of the same decision". He sees organisational authority as a "relation that serves by subordinating the decisions of the individual to the communicated decisions of others". Within a department these may be seen as the functions of the equivalent of a "line manager" in industry, and at inter-departmental level through the medium of interdepartmental committees and the informal relations of civil servants.

(b) *Executive level.* This involves co-ordination through Treasury responsibility and control, and now through the co-ordinating functions of the Civil Service Department.

(c) At the *political level* co-ordination is carried out through the Cabinet, the Cabinet secretariat, and Cabinet committees.

NOTE: A further co-ordination problem occurs in devising means whereby external values may be inculcated in those working with within the department in order to enable functions to be carried out in the light of the beliefs in which the State should exercise its functions. This will be manifested through indoctrination training, or more formally through financial controls, appeals system, and obligatory consultation procedures.

16. Problems arising from functional approach. A certain amount of friction is caused by this approach in the area of interdepartmental responsibilities. Such disputes are not generally amenable to Treasury co-ordination owing to the limited number of departments involved, and the often specialised nature of the problems. Such problems in practice may be resolved by the following.

(a) *Periodical reallocation of duties.* This will occur in order to concentrate decision-taking responsibility at a single point.

(b) *Informal elements.* The informal activities of senior civil servants.

(c) *Formal methods.* These will include the use of formal interdepartmental committees or conferences, though these are subject to certain disadvantages in that they are subject to a *liberum veto* of members, and may tend to achieve co-operation at the level of the lowest common denominator.

17. Control of policy execution. Simon distinguished procedural and substantive co-ordination in the following terms "By procedural is meant the specification of the organisation itself—that is, the generalised description of the behaviours and relationships of the members of the organisation. Procedural co-ordination establishes the lines of authority and outlines the spheres of activity of each organisation member, while substantive co-ordination specifies the content of his work." These functions may be considered in the light of the work of the Treasury and the Civil Service Department.

18. Treasury control. Details of Treasury control are dealt with in detail in VII, but its main functions in this area may be stated as follows:

(*a*) financial control for the purpose of *substantive co-ordination* to ensure that policy objectives are achieved;

(*b*) the rule that no legislation requiring expenditure may go before the House of Commons without the support of a Treasury minister;

(*c*) the maintenance of agreed procedures and methods of working, e.g. in relation to the form of departmental accounts and the method of the presentation of estimates (*procedural co-ordination*).

19. Civil Service Department. The Department's main area of concern lies in the standardisation and development of personnel and management functions within departments, as compared with the Treasury which is more concerned with overall manpower policy.

20. Co-ordination of policy-making. This entails co-ordination over the development of new policy, political strategies, and new methods of working through individual departmental constituents of the overall government machine.

21. The Cabinet's general role as co-ordinator. The Cabinet is effectively the centre of the administrative system and is the major instrument of government in Britain. Its central role takes three forms.

(*a*) *Constitutional.* The administration derives its authority from the Cabinet.

(*b*) *Hierarchical.* Cabinet decisions and the minutes in which they are recorded constitute the primary administrative documents.

(*c*) *Administrative.* Formally, at least, major decision-making originates in the Cabinet and initiates chain reactions (*see* V). In addition, the Cabinet exercises vital administrative functions in its role as co-ordinator, director, planner and supervisor.

NOTE: The political functions of the Cabinet necessarily colour all its relations with the administration.

22. Methods of co-ordination by the Cabinet. The Cabinet provides formal machinery for co-ordination in its role as "final court of administrative appeal" and, below Cabinet level, with the exception of the Treasury, co-ordination is largely informal. Devices which have been adopted by the Cabinet for the achievement of administrative co-ordination may be summarised as follows:

(*a*) *ad hoc* committees;

(*b*) standing committees;

(*c*) "overlords";

(*d*) creation of co-ordinating departments;

(*e*) amalgamation of departments into super-departments under a single head.

23. Cabinet committees. These are one of the major postwar developments in the field of government administration. They may be of an *ad hoc* nature, being constituted temporarily to deal with specific problems or, more commonly, be standing committees, permanently constituted, dealing with specific areas of government e.g. social services, economic policy, etc. Originally it was the practice for senior non-departmental ministers to preside over such committees, though it is now more common for Cabinet ministers with departmental responsibilities to preside, e.g. in 1978 the Chancellor of the Exchequer presided over the Public Expenditure Scrutiny Committee, while Harold Wilson, when Prime Minister, presided over two or three Cabinet committees.

The committees are empowered to deal with particular inter-departmental matters and in many cases have the power to make binding decisions without recourse to the Cabinet. Despite their importance the work and existence of these committees is formally secret, though the "COBRA" emergency committee was given unusual prominence during the 1984 "siege" of the Libyan People's Bureau.

24. "Overlords." The period 1951–55 saw the use of "overlords" as the primary co-ordinating agency, i.e. non-departmental ministers were responsible for the co-ordination of food and agricultural policy, and for transport, fuel and power.

The method was criticised for the following reasons:

(*a*) it detracted from the status of departmental ministers;

(*b*) it raised problems of ministerial responsibility;

(*c*) difficulty was occasioned in defining the actual role of "overlords", i.e. whether they were to be directors or merely advisers and co-ordinators.

25. Co-ordinating departments. Constitutionally it is a logical progression from the use of overlords to that of setting up departments with terms of reference defining the division of responsibilities between the overall department and the sub-departments it is established to incorporate; e.g. the Department of the Environment combines under its general authority two hitherto separate departments with often overlapping functions and consequent problems of co-ordination and demarcation. The overall department becomes responsible for the achievement of the general policy objectives for which they share responsibility. In fact Tory policy in the early 1970s was aimed at integration as a means of co-ordination rather than the mere establishment of formal independent co-ordinating machinery.

26. Cabinet secretariat. The secretariat performs co-ordinating functions in addition to its Cabinet and Cabinet committee servicing functions. It achieves this principally through its duties of following up Cabinet decisions and making such decisions known to departmental ministers involved.

27. Organisation at the centre of government. In many countries there is a Prime Minister's department dealing with central policy questions and co-ordination. In the United Kingdom there are two relevant departments: the *Cabinet Office* and the *Treasury*. The Prime Minister carries responsibility for both as Minister for the Civil Service, First Minister in the Cabinet and First Lord of the Treasury. The permanent secretaries of the Treasury and the Cabinet Office have direct access to the Prime Minister and may be regarded as perhaps the most influential officials in the administration (*see* II, Fig. 2).

As an individual the Prime Minister also has the staff of the *Prime Minister's Office* which is a high-powered unit of civil service staff on secondment from various departments headed by the Principal Private Secretary, who is of deputy secretary rank. Also included as part of the office are the Prime Minister's political staff—parliamentary secretary and political advisers (*see* **14** (*f*)). The operation of the office depends on personal relationships rather than a formal structure and it represents the main device through which the Prime Minister is able to keep abreast of the political and administrative systems she or he heads.

PROGRESS TEST 4

1. How may departments be classified? (**3**)
2. Explain the theory of allocation of functions. (**4–5**)

3. What are the main features of the White Paper on the Re-organisation of Government 1970?   **(7–10)**

4. How are departments organised internally?   **(14)**

5. What are the main problems of co-ordination of central government?   **(15–16)**

6. Explain the administrative arrangements for co-ordinating the work of government.   **(20–27)**

CHAPTER V

Central Administration
II: The Policy-Making Process

INTRODUCTION

1. Policy and administration. Public administration theorists were for a long period concerned with attempts conceptually to distinguish policy and administration. The distinction, which was probably based on a confusion of politics and administration, and the desire to keep the former out of the latter, has always been somewhat fictional. Nevertheless the theory of separation of these functions has been reflected considerably in British constitutional practice, particularly in the doctrine of ministerial responsibility, i.e. the minister is conceived of as being solely responsible on the political plane for policy-making and is aided by a neutral, non-policy-making bureaucracy which solely administers the policy decisions of the minister, and is effectively divorced from the intricacies of policy-making by its non-professional status.

NOTE: This distinction was not totally unrealistic in the period when legislatures still retained the initiative in policy-making and the executive branch of government was comparatively small and inexpert. However, the growth in administrative discretion, and the inability of legislatures to solve all problems by legislative means, has markedly shifted this emphasis. "The exercise of discretionary power, the making of value choices, is a characteristic and increasing function of administrators and bureaucrats; they are thus importantly engaged in politics" (W. S. Sayre, R. Carson and T. Harris, *Public Administration in Modern Society*, McGraw-Hill, 1963).

2. The new emphasis. "The increasing volume and complexity of government has had two important results from the standpoint of administrative responsibility. It has shifted the initiative in legislation to the administration, and it has vastly increased the amount of legislating by the administration itself" (Simon—*see* III, **45**). As will be seen (*see* **9–11**), this change in initiative gives the administration considerable power in choosing the goals and values by which its decisions will be guided.

POLICY-MAKING

3. The nature of policy. Policy has been defined as "a matter of either the desire for change or the desire to protect something from change" (J. D. B. Miller, *The Nature of Politics*, Penguin, 1965) or, more fully, as "policy-making occurs in the determination of major objectives, in the selection of methods of achieving these, and in the continuous adaptation of existing policies to the problems that face a government" (N. Johnson, "Who are the Policy Makers?" *Public Administration*, 1965).

There are therefore two principal features of policy, which may be identified as follows.

(*a*) Policy is concerned with either change (its dynamic aspect), or with the preservation of the *status quo* (its static aspect).

(*b*) There is no clear distinction between policy and administration and both contain dynamic elements. The existence of a passive executory administration is no longer a justifiable assumption.

4. Policy-making in a democracy. In an open political system policy-making is a complex process involving individuals and organisations outside as well as within the formal political institutions. It must be remembered that all political activity is directed towards influencing the decision-making process. The following factors are significant.

(*a*) *Party*: the party machines determine policy though generally only in the broadest outline.

(*b*) *Government.* The Prime Minister, ministers and the civil service.

(*c*) *External.* Many political forces play upon the decision-making processes of government including: pressure groups; foreign governments; international associations, e.g. EEC and NATO; public opinion; media comment; and public opinion, such as shown through opinion polls (*see* XV).

5. The policy-making hierarchy. Four levels of policy-making hierarchy have been identified.

(*a*) *Political or general policy-making level.* This consists of the determination of major policy objectives in broad terms, these being manifested in the party political programmes. The effect of such broad policy is to provide a general framework within which effective policy may be worked out.

NOTE: It must be doubted whether such a broad policy classification can be truly regarded as policy at all, but consists rather of a comparatively undefined, non-binding set of ideals.

(*b*) *Executive policy.* This is regarded as the effective reduction of general or political policy into concrete, practical objectives, and manifests itself as Cabinet policy.

(*c*) *Administrative policy.* The form in which the ministerial administrator carries the executive policy into operation.

(*d*) *Technical policy.* The day-to-day policy adopted by officials in working out administrative policy.

6. Defects in the hierarchical theory. The following points should be noted.

(*a*) The theory tends to ignore inter-relations of various groups in the policy-making process, e.g. ministers and civil servants acting together.

(*b*) It fails to incorporate an effective definition of policy.

(*c*) It does not attempt to locate the point of effective policy-making i.e. to assess the relative importance of the various hierarchies.

(*d*) It fails completely to illustrate the upward movement in policy-making and regards policy-making as a downward progression from the general to the particular.

7. The elements of policy. Policy-making is effectively a two-part process.

(*a*) *Analysis and choice presentation.* This involves the primary determination of problem areas, definition of the issues involved therein and an examination of the methods of problem-solving.

(*b*) *Decisions on policy.* This involves the making of the actual decision as to the implementation and choice of alternatives presented.

8. British constitutional theory. In theory the application of the elements of policy-making (*see* **7**) implies a separation of people and of positions in time. It is, however, in the assessment of the relative importances of these functions that the location of policy-making power can be found. In strict theory the civil service has no policy-making power, but exists merely to advise ministers and to carry out policy determined by the minister.

LOCATION OF POWER

9. Power in the formulation role. The strategic position of the official and the comparative weakness of the minister have been summed up by Lord Bridges: "There is an early stage in any project when things are fluid; when, if you are in touch with those concerned and can get hold of the facts, it is fairly easy to influence decisions. But after a scheme has been worked on ... it is very difficult to do anything but approve, or throw it overboard" (quoted by N. Johnson, "Who are the Policy Makers?" *Public Administration*, 1965, p. 284).

Thus the process of analysis and presentation may be divided into the following stages.

(*a*) The fluid stage where opinions are open and influence is of greatest importance.

(*b*) The post-research stage where alternatives are presented and modification and influence replaced by acceptance or rejection.

Evidence of the power of the administration in the decision-making process is to be seen in the extent to which it attracts the attention of interest groups. Influential groups such as the National Farmers Union, for example, deal extensively with officials both in the Ministry of Agriculture, Fisheries and Food, and in the Commission of the EEC. The NFU rarely engages in any overt manifestation of political will such as demonstrations, preferring to use its contacts at the official level.

NOTE: It is thus in the preparation and presentation of alternatives (i.e. the true role of the civil servant) that the official may achieve something approaching absolute policy-making power. The role of a minister may thus be confined to exercising choices between presented alternatives.

10. The position of the minister. The weak position of the minister in policy-making is illustrated in the following ways.

(*a*) *Weakness of the constitutional doctrine.* The theory (*see* **8**) is based on the false assumption that a minister has time, energy and experience to master the great range of policy issues facing a modern department and can thus effectively control all aspects of that department's work.

(*b*) *Pressures on the minister.* The weakness of the minister might to an extent be alleviated if he was not overburdened with matters other than policy-making. However, he is concerned also with non-departmental matters, party political duties, official engagements, etc. These result in his having to rely heavily on advice from senior civil servants, and particularly from his Permanent Secretary (but note role of Senior Policy Advisers recommended by Fulton Committee—*see* VI). Such advice tends often to reach him in the form of a *fait accompli.*

(*c*) *Rejection of advice.* The minister's role is largely confined to choosing between alternatives presented to him, unless he is exceptionally astute or has outside advisers. Unless this is the case he is not likely to be aware of alternatives which have been rejected during the policy analysis stage. Thus it is probable that a minister is only presented with a real choice in the event of civil service disagreement.

11. Strategic position of civil servants. The following points should be noted.

(*a*) A minister will be unlikely to reject advice owing to his dependence on civil service co-operation, for the following reasons in particular:

(*i*) the officials may be his only source of advice—the extent of the special adviser network is very limited in the United Kingdom, by contrast to the *Cabinet* of a French minister.

(*ii*) officials are in the best position to carry out inter-departmental negotiations and liaison with the Treasury which may be necessary for the effective implementation of policy.

(*b*) Policy is often formed at inter-departmental meetings of civil servants, and minutes of ministerial proceedings are prepared by civil servants; the Private Secretary post is regarded as a promotion position and thus encouragement of frank relay back to the minister is discouraged; and the Permanent Secretary may tend to develop what he conceives to be the true role of his department, and is thus likely, consciously or unconsciously, to lead the minister.

"I have known a few cases where fairly senior officials have kept a Minister in the dark about the fact that there was quite a lot of debate further down the line" (Boyle).

(*d*) The official is in a strategic position (*see* **10**).

(*e*) The tradition of civil service anonymity protects the official from outside examination.

12. The role of the minister. Despite the predominance of the official the minister still retains an important role as follows.

(*a*) A strong minister may be able to impose his will on his department.

(*b*) Ministers are still the "accountable persons" and the civil servants must therefore be constantly aware of the political environment in which they function.

(*c*) The legislative context of the ministerial role must be taken into account. Policy must manifest itself in legislation and a department thus must rely on the political ability of its minister to steer such legislation through the House.

(*d*) The role of the minister is strengthened by collective involvement in Cabinet, Cabinet committees, and *ad hoc* meetings with the Prime Minister.

Thus it is fallacious to regard a minister as playing a purely passive role in the policy-making process and his position must be viewed in the light of his political role and the exigencies thereof.

13. Strengthening the ministerial role. The minister's position *vis-à-vis* officials could be strengthened, however, by use of all or some of the following:

(*a*) Provision of the minister with more expertise outside the single chain of command, e.g. greater use of "personal" appointments, use of a French style "Cabinet", etc.;

(*b*) an extension of the committee procedure of the House of Commons along the lines of the US Congressional Committee of Inquiry system;

(*c*) direct access of the professional hierarchy in a department to the minister (*see* VI).

(*d*) By use of management tools such as the MINIS system (Management Information for Ministers) introduced by Michael Heseltine when at the Environment Department. MINIS is a system for collecting and evaluating information about departmental activity and determines priorities, thus improving the minister's perception of problems

14. The role of the Treasury. Within the power structure of policy-making the Treasury is predominant on the official side. This domination is a result of the following:

(*a*) the representation on all inter-departmental committees of Treasury representatives;

(b) the role of the Treasury in the control of expenditure and the important relationship of policy and finance;

(c) the responsibility of the Treasury for fiscal and monetary policy which are the two main instruments of government economic policy.

15. Criticisms of civil servants as policy-makers. The following points should be noted:

(a) their tendency to compromise;
(b) their lack of professionalism;
(c) their lack of long-term strategies;
(d) their failure to make effective use of professionals.

(*See also* VI where these matters are more fully developed.)

16. Think tanks. Bodies of academic and other experts are sometimes referred to as *think tanks*.

(a) *The Central Policy Review Staff (CPRS) 1971–83.* Known as *the think tank*, this was set up following the 1970 White Paper on the Reorganisation of Government; it is a multidisciplinary research team whose role was to help integrate government policy through a programme of research into key policy areas. Its investigations have included studies on Concorde, government research and development, regional policy and the computer industry. Its brief was to consider the longer-term implications of decisions.

The CPRS was established as an integral part of the Cabinet Office and was thus at the disposal of the government as a whole. Its aim was to help ministers make better policy decisions by working out the implications of their strategies and the policy consequences and priorities that would result. The rationale for its abolition was the development of departmental policy units and the policy unit within the PM's office.

(b) *Other think tanks.* There are various institutes, not a part of the structure of government, that specialise in monitoring the decision-making processes of the government. Although not a part of the formal decision-making process of the administration they are considered to be influential—if only by providing effective and authoritative ammunition for the opposition. Amongst these would be included the National Institute for Economic and Social Research (NIESR), which is best known for its work in connection with economic forecasting. Similarly there is the Institute for Strategic Studies (ISS) which monitors the implications of decisions in the field of defence policy.

These, together with the work of many university departments are a source of ideas, analysis and criticism of government policy formulation.

A COMPARISON WITH LOCAL GOVERNMENT POLICY-MAKING

17. Difficulty of precision. At least from an internal point of view central policy-making is comparatively clear-cut compared with the practice in local government. The difficulty in arriving at a clear picture arises for the following reasons.

(*a*) Differences in size of local government units involve consequently differing relations between elected representatives and officials.

(*b*) More important figures are involved in the local government situation compared with the central position which is essentially a relationship between minister and Permanent Secretary.

(*c*) All members in local government have access to chief officers, whereas in central government the Opposition are denied access to senior civil servants.

(*d*) Personalities play a much greater role in local government.

18. Constitutional theory. This is the same as for the central government, i.e. officers advise and councillors decide policy. But this again ignores the following facts.

(*a*) Officers prepare matters for the council.

(*b*) Officers are the trained and experienced parties.

(*c*) Officers are in the best position to measure the impact of existing policy, to possess knowledge as to the adequacy of resources, and to estimate the future effects of policy decisions.

19. Committee on Management in Local Government. Research carried out for the Committee identified various elements concerned in the initiation of policy, namely, "policy committees", party groups and intra-party influence groups, individual committees, individual committee members, relationships between committee chairmen and chief officers, and the contributions of officers.

The Committee's report seemed unable to identify any readily definable source of policy initiation. In general its research showed a predominance of officer-initiated policy, this being explained as inevitable consequence of the technicalisation of local government work.

A comparison was drawn between "sowing seeds" and actually defining policy, the responsibilities being those of officers and members respectively. However, a bald statement such as this could theoretically be applied also to the central government situation and would tend to obliterate the realities of the situation.

20. The Bains Report. (*See* also XVII, **19–25**.) The Bains Working Group on Local Authority Management Structure reported in 1972, and most of the local authorities established on reorganisation in 1974 have accepted its proposals to a substantial extent. In essence its recommendations were based on the desirability of developing a Corporate Management approach in local government. In broad terms its main proposals may be summarised as follows.

(*a*) *Member structure.* On the member side it recommended a rationalisation of the committee structure, away from the concept of service committees and into programme committees dealing with related functions of the authority. At the apex of the committee structure there is now universally a policy and resources committee which sets the main strategic pattern for the local authority, though final policy decisions rest with the council. The policy and resources committee is supported by four subcommittees, namely land, personnel, finance, and performance review.

(*b*) *Officer structure.* The Bains Report did not advocate extensive reorganisation of the departmental structure, and indeed local authorities have proved resistant to suggestions of this nature. However the Report suggested, and this has generally been adopted, that co-ordination of policy on the officer side should be achieved through a system to some extent mirroring the member structure, viz. an officer's management team presided over by a non-departmental executive officer.

The creation of the post of Chief Executive has, by placing in the hands of a single official, responsibility for all aspects of an authority's work, perhaps shifted the balance of power between councillors and officials further towards the officials.

PROGRESS TEST 5

1. Compare the meanings of policy and administration.   (**1, 2**)

2. What do you understand by policy-making?   (**3, 4, 7**)

3. Comment on the hierarchical theory of policy-making.   (**5, 6**)

4. Comment on the respective positions of the minister and civil servants in policy-making.   (**9–13**)

5. What are the functions of the Central Policy Review Staff. (**16**)

6. Outline the policy-making process in local government. (**17–19**)

7. What were the main organisational recommendations of the Bains Report?   (**20**)

CHAPTER VI

The Civil Service

INTRODUCTION

1. Definition. The civil service was defined by the Tomlin Commission as "those servants of the Crown, other than political or judicial office holders, who are employed in a civil capacity, and whose remuneration is paid out of money provided by Parliament".

2. Some underlying concepts. Any appraisal of the problems confronting the civil service must bear in mind the following points.

(*a*) Despite criticisms of organisation, selection and power, the civil service has an unparalleled achievement of impartiality, integrity and incorruptibility.

(*b*) The civil service is not on an exact parallel with organisations in the private sector and the tradition of political accountability and responsibility of political heads of departments necessarily results in a greater degree of bureaucratic procedure than might otherwise prevail. This manifests itself in a reluctance to delegate and consequent centralisation of decision-taking functions, in excessive and repeated checking of procedures and actions at lower levels and in a tendency to elevate the importance of maintaining the status quo.

(*c*) Considerable effective policy-making power lies with the civil service (*see* V) and any discussion of the defects in the service must not be allowed to hide behind the practices of anonymity and ministerial responsibility.

(*d*) In the existing context of public administration the civil service must be judged as a management organisation and its effectiveness assessed as far as possible on principles which would be applied to management organisations, subject, however, to allowance for the constraints to which public administration is subject (*see* III).

3. Requirements of the civil service. The Fulton Committee stated the requirements of civil servants under modern conditions to be:

(*a*) practical judgment and negotiating skill;
(*b*) knowledge of economic and industrial factors;
(*c*) numerate skill;
(*d*) professionalism.

NOTE: The Committee distinguished as follows between the two types of "professionalism" in the context of the civil service. (1) Specialism in the professional capacity sense. The Committee considered that the civil service had been consistently neglectful of this, and in particular had failed to give specialists the equivalent status and responsibilities they would have enjoyed in private business, particularly by the policy of organising specialists in separate hierarchies and by reserving policy and financial control to generalist administrators. It will be seen that the English Committee (*see* **26–27**) took the attitude that in 1977 this problem had not been adequately overcome. (2) Professionalism among generalists in the sense that generalist administrators tended to lack expertise in any particular area, and that this consequently inhibited effective policy-making, prevented fundamental policy evaluation, and led to inadequate relationships with outside organisations.

HISTORICAL DEVELOPMENT

4. The Northcote–Trevelyan Report 1854. The *Report on Organisation of the Permanent Civil Service* was of great importance in establishing the underlying principles of the civil service until the post-Fulton Committee reforms in the late 1960s to early 1970s. Until this latter period the civil service was largely anchored by the Northcote–Trevelyan concepts of career service and predominance of the generalist, despite the fact that fundamental changes had taken place in the nature of government since 1854, and in particular:

(*a*) the change from passive regulation to active participation;
(*b*) the development of new decision-making techniques;
(*c*) rapid technological progress;
(*d*) the blurring of public and private sector functions;
(*e*) the extension of the decision-making time factor through complexity, etc.;
(*f*) increasing international involvement.

5. Defects prior to Fulton. The Fulton Committee was appointed in 1966 to "examine the structure, recruitment and management, including training, of the Home Civil Service, and to make recommendations". Stated briefly the major deficiencies found by the Committee were:

(a) the overriding predominance of the generalist philosophy;
(b) the work-impeding factors of the class system;
(c) lack of opportunities, responsibilities and authority given to specialist groupings;
(d) inadequacy of the use of skilled managers;
(e) inadequacy of contact between the service and the public;
(f) inadequate personnel management.

6. The Fulton Committee recommendations. These may be examined in outline under the classifications of:

(a) recruitment and training;
(b) mobility and career service;
(c) the structure of departments;
(d) the structure of the overall service;
(e) the central management of the civil service;
(f) the civil service and the community.

7. Recruitment and training. The principal recommendations of the Committee were:

(a) the integration of responsibilities for recruitment and training;
(b) the establishment of a new Civil Service Department;
(c) recruitment should be for a specific function;
(d) more emphasis on recruitment by departments involved;
(e) the establishment of a civil service college.

8. Mobility and career service. The Committee were anxious to preserve the career service nature of the civil service and they felt it led to a professional and experienced service; it encouraged loyalty; and it led to less constraints on giving forthright and impartial opinions. The Committee however recommended that:

(a) advantages would accrue from temporary and short-term appointments and from an interchange of staff with industry and commerce;
(b) there should be greater consideration given to facilitating movements into and out of the service.

9. Departmental structure. The Committee considered that the common organisational need of defining responsibility and decision-making authority in the civil service was difficult as decisions invariably had to be referred for confirmation to an unnecessarily high level, and that delegation was difficult due to decisions often overlapping departments. Nonetheless they recommended that:

(*a*) accountable management should be established in order to identify parts of an organisation to which cost and other performance measurement might be applied;

(*b*) high-level management services and techniques should be applied;

(*c*) long-term planning and research units should be established and these should be responsible for the identification and study of long-term problems; suggesting appropriate policies; and relating short-term decisions to future developments.

10. Civil service structure. The Committee considered that the defects in the then existing structure were that the class system was invalid; the occupational divisions between separate divisions and specialisms caused strain; the structure prevented the most efficient use of staff; the structure led to the inefficient organisation of work; effective job analysis was inhibited; and accountable management was made difficult. In response to these criticisms the Committee made two fundamental proposals for change.

(*a*) Class divisions should be abolished and a continuous grading structure substituted for each occupational group.

(*b*) The best man for the job must apply to the civil service irrespective of occupational groupings or educational qualifications.

NOTE: These recommendations implied the need for a unified classless structure. A number of successive grading levels embracing all jobs in the service was required, and the salary range in each grade should be relatively broad and overlapping between grades.

11. Central management of the civil service. Prior to Fulton the Treasury was responsible for the central management of the service. This function was discharged through the Pay and Management Group. This, however, was never a fully developed body with overall management responsibility, e.g. recruitment was shared with the Civil Service Commission, and responsibility for personnel management and management services tended to be more advisory than directive.

Consequently the Fulton Committee recommended that two major institutional changes were required.

(a) Responsibility for recruitment, selection and other functions of central management should be brought together in a single department.

(b) The expanded and unified management functions should be made the responsibility of a new department created specifically for that purpose, particularly as central management is not an appropriate function for a central finance department such as the Treasury.

12. The civil service and the community. The Committee advocated greater participation in the decision-making process; that civil service anonymity was no longer a valid principle; and on a broader scale that Ministers should become more involved in the decision-making process, e.g. by the use of personal appointments and senior policy advisers.

THE PRESENT STRUCTURE

13. The Civil Service Department (CSD). The CSD was established post-Fulton to take over the Treasury's responsibilities. The PM was in direct control, though most responsibility was taken by another Cabinet minister, the leader of the House of Lords. After thirteen years of operation the Government decided to abolish the CSD and to divide its functions between the Treasury and a Management and Personnel Office (MPO) within the Cabinet Secretariat structure. The reasoning behind the abolition was that the separation of manpower planning and central control of financial resources caused problems, particularly at a time when the Government was committed to reducing civil service numbers and expenditure.

Fulton principles were still recognised as valid in this reorganisation and it is important to appreciate that control does not lie exclusively with the Treasury. The division of responsibilities is:

(a) *The Management and Personnel Office.* This is formally headed by the PM as Minister for the Civil Service with the Chancellor of the Duchy of Lancaster (Leader of the House of Lords) effectively the Minister of State. The Cabinet Secretary serves as Permanent Secretary. The functions of the MPO include:

(i) management systems and organisation;

(ii) the "Rayner" efficiency unit (since 1983 under a permanent civil servant);

(*iii*) cost-cutting studies;

(*iv*) personnel management;

(*v*) Civil Service College;

(*vi*) Civil Service conduct and security;

(*vii*) Civil Service Commission, whose commissioners retain their traditional independence over selection.

(*b*) *The Treasury*. In the reorganisation, a Minister of State's post was transferred from the CSD to take the day-to-day responsibility for those Civil Service functions returned to the Chancellor of the Exchequer. The civil service functions of the Treasury include:

(*i*) manpower numbers;

(*ii*) remuneration;

(*iii*) conditions of service;

(*iv*) The Central Computer and Telecommunications Agency.

The Civil Service is now jointly headed by the Secretary to the Cabinet and the Treasury Permanent Secretary.

This reorganisation is typical of many—changes are made to solve problems as they are identified, i.e. it reflects the need for a more independent, management-oriented approach to controlling the Civil Service. The change led to further problems, e.g. the divorce between manpower planning and financial control. The result was a further compromise change: Treasury influence was reintroduced but the key policy development and planning functions were retained under the PM within the Cabinet Office.

14. Staffing structure. There are nearly three-quarters of a million civil servants in the United Kingdom employed in a great variety of tasks. The *administrative group* of about 250,000 provides the administrative, executive and clerical services that dominate the central departments. Figure 4 shows the promotion structure of the administrative group. Since 1971 there has been a single promotional ladder, whereas before there were three distinct "classes" —administrative, executive and clerical—and movement across the class barriers was difficult and unusual. There remain, however, different points of entry into the system that coincide with the entry points for the old classes.

15. The higher civil service. There are about 600 civil servants of the rank of permanent secretary, deputy secretary, under-secretary or equivalent who are referred to as the higher civil service. Their appointment and promotion is monitored directly by the head of the Civil Service and the Prime Minister. The fact that there are

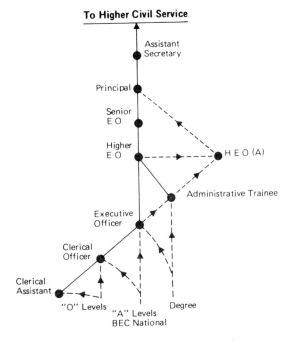

FIG. 3   *Entry qualifications and promotional routes in the*
Administrative Group of the Civil Service.

approximately 3,500 civil servants of assistant secretary or equivalent grade indicates the difficulty of breaking into the higher
group.

The creation of a unified administration group presented a recruitment problem in that high-quality applicants might well have
been deterred by the prospect of having to work their way slowly
upward through the ranks. Thus a "fast-stream" promotion channel was created—the Higher Executive Officer (A) grade. HEO (A)
posts are designated in sections and departments where the holder
of the post gets a broad picture of the work of the department
or the civil service as a whole. Such posts might well exist in
minister's private offices, the Cabinet secretariat or at other key
policy-making positions in the system. Successful holders of HEO
(A) posts can expect to move directly to principal at a relatively
early age. Balancing the numbers of principals appointed from
SEO and HEO (A) posts remains a constant manpower planning
problem and is kept under continuous review.

16. Departmental classes. These consist of certain officers carrying out functions, although of a similar level to that performed by the administration group, are of a comparatively specialist nature, e.g. customs officials and tax inspectors.

17. Scientific and specialist groups. These groups consist of civil servants with technical and professional qualifications and functions, e.g. scientists, engineers, architects, statisticians and data programmers. The Fulton intention of integrating these into the mainstream is by no means achieved as yet.

18. Allocation of functions. Although the civil service is now "classless" an examination of the functions of the old classes gives some indication of the type of work carried out at particular levels in the civil service.

(*a*) The *administrative* class which now corresponds broadly with the top of the administration group, and with under undersecretaries and above, though predominantly with the latter, was concerned broadly with the exercise of financial control over departmental work, the development, setting out and execution of government policy, and with what might generally be described as "management functions".

(*b*) The old *executive* class was principally responsible for the more important work of supply and accounting departments, for casework, and for matters of internal organisation and control. In addition executive officers were concerned with the supervision and management of large blocks of clerical work, the management of local and regional offices, and such important matters as government accounting, contract negotiation, organisation and method work, and automatic data processing.

(*c*) The *clerical* class was concerned essentially with the performance of routine day-to-day functions.

PARTICULAR PROBLEM AREAS

19. Weakness of line management functions. The "line manager" in the civil service is subject to the following constraints which would be very rare in a commercial or industrial undertaking.

(*a*) *Motivational constraints.* Unlike the line manager in a non-public administration context, the line manager in the civil service is deprived of many of the motivational incentives and sanctions normally associated with his post, e.g. he does not have powers to hire and fire, to award bonuses, to promote, etc. The only "establishment" type function he can exercise is in respect of the annual employee report which again is modified in effect as a result of the civil service convention of "fair play".

(b) *Financial control weaknesses.* Where financial authority is delegated to persons in line management situations such persons are subject to constraints imposed by central management functions. This results in excessive caution, reference of decisions to the highest level to guarantee support for decisions and excessive detailing of decisions.

(c) *Management control and techniques.* The concept of management control in the civil service is given limited interpretation. Unlike an industrial manager, who may be responsible for the organisation and cost effectiveness therein, the civil service manager exercises a passive role in controlling costs based on a public accountability for expenditure basis, rather than a positive approach of using management techniques to improve departmental efficiency. There is comparatively little encouragement in the system to express quantitatively required standards of achievement.

20. The specialist-versus-generalist controversy. Although the controversy is somewhat mitigated in respect of the civil service as a result of the Fulton Report it still merits serious consideration in that:

(a) the English Committee Report (*see* **26–27**) suggests that the higher posts in the civil service are still filled by generalist administrators, and there is still a bias in recruitment in this direction;

(b) the controversy goes beyond the civil service and may be seen as having broad application in public administration, particularly in the local government service.

21. The theory. The theory of the preference for the generalist administrator is that their broad academic background effectively enables them to reflect the views of their political head, who in turn is non-specialist, and that, by virtue of their in-service training, they are able to deal with a wide range of matters.

22. The case for the administrator. The following points should be noted.

(a) The "administrative function" it is claimed does not depend on the possession of particularised technical expertise. "Since administrative decisions are never of the same character as technical decisions, the technical expert does not in principle have any merits over other persons as a performer of the administrative function" (Paul Meyer, *Administrative Organisation*).

(*b*) The specialist is likely to give undue weight to technical considerations.

(*c*) Specialists have a greater tendency to ride "hobby-horses".

(*d*) The view was expressed in the Northcote–Trevelyan Report, that men who have followed no formal technical education or who have exercised no specific business background "will generally be found in business of every profession superior ... to those devoted to the special studies of their calling".

23. The case for the specialist. The following points should be noted.

(*a*) The concept of the "administrative" function (*see* **24**) tends to underestimate the considerable technical element that may be contained in what is superficially considered to be a purely administrative decision.

(*b*) Technical knowledge may often prove more important than mere administrative skill alone.

(*c*) There is no reason, as illustrated by the experience of the French Civil Service (*see* **28–32** below) to assume that a specialist is incapable of acquiring administrative techniques.

(*d*) There has been a failure of generalists to identify the key long-term problems of administration.

(*e*) Administrative skill nowadays is in fact a specialist matter involving the application of sophisticated management techniques, and thus, of itself, requiring specialised training and experience.

24. Is there an "administrative function"? As seen above a key element in the generalist case has been the ability to identify a separate administrative function. Essentially the case for reserving the higher policy-making and control positions for generalist administrators rests upon the presuppositions of the existence of this separate function. This has been defined as the "bringing together of the disparate issues involved in taking major decisions of policy, advising on what the decisions should be, and subsequently putting them into effect" (evidence of First Division Association to the Fulton Committee). British practice has consequently been to evolve a false distinction between administration and management to the detriment of the management role. This view of administration as an art rather than a science leads to the relative disrespect for management control and operational techniques.

25. The civil service and economic policy-making. Economic policy-making at the official level is the result of the combined efforts of various officials, namely, administrators, economic advisers, and administrators who are at the same time economists. In practice, however, because of numerical and hierarchical factors, there has tended to be a concentration of authority in this field in the hands of the generalist administrators compared with the authority wielded by the "irregulars", i.e. the professional economists. Despite the drafting into the civil service of large numbers of economists, particularly during the Labour administration of 1964–70, mistakes were made which prevented the redress of the balance in favour of the professionals, and this position still applies to a considerable extent despite the recommendations of the Fulton Committee.

(*a*) The specialist economists were spread too thinly between departments, and generally too low in the administrative hierarchy to give them either collective or individual authority.

(*b*) The tendency still remains to leave generalist administrators in the final decision-making position in the hierarchy.

(*c*) Considerable importance was still attached to the non-economist lobbies.

THE ENGLISH COMMITTEE REPORT

26. The English Committee. The English Committee, technically part of the House of Commons Expenditure Committee, mounted in 1977 the first proper and independent inquiry into how the civil service had implemented the reforms thought essential by the Fulton Committee. Its report (the Eleventh Report of the Expenditure Committee) was highly critical and in general terms it considered that the Civil Service had failed to implement the major recommended reforms (*see* also **33–36** below). The report was significant in that it represented the first investigation into the public service by a parliamentary, as distinct from governmental, committee for 104 years.

27. The main recommendations.

(*a*) Responsibility for efficiency and manpower requirements of the service should be returned from the Civil Service Department to the Treasury. The basic reason for this view was that, in the Committee's opinion, there had occurred an indefensible separation of control over public service expenditure, exercised by the Treasury, from responsibility for efficiency and manpower requirements, exercised by the Civil Service Department.

(b) Parliamentary committees should be established specifically related to departments and manned by back-benchers.

(c) The doctrine of ministerial responsibility should be relaxed with reference to accountable units so that civil servants could be publicly accountable for management, but not political, decisions.

(d) The present limit on ministerial advisers of two per Cabinet member should be scrapped and the ministers should be free to adopt any organisation they think fit.

Parliamentary committees are often critical of the civil service; the 1980 report of the Treasury and Civil Service Committee provided evidence relating to civil service pay increases that strengthened the resolve of the government to resist pay claims made by the civil service staff association in 1981.

A COMPARISON WITH THE FRENCH CIVIL SERVICE

28. Background. In considering the significance of differences in organisation and operation between the two civil services the following background points must be borne in mind.

(a) The two civil services had developed against different concepts of the role of the state; namely, the British civil service developed during the period of *laissez-faire* and the "nightwatchman" theory of the role of the state, whereas the French civil service developed in a state where there has been for a considerable period marked emphasis on state intervention on a wide scale.

(b) The French system of government involves considerable administrative de-concentration, including the running of what in Britain would be considered local government services and consequently involves considerable functional specialisation and expertise.

(c) French higher education is more career-orientated than the British system. The use of civil service schools and specialised post-entry training in schools attached to ministries results in the training of the French specialist classes taking place outside the traditional university system.

(d) France has never experienced or encouraged the separation between careers in public administration, business management and technology which is found in Britain.

(*e*) The policy of the French technical schools is from the outset to recognise the need for the training of specialists to encompass both technical and administrative training.

29. The use of specialists. The French civil service places predominant reliance on prescribed qualifications. These qualifications in specialists take the form, however, of civil service rather than professional body qualifications as in the British specialist classes. In addition, in France most *corps* (*see* **32**(*b*)) are truly departmental and specialise and carry responsibility for specific areas of departmental work. However, French specialists are regarded as both technical personnel and potential administrators and both technical and administrative *corps* members may be promoted to administrative positions.

The reliance within France upon examination performance to select senior staff in many areas other than the civil service is thought by many to create a much more coherent élite of senior policy-makers including politicians. This is not to say that there is a perfect administrative system free from the problems of bureaucracy, and recently a minister responsible for administrative reform has been appointed.

30. Structure of the service. The French civil service is structured in the following ways.

(*a*) *Classes.* The service is horizontally divided into four classes, based essentially on educational background, which deal with broad functions, e.g. Category A deals with "policy and direction". Promotion barriers exist both between and within classes, e.g. between the divisions of Category A into higher and secondary *corps*.

(*b*) *Corps.* All civil servants are appointed to *corps* within which their particular careers lie. In comparison, classes have relatively little importance. *Corps* have been defined as groups of civil servants governed by the same regulations and qualifications for the same grades. Each *corps* is a watertight unit.

(*c*) *Services.* These represent the vertical divisions of the civil service. A service consists of a series of vertically related *corps*, and results in the unification of policy-making and field services through the top management sections in Paris.

(*d*) *Grades.* These exist within each *corps*.

31. Recruitment and promotion. Recruitment is generally based on examinations and little emphasis is placed on character, proven ability, etc. In the technical *corps*, examinations are usually theoretical in order to test intellectual ability. Recruitment to the *corps* in Class A requires admission to post-entry schools, i.e. the National School of Administration or the École Polytechnique, and graduation from these.

Promotion is by "objective" examination procedures to the higher *corps*. Within *corps*, promotion is usually by seniority, though at the higher grade level procedures are more formalised.

32. Conclusion. The following characteristics of the French civil service may be identified:

(*a*) career orientation;

(*b*) allegiance to *corps* rather than to the service;

(*c*) use of specialists as administrators (*see* **29** above);

(*d*) little distinction between technical and advisory functions;

(*e*) fluid movement in and out of the service, particularly in the higher *corps*.

IMPLEMENTATION OF THE FULTON PROPOSALS

33. Government White Paper. The English Committee was very critical of the extent to which the Fulton proposals had been implemented (*see* **26–27** above). Subsequent inquiries have been less pessimistic than the English Committee about the degree of implementation of Fulton. The Fulton Committee reforms essentially centred on the concept of professionalism, the need to overhaul recruitment, and the need to create greater opportunities for non-graduates and specialists. Recently concern has been about the overall size of the Civil Service rather than structure and operation.

The White Paper stated that "the acceptance of Fulton resulted in a number of radical changes in the organisation and management of the civil service". On the other hand Lord Crowther Hunt commented "in general, the civil service has implemented those parts of Fulton it liked and which added to its power, and failed to implement the ideas that would have made it more professional, and more accountable to Parliament and the public". It is thus necessary to attempt an assessment of these conflicting views.

34. Quantifiable results.

(*a*) *Civil service should be less "Oxbridge" dominated.* In fact the "Oxbridge" graduates as a proportion of external recruits to the administrative grade marginally increased during the decade following the report.

NOTE: It is also clear that where recruitment is from other universities it fails to reflect the composition of such universities, being heavily weighted in favour of those with a public school background.

(b) *Civil service intake to be less dominated by arts graduates.* Arts graduates as a proportion of recruits to the administrative grades only decreased from 59 per cent (1966–68) to 56 per cent (1975–77).

(c) *More specialists should get top jobs.* The background of under-secretaries and above was in the proportion 62:38 per cent, generalists to specialists, in 1970, and in 1978 had only changed to 59:41 per cent.

(d) *More qualified accountants in the civil service.* The number of qualified accountants had only increased from 309 in 1967 to 367 in 1978.

(e) *Substantial exchange of staff with industry and local government.* The mumber of civil servants seconded to industry, commerce and local government had increased from twelve in 1968 to twenty-five in 1975.

35. Comments on the statistics.

(a) The apparent biases in recruitment of élite administrators were still as evident as ever.

(b) The hold of generalists on the 800 most senior jobs at under-secretary level and above was still maintained.

(c) The number of accountants, although growing in absolute numbers, was growing less slowly than the civil service as a whole.

(d) The flow of civil servants to commerce and industry on secondment was misleading. The White Paper pointed out that "the rise in these figures ... indicates an improvement in data flow from the departments rather than a real increase in activity". Even allowing for this the figures involved were extremely low in relation to the total number of civil servants employed.

36. The English Committee. The committee stressed in particular the need for:

(a) more professionalism;

(b) a complete overhaul of administrative training;

(c) greater control over Whitehall by ministers and by Parliament.

37. Defects in the White Paper. The crucial criticism of the White Paper was that it totally failed to respond to many of the major issues raised by the English Committee, in particular, the following.

(*a*) *Recruitment.* No response appeared to the English Committee's comment that "it looks as if the Civil Service Commission not only reinforces an Oxford and Cambridge bias, but (even where it does take from other universities, tends to prefer public school boys) and so also creates a bias which either does not exist in other universities or is much smaller there".

(*b*) *A classless civil service.* The Wilson Government accepted the Fulton recommendation that all barriers to career progress in the civil service should be scrapped and a "unified grading structure" created. However unified grading had only so far been applied to the 800 senior civil service posts. The Committee commented that "for reasons that are not very clear, progress on this ceased in October 1975. Incomes policy was given as one reason but does not seem to be wholly relevant and another reason given that it would take the time of staff inspectors, seems merely to mean that this matter is given no priority."

(*c*) *Professional accountants.* "The Fulton recommendation on the employment of accountants on an increasing scale in the civil service does not seem to have had much effect".

(*d*) *Cash limits.* These "render the present division of responsibility between the Treasury and the Civil Service Department obsolete; by investing the Treasury with an interest in the efficiency of departments, they destroy the 'raison d'etre' for a second department which is also concerned with efficiency".

(*e*) *Ministerial power.* "Many departments are large and it is not difficult to push forward policies without a Minister's knowledge ... further it is often said to be extremely difficult to launch a new policy initiative which is not to the liking of the Department ... there seems to us to be no justification for any of these practices".

PROGRESS TEST 6

1. What is meant by "professionalism" in the context of the civil service? (**3**)

2. Outline the changes in government which affected the role of the civil service between 1854 and the Report of the Fulton Committee. (**4**)

3. What did the Fulton Committee consider to be the main defects in the civil service? **(5)**

4. Outline the main recommendations of the Fulton Committee. **(6–12)**

5. What is the role of the Civil Service Department? **(13)**

6. How has the staffing structure of the civil service altered since the Report of the Fulton Committee? **(14–17)**

7. What are the main constraints imposed on a "line manager" in the civil service? **(19)**

8. Compare the cases for the generalist administrator and the specialist in the civil service. **(20–24)**

9. What were the main recommendations in the English Committee Report? **(26–27)**

10. Compare the structure of the British civil service with that of the French civil service. **(28–32)**

11. To what extent have the main recommendations of the Fulton Committee not been implemented? **(33–35)**

12. Outline the defects in the 1978 White Paper on Civil Service Reform. **(37)**

CHAPTER VII

Bureaucracy

CHARACTERISTICS OF BUREAUCRACY

1. A definition of bureaucracy. The difficulty in arriving at an adequate definition of bureaucracy is the necessary elimination of certain derogatory or subjective and emotive descriptions. Various meanings which have been given to the term include the following.

(*a*) *Institutional meaning.* The term "bureaucracy" may refer to government by officials as opposed to government by elected representatives. Alternatively, it may be used to indicate that, although representative government exists, the dominant role is held by the officials. These definitions, however, tend to be inadequate in that they fail to distinguish those common situations where government consists of a combination of elected and non-elected members and officials.

(*b*) *Activity of officials.* In contrast a definition may be attempted from the aspect of what officials do or how they behave. In this respect the following interpretations exist.

(*i*) *Derogatory.* The synonymous use of "bureaucracy" and "red tape", resulting from the real and supposed difficulties of dealing with the official environment.

(*ii*) *Regulated system.* A regulated administrative system operating through complex interrelated organs.

(*iii*) *Methodological.* A study of methods based on either (*i*) or (*ii*) above.

For the purpose of this chapter the definition at (*b*)(*ii*) above as a regulated system will be adopted. This is due to its objective and analytical nature, the other definitions being associated with subjective or disparaging overtones. Bureaucracy is thus conceived of as a form of organisation.

2. Weber's definition of bureaucracy. Max Weber, the German sociologist, principally developed the organisational definition of bureaucracy, and conceived of the concept in two aspects, namely:

(*a*) the social mechanism that maximises efficiency in administration;

(*b*) a form of social organisation with specific characteristics. Peter M. Blau has described this social organisation as "institutionalised strategies for the achievement of administrative objectives by the concerted efforts of many officials" (*Bureaucracy in Modern Society*, Random House).

3. Weber's characteristics of bureaucracy. Weber specified the following characteristics or conditions that an organisation must possess before properly being called a bureaucracy.

(*a*) The regular activities required for the purpose of the structure are distributed in fixed ways as official duties.

(*b*) Specified spheres of competence have been marked off as part of a systematic division of labour.

(*c*) The official is subject to strict and systematic discipline and control in the conduct of his office.

(*d*) All operations are governed by a consistent system of abstract rules.

(*e*) There is consistency in the application of the rules to specific cases.

(*f*) The organisation of offices follows the principles of hierarchy, i.e. each lower office is under the control and supervision of a higher one.

(*g*) Officials are subject to authority only with respect to their impersonal official obligations.

(*h*) Candidates are selected on the basis of technical qualifications. In the most rational cases this will be tested by examinations, or guaranteed by diplomas certifying technical competence, etc.

(*i*) Being a bureaucratic official constitutes a career, and there is a system of promotion according to seniority or merit, or both.

4. Weber's conclusions. Weber concluded that a fully developed bureaucracy has the advantages of speed, precision, unambiguity, continuity, discretion, unity, strict subordination, and reduction of friction and of material and personal costs. He considered that its specific nature develops more perfectly the more it is dehumanised, i.e. "the more completely it succeeds in eliminating from official business all purely personal, irrational, and emotional elements which escape calculation".

The organisation conceived by Weber is therefore designed to achieve a rational orientation towards tasks which are conducive to efficient administration.

5. Etzioni's view. Etzioni considered that organisations are characterised by the following:

(*a*) division of labour, of power, and of communication responsibilities, such divisions being deliberately planned to achieve certain goals;

(*b*) the presence of power centres which control the concentrated effort of the organisation and continuously review its performance and repattern its structure, where necessary, to increase its efficiency;

(*c*) the classification of personnel.

This view is based on Weber's classical view of bureaucracy.

BUREAUCRATIC PROCEDURE

6. Nature. Bureaucratic procedure dictates a course of action governed by a prescribed set of rules, in order to achieve uniformity. Such rules are abstract in order to guide the different courses of action necessary for the accomplishment of the organisation's objectives in diverse conditions. The rules become more detailed at the lower points in the organisation's hierarchy, though at the point of execution modification may be necessary in the interests of administrative efficiency.

7. Modification. This involves modifying procedures to focus them on their intended objectives and on existing conditions. Such modification may be induced by internal or external factors and may involve the following.

(*a*) *Redefinition.* The sacrifice of one objective of procedure in order to achive another more effectively.

(*b*) *Amplification.* The redirection of operations towards objectives which are in danger of neglect.

NOTE: Modification gives bureaucracy a dynamic aspect and enables an organisation to serve the needs it was created to serve.

8. "Sine ira et studio." Weber stated that bureaucratic officials will approach the public "in a spirit of formalistic impersonality without hatred or passion, and hence without affection or enthusiasm". He conceived of this requirement as intended to assure equitable treatment of clients, and rational rather than emotionally dominated administration.

In practice, however, this approach is not always operable as demonstrated by Blau in his research on the treatment of Negro clients by US agencies. However, personal motives and prejudices may largely be eliminated by an evaluation system of focusing interest, e.g. by statistical records.

THE CASE AGAINST BUREAUCRACY

9. Nature of the case. The principles of the case against bureaucracy stem from its supposed mechanistic nature, i.e. its regimentation and predictability. Thus, in essence, the very advantages claimed by Weber are turned against bureaucracy by its critics.

10. Disadvantages of bureaucracy. The following points should be noted.

(*a*) Men in bureaucracy fulfil merely segmental roles over which they have no control.

(*b*) In consequence, they have little or no opportunity to exercise individual judgment, with the result that an employee feels separated from his work.

(*c*) In order to be effective, bureaucratic personnel must behave consistently and follow regulations strictly. This automatically limits a bureaucrat's capacity to adapt to changing circumstances not envisaged by those who drew up the rules.

(*d*) The general rules which may make for overall efficiency produce inefficiency and injustice in individual cases.

(*e*) The impersonal treatment of clients envisaged by Weber has harmful effects *vis-à-vis* such clients.

(*f*) Weber's view that bureaucrats should not become closely involved in personal relations with colleagues has undesirable practical effects and according to research carried out by Blau (*The Dynamics of Bureaucracy*, University of Chicago Press, 1955), the "ritualistic" behaviour of bureaucrats stems more from the instability of established social relationships within the organisation than from over-identification with rules.

(*g*) The key limit on the efficiency of bureaucratic administration lies in the difficulty of coping with uncertainty and change. Bureaucracy thus rests upon tasks being convertible into routine. Blau has pointed out, however, that unfavourable conditions of operation may in fact generate favourable attitudes to change.

"Nobody can at the same time be a correct bureaucrat and an innovator. Progress is precisely that which the rules and regulations did not foresee; it is necessarily outside the field of bureaucratic activities." (Von Mises)

NOTE: Blau (*see* (*f*) above) considered that a categorical statement as to the antipathy between bureaucracy and innovation was not justified. He found that bureaucratic operations can be instrumental in promoting social change, but that a member of the bureaucracy is not capable of changing procedures on his individual initiative.

11. Chester I. Barnard's view. Chester Barnard criticised Weber for failing to analyse and compare the correspondence of behaviour in organisations with organisational blueprints. In particular he failed to account for the fact that in the course of operations new elements arise in the structure which will effectively influence subsequent operations. Such "informal organisations" were considered by Barnard to be necessary to the operation of formal organisations as means of communication, cohesion, etc.

12. The failure of bureaucracy. Warren G. Bennis (*The Functions of the Executive*, Harvard University Press, 1938) considered that bureaucracy no longer works, and advanced the following reasons.

(*a*) It suffices only for simple tasks under simple conditions. In existing conditions of change Bennis considers that "survival is dependent on the institutionalisation of perpetual change ... and democracy becomes necessary".

(*b*) Change is accelerated by the growth of science, research and development activities, and intellectual technology. In addition the increase in transactions with social institutions, e.g. trade unions, has a profound influence and militates against the conditions suitable for the effective working of bureaucracy (i.e. stable conditions of environment are displaced).

(*c*) Formal education of employees alienates them from bureaucracy. In particular, hierarchy and bureaucracy are anathema to the professional. In addition a scientific attitude can only flourish in a democratic environment.

NOTE: Bennis considered that future organisations will tend to consist of temporary project teams to solve specific problems, with executives functioning as co-ordinators rather than as hierarchial supervisors.

13. Personal factors. A further disadvantage of bureaucracy is that personal factors associated with it tend to reinforce reaction against change. In particular, the following should be noted.

(*a*) An organisation set up to achieve change may have its objectives compromised by administrators in the organisation if the achievement of such objectives tends to threaten their tenure or the overall stability of the organisation.

(*b*) Identification with existing bureaucratic apparatus creates a tendency to sanctify procedures, and thus to resist changes in them even though conditions may call for such adjustment.

BUREAUCRACY AND PUBLIC ADMINISTRATION

14. Public administration as a large-scale organisation. Initially, it is important not to confuse defects in bureaucracy with defects in large-scale organisation. Defects in co-ordination and organisation inherent in large-scale organisations may apply whether the organisation is bureaucratic or not. In addition, criticisms of complexity of organisation, the subordination of the individual, conformity, and the stifling of initiative must be accepted as applicable to most large-scale organisations and not merely as characteristic of bureaucracy.

15. Efficient public administration. The more disadvantageous effects of public administration may be diminished by the presence of certain features:

(*a*) effective external political control;
(*b*) flexibility of organisation;
(*c*) good leadership and management;
(*d*) maximum internal delegation;
(*e*) just personnel management;
(*f*) maximum internal co-operation;
(*g*) continuous review of, and research into, objectives, methods and results;
(*h*) a professional morale antipathetic to bureaucratic methods;
(*i*) effective publicity;
(*j*) widespread outside understanding.

16. The civil service and bureaucracy. The civil service has been accused of containing a "bureaucratic, hierarchically organised, and tightly knit élite" (A. M. Hanson and M. Walles, *Governing Britain*, Fontana, 1973). On the other hand, it has been stated that bureaucracy is a means of institutionalising clear, universal and impartial procedures for the administration of authority ... infinitely preferable to most of its historical alternatives". What must therefore be considered is the extent to which the British civil service combines the more preferable aspects of bureaucracy with subjugation of the more harmful aspects. In this respect two important aspects must be borne in mind as background, rendered all the more important in industrial society, namely:

(*a*) the administration of modern technology greatly magnifies the tasks of administrative bodies;

(*b*) the process of decision-making becomes increasingly technical as the amount of necessary information multiplies.

In order to determine the bureaucratic elements in the British civil service it is proposed to analyse its nature against Weber's principles, and then to consider it in the light of the principles of efficient public administration outlined above (*see* **17**).

17. Comparison with Weber's principles. Superficially, the British civil service accords with many of Weber's characteristics, yet close analysis reveals that in actual practice such accordance is not predominant. The following points should be noted.

(*a*) The civil service follows the principles of hierarchy with supervision and control of lower offices by higher ones. In practice this control tends to be less than real, with considerable independence of action delegated to individual civil servants, though often exclusively at higher levels.

(*b*) Selection of candidates on the ground of technical qualifications determined by examination, etc., has long been a cardinal principle of civil service entry, at least prior to interview stage. However, such entry has not been exclusively predetermined on the grounds of technical competence and qualifications.

(*c*) The systematic division of labour exists to a large extent and was typified in particular by the old class system and the strict division between specialist and generalist. However, within classes the regular rotation of staff (again largely administrative class) operated against this.

(*d*) The civil service constitutes a career for most officials, with little or no movement between the service and industry, as exists for example in the US civil service.

(*e*) Detailing of duties in specific form certainly exists at most executive levels and is particularly prevalent amongst lower grades.

(*f*) As has been explained in V, the policy-making function of higher civil servants is a marked departure from bureaucratic practice. However, this is limited to a comparative view of the very top ranks.

(*g*) The emphasis on public accountability contributes to bureaucratic procedure by enforcing double checking, reference to higher authority, etc.

18. Comparison with principles of efficiency. The consistency of the civil service with these principles is largely dealt with elsewhere in the book as follows:

(*a*) effective political control (*see* II);
(*b*) flexibility of organisation, etc. (*see* VI);
(*c*) effective publicity and outside understanding (*see* VI);
(*d*) leadership and management, etc. (*see* VI).

19. Conclusions. The bureaucratic tendencies in the British civil service are probably overestimated and exist more at lower grade levels, though of course this has effects resulting in public frustration.

A key to principles of efficient administration and reaction against bureaucratic tendencies lies in the adoption of the Fulton recommendations (*see* VI), which aim at increasing efficiency, enlarging external relations, minimising hierarchical tendencies, bettering personnel management, and generally increasing the flexibility and initiative of the service.

PROGRESS TEST

1. What is meant by "bureaucracy"?   (**1, 2**)
2. What did Weber consider to be the characteristics and advantages of bureaucracy?   (**3, 4**)
3. Outline the case against bureaucracy.   (**9–13**)
4. How far do you consider the civil service to be a bureaucracy?   (**16–18**)

CHAPTER VIII

Public Expenditure

INTRODUCTION

1. Definition. Public expenditure may be defined as all expenditure which has to be financed from taxation, national insurance contributions or government borrowing. It includes current and capital items of central and local government and loans to nationalised enterprises. In total public expenditure accounts for about 40 per cent of Gross Domestic Product and will exceed £100 billion during the year 1981–82. Public expenditure involves the Government in three basic tasks of administration:

(*a*) deciding what total should be planned, and how it should be allocated between programmes and parts of the public sector;

(*b*) controlling actual spending, so that outcome matches plan, and to fulfil the requirements of parliamentary control over public spending;

(*c*) arranging for actual expenditure to be prepared, audited and examined.

It is an integral part of democratic control that the finance of government is as much under public scrutiny as the acts of policy that lead to the spending. Thus control, particularly through the parliamentary system, is a key feature of the financial planning arrangements in the United Kingdom.

Public expenditure may be regarded from three main viewpoints.

(*a*) *Legal.* This involves ensuring that public expenditure is incurred only in respect of those matters for which there is express approval, and then only within specified limits.

(*b*) *Managerial.* This is the control aspect which consists of ensuring the efficient carrying out of policies and the elimination of the waste of public funds.

(*c*) *Strategic.* This means devoting resources to objectives that are most effective in reaching goals which have been predetermined after critical policy analysis.

2. Public expenditure and Parliament. The legal framework of parliamentary involvement consists of the following.

(*a*) Estimates of expenditure are presented to Parliament, and, where appropriate, supplementary estimates.

(*b*) Estimates are divided into "votes" in respect of particular items of expenditure, and all votes in particular fields are grouped together in "classes" of which there are twelve in all, e.g. defence estimates.

(*c*) Parliament theoretically scrutinises the votes, and at this point could exercise the managerial function. This, however, is in fact precluded by lack of time and the preference for treating Supply Days as occasions for debates on matters of general policy. In addition, votes are insufficiently detailed to allow effective exercise of this function.

(*d*) Votes, when approved, go into the Appropriation Act.

(*e*) The Appropriation Accounts are audited by the National Audit Office under the Comptroller and Auditor General who is now independent of the executive as a servant of Parliament (in the same way as the Parliamentary Commissioner).

(*f*) The report of the Public Accounts Committee completes the cycle.

NOTE: Although concern has been expressed at the perfunctory examination which the estimates receive it would appear that the procedure suits both government and opposition parties, as formal approval with minimum discussion permits concentration on political–capital-making aspects. In addition the House exercises more effective detailed control through the medium of its supporting committees.

CONTROL THROUGH COMMITTEE STRUCTURE

3. Introduction. The major reforms of control of finance exercised by Parliament are through the media of the Public Accounts Committee, and the new investigatory select committees, especially the Treasury and Civil Service Committee (*see* II).

4. The Public Accounts Committee. Although theoretically appointed to exercise the *legal* aspect of control, the Committee has, in recent years, concentrated more on the elimination of waste, the encouragement of sound practices in estimating, contracting and financial administration generally and the need to obtain value for money, e.g. the inquiry into and the subsequent repayment of excess profits in the Ferranti Case. Its *formal functions* are:

(*a*) to audit the accounts and to guard the procedures and priorities of control by Parliament;

(*b*) to act as an outside audit on the propriety and honesty of departments' operations.

5. Importance of the Committee. The Committee has achieved great esteem and effectiveness, although it has no executive power, and its examination of accounts is two years behind their presentation; it has been the most important Committee for controlling the executive for the following reasons.

(*a*) It has high political status being chaired traditionally by a senior Opposition chairman, currently Joel Barnett, former Chief Secretary to the Treasury.

(*b*) Its criticisms are highly respected in Whitehall, more from the aspect of their political repercussions than in the normal auditing sense, particularly as civil service reputations are seen as being at stake in appearances before the committee.

(*c*) It is essentially concerned with efficiency rather than strict legal control and is regarded as a major check on bureaucratic mismanagement.

(*d*) Its work has led to direct improvements in government procedures, e.g. the practice of development contracting in government departments was introduced and still operates as a result of the Committee's criticisms of the previous practice, in 1968, between Bristol Siddeley Engines and the Ministry of Aviation.

(*e*) Publicity attracted to its findings when large-scale overspending or other errors are revealed is a part of the discipline upon the government to maintain tight financial control to avoid such embarrassment.

6. Criticism. Despite its considerable authority and achievements the machinery of the Committee is not appropriate for checking the efficiency of departments and the avoidance of waste. This is essentially a responsibility which must lie with the departments themselves and with the Treasury. In addition it is often difficult to distinguish the role of the Public Accounts Committee from that of the Expenditure Committee and in fact both Committees have on occasions produced reports covering the same areas, e.g. the Expenditure Committee's Report on public investment in the private sector had shortly before been dealt with by the Public Accounts Committee.

EXPENDITURE COMMITTEES

7. Scrutiny of public expenditure and administration. To follow up the annual expenditure debate, the Select Committee on Procedure recommended that there should be instituted an Expenditure Committee empowered to effect more detailed scrutiny. The Committee, which was set up in early 1971, replaced the old Estimates Committee and has the power to investigate the whole field of public expenditure, unlike the Estimates Committee which was limited to that part specifically covered by the estimates. The work of the Committee has now been taken up by the new investigative Committees (*see* II and **10** below), which are charged with examining the expenditure, administration and policy of their respective departments and associated public bodies.

8. The development of control through select committees. The old Estimates Committee, although since 1971 is only of historical significance has certain points relating to its functioning which are worthy of mention. Implied in its formal terms of reference were the duties to determine whether administration was effective and economical, and critically to examine policy without challenging such policy. This seemingly contradictory latter point effectively meant that the Committee could ask whether the financial demands of policy were reasonable and if the policy was effectively being carried out, but not whether such policy was in fact initially justified. The Expenditure Committee is not subject to this limitation.

The main achievements in broad terms of the Committee were improved costing in departments; better use of management techniques, and the establishment of the Fulton Committee. The Committee however suffered from the following limitations:

(*a*) amateurism and a reluctance to introduce subject specialisation;

(*b*) lack of planning in approach to inquiries;

(*c*) absence of specialised support staff—the Public Accounts Committee (PAC) always commanded greater respect in the departments, being backed by the Exchequer and Audit departmental staff;

(*d*) inability to pinpoint individual responsibility as compared again with the PAC;

(*e*) failure to follow up because of inadequate staff;

(*f*) failure to develop means of commenting on the forward expenditure programmes of the government.

9. The Select Committee on Expenditure. As compared with the Estimates Committee which it replaced the following points of importance emerge.

(*a*) One of its functions was to examine the annual expenditure White Papers (*see* **13–16**), thus putting it in a position to elucidate information on gaps and other deficiencies in such White Papers, and to discourage further deficiencies.

(*b*) Whereas the Estimates Committee was limited by the annual nature of the estimates, the Expenditure Committee was able to examine forward projections of public expenditure, to question the basis of their preparation and to require justification by the departments of the priorities contained therein. It was thus a *policy* committee as opposed to the Estimates Committee.

The Committee worked by investigating the government's spending commitments rather than simply expenditure on the basis of annual departmental estimates. It operated through six sub-committees, one for general public expenditure, the others related to particular areas, for example trade and industry, defence and external affairs, and education and the arts.

10. The current pattern. When the Expenditure Committee was set up it was considered an important step towards more open government because of its public hearings and policy role. In that it divided its operations among six policy area sub-committees, it can be seen as a forerunner of the new system of fourteen investigative select committees. The Treasury and Civil Service Committee can be seen as perhaps the equivalent of the public expenditure sub-committee. Its sphere of interest extends to the two revenue departments—the Inland Revenue and the Customs and Excise. Its sub-committee will be primarily concerned with civil service and taxation matters, while the full Committee concentrates on major questions of economic policy.

Despite the step these Committees make towards more open government, the considerable secrecy within which British government and administration is conducted acts as a barrier to their effectiveness. For example during 1980 the Defence Secretary failed to inform the Defence Committee of the Cabinet's decision to buy the Trident missile—the largest single financial commitment of the year. *New Society* (15th January 1981) considered that "already committees have found themselves frustrated and angry in their search for truth and enlightenment".

11. The case for a Taxation Committee. As long ago as 1967 the Select Committee on Procedure suggested the establishment of a Committee to examine proposals for new forms of taxation and for changes in the structure of existing taxes in advance of the budget. It was envisaged that the Committee would be a sub-committee of the Select Committee on Expenditure. Although never established within the Expenditure Committee structure and opposed by the Treasury it may be that the sub-committee of the Treasury and Civil Service Committee may adopt a role of this sort.

12. The need for a committee to consider taxation.

(*a*) The Treasury view that such a Committee would be inconsistent with "the existing constitutional framework" is not relevant as the Committee would be concerned with the long-term view and not on current short-term proposals, and thus would not impinge on the necessary confidentiality of taxation changes.

(*b*) "Many of the issues would be highly politically charged and political tension might arise within the Committee which would inhibit the objective examination of proposals. . . ." However this Treasury argument has not been advanced against the Expenditure Committee, and would in any case be offset as a result of its reports leading to better informed debates in the House.

(*c*) The Treasury objection that the Committee would stray into the field of policy formulation may be countered by techniques enabling the separation of analysis and decision-making, the latter in any case hardly being the province of a committee of this nature.

THE EXPENDITURE WHITE PAPER

13. The concept. Both the Plowden Report on the Control of Public Expenditure (Cmnd. 1432, 1961) and the Report of the Select Committee on Procedure (*Scrutiny of Public Expenditure and Administration*, 1967) drew attention to the shortcomings of the traditional form of presentation of public expenditure policy. In response to the Plowden Report, White Papers on Public Expenditure appeared from 1963–69, though all essentially represented special products designed to meet particular situations, and the normal parliamentary business of dealing with public expenditure continued to be related to the annual supply estimates.

14. The Green Paper (1969): Public Expenditure—A New Presentation. It had become clear by the end of 1969 that the annual surveys were constituting the framework within which the government were taking major decisions on expenditure, and the Green Paper recommended that there should be an annual White Paper showing the results of each year's public expenditure survey by the government. The presentation of the White Paper should be an integral part of the annual parliamentary financial cycle.

15. The White Papers. These have been produced annually since 1969 based on the annual "PESC" (Public Expenditure Survey Committee (*see* **21** below)) exercise. The White Papers contain figures for the preceding, the current, and four succeeding years, though of course after the first succeeding year the figures are only of a broad indicative nature. Expenditure is then broken down in four ways.

(*a*) By programme, e.g. defence, social services, debt interest.

(*b*) By spending authority, i.e. the branch of government concerned.

(*c*) By economic strategy. This shows the effect of state spending on the national income and expenditure in the economy, broken down into current and capital expenditure.

(*d*) By demand on output. This tries to work out the true effects of government spending on national demand.

NOTE: The figures have to be treated with caution as each figure is estimated on the basis of prices ruling when the estimate is made, and, as the figures are compiled over a period of months the use of different price bases at the time of rapid inflation makes the total of different types of expenditure meaningless. Criticisms of the approach are dealt with further below in relation to PESC.

16. Role of estimates. White Papers are supplementary to existing procedures, and the consideration in depth of actual policy remains a matter for separate presentation and debate on Supply Days, introduction of Green Papers, etc. The estimates thus retain their independent role in the context of the House's formal legal control.

PUBLIC EXPENDITURE MANAGEMENT

17. The official side. Having examined Parliament's role in relation to public expenditure it is necessary, in order to present a clear picture, to examine the major forms of organisation and process on the official side. It must be borne in mind however that the process of public expenditure is a joint process and it concerns essentially the Cabinet at the political level, and the Cabinet Office, the Treasury, and the Civil Service Department at the official level. In addition to the structure at the centre the question arises as to the relationship of the centre with the major departments.

18. Central control of public expenditure. The central departments —Cabinet Office and Treasury (*see* IV, **27**)—headed by the most senior civil servants may conveniently be regarded as a single group, though in practice the degree of their interrelationship varies according to changing political circumstances. The expenditure functions of these bodies may be summarised as:

(*a*) the *Cabinet Secretariat* which exercises a co-ordinating role and is responsible for advising the Prime Minister on the machinery of government as well as controlling key policy questions about the civil service.

(*b*) the *Treasury* which is concerned with the management of the economy; home and overseas finance; fiscal policy; Civil Service manpower and pay; and coordination of economic policy.

19. The centre and the departments. The functions of the centre in relation to the departments are:

(*a*) analysis of issues for the Cabinet by the Central Policy Review Staff;

(*b*) public expenditure allocation carried out by the Public Expenditure Survey Committee (PESC) of the Treasury through its public sector divisions;

(*c*) control of departmental manpower requirements by the CSD.

The role of the centre impinges on the role of departmental ministers in that decisions are taken which impose constraints on the departments; these constraints are determined by the Cabinet, and the centre must make sure that the departments comply with the constraints. This is a joint responsibility and the relationship should be, according to the Plowden Committee, "one of joint working together in a common enterprise; it should be considered not in terms of more or less independence of the departments from control by the Treasury, but rather in terms of getting the right balance and differentiation of function."

20. PAR and PESC. These are essentially related operations in a large overall process aimed at enabling the government to:

(*a*) create an overall policy for resource use;

(*b*) establish departmental objectives and priorities;

(*c*) establish a framework for allocation between departments;

(*d*) ensure departments keep within their allocations;

(*e*) provide an effective means of making day-to-day decisions within the overall strategy.

21. PESC. This is the principal means of inter-departmental co-ordination under Treasury chairmanship. PESC is responsible for the assessment of programmes and their implications for public expenditure as a whole against the background of medium-term economic analysis, and for producing the annual report for ministers on which basic decisions on public spending are taken, and on which the subsequent White Paper is founded.

22. The Programme Analysis and Review (PAR) experiment. The 1970–74 Conservative government introduced the PAR technique. It was operated under the Chief Secretary to the Treasury by the subsequent Labour administration but abandoned in 1979 as part of a programme of reducing government expenditure in the shorter term.

While PESC is concerned with the allocation of resources on a medium and long-term basis, PAR had a more fundamental role and was concerned with an appraisal of the priorities and objectives stated by the Departments before the process of allocating finance had begun. The primary objective of the scheme was to evaluate more rationally the conflicting demands for funds of each Department's programmes.

Although since abandoned, some form of PAR is likely to reappear as the underlying trend towards corporate and overall planning is unlikely to be reversed.

23. Some failings of the PESC system. In determining the public expenditure forecasts particular problems have become apparent which have led to difficulties in controlling public expenditure.

(*a*) Although the calculations involved indicate the volume of spending no system has been evolved whereby accurate long-range forecasts can be made.

(*b*) It works on the assumption that taxation policies will remain static and thus separates public spending decisions from tax decisions.

(*c*) The existence of unexpected contingencies cannot be allowed for.

THE TREASURY

24. The Treasury structure. The work of the Treasury is divided into four main sectors. At the head of the Department is a permanent secretary. Three of the divisions are headed by a second permanent secretary and the other by the Chief Economic Adviser.

(*a*) *The Chief Economic Adviser's Sector*. This consists of economists who deal with economic forecasting and the use of the Treasury's macro-economic model for the simulation of the effects on the economy of major economic policy options.

(*b*) *The Overseas Finance Sector*. This deals with international monetary policy, the financial aspects of EEC membership, exchange control, reserve management, balance of payments, overseas aid, and export finance.

(*c*) *The Domestic Economy Sector*. This sector has two main areas of responsibility. Firstly, it has a close relationship with industry aimed at relating government policy effects with industrial decision-making. Secondly, it is concerned with counter-inflation policies, taxation policy, and monetary policy.

(*d*) *Public Services Sector*. This is responsible for control over public expenditure and the annual public expenditure survey.

NOTE: Co-ordination of the sectors is provided through the medium of a Central Unit, the unit also taking responsibility for areas of policy which transcend sector boundaries, e.g. budget preparation.

25. Treasury control. The Treasury fills an almost unique role amongst central finance departments in being the sole ministry of finance. Prior to the creation of the Civil Service Department it combined financial control with control over government personnel, and over civil service organisation and methods.

NOTE: The Treasury still retains an influential role in civil service matters (*see* VIII).

Treasury control is exercised through the media of co-ordination of financial policy (*see* **26–27**), co-ordination of economic policy (*see* **29–30**) and influence over the nationalised industries and the civil service (*see* **36**). It also holds a vital role in the whole decision-making process (*see* V).

26. Co-ordination of financial policy. This may be broken down into the following aspects.

(*a*) *The requirement of prior approval.* Departments are obliged to obtain Treasury approval of any variation in their activities that has a financial aspect. In general it is departmental practice to consult the Treasury during the planning stage of new activities and, while Treasury attention centres mainly on proposed new services, recurrent expenditure and services are only accorded freedom from Treasury control to the extent that the Treasury sees fit.

(*b*) *Criticism of new legislation and policy.* Although the requirement of prior approval (coupled with approval of estimates) is the foundation of the Treasury's power to co-ordinate financial policy, the Treasury possesses the further right of examining and criticising new policy proposals before they reach Cabinet level. Control of this nature is reinforced by the following:

(*i*) the Chancellor's power to delay Cabinet decisions until his officials have prepared a brief;

(*ii*) the usual practice of early consultation between departments and the Treasury;

(*iii*) the Cabinet rule that no proposals are circulated until the Chancellor's sanction has been obtained. This rule affords the Treasury an opportunity of pointing out financial consequences and thus enables it to act, in practice, as a staff agency advising departments on the formulations of policy.

(*c*) *Priorities in expenditure.* The annual review of departmental estimates is submitted to the Treasury before submission to Parliament. The Chancellor, with the aid of the Treasury and in consultation with the ministers concerned, determines in advance the relative orders of magnitude which he proposes for different sections of government expenditure.

(*d*) *Annual review of estimates.* The detailed patterns of expenditure are reviewed in the annual estimates of expenditure. The Treasury, in addition to first examination of the estimates, also receives forward estimates from the departments. This provides it with an enlarged perspective from which the annual estimates may be regarded.

27. The importance of financial control. Treasury control operates as an effective safeguard against the misuse of executive powers, and provides an administrative balance against the powerful position of the executive under the British system of Cabinet government (*see* II). In particular, the following points should be noted.

(*a*) The requirement of prior approval does not mean automatic approval of the estimates, and neither does approval of the estimates dispense with prior approval. The requirement of prior approval involves a more detailed examination of proposed expenditure than does the estimates, and also relates to future expenditure.

(*b*) Although legally the Appropriation Act does not bind the departments to sub-heads and items in the original estimates, freedom is diminished by Treasury safeguards. Deviation from sub-heads is only permitted in the civil departments with Treasury approval, and the Treasury decides whether proposed deviations are of such significance as to require bringing to the notice of Parliament.

NOTE: The service departments have freedom to transfer items, but may transfer between sub-heads only with Treasury approval.

(*c*) The importance of Treasury control is emphasised by the weakness of parliamentary control. In compelling circumstances the executive can legally incur future expenditure not provided for in the Appropriation Act. The Treasury, however, is able to examine future implications of policy, and its approval is needed for activities involving contingent future liabilities. This involves interaction between Treasury and departmental officials.

(*d*) By reason of its scope, Treasury control tends to induce ministers to look beyond immediate problems.

(*e*) It provides valuable staff assistance to the departments with regard to the implications of future policy.

28. Ensuring economy. The traditional "housekeeping" functions of the Treasury are still exercised but the trend is away from the detailed control of the prewar period towards delegation to the departments. The Treasury devises and operates monitoring systems to ensure that departments are operating satisfactory systems internally.

NOTE: In this respect, there is a division of responsibility between the Treasury and departmental officials, and between the Treasury and the Public Accounts Committee.

29. Co-ordination of economic policy. The responsibility for the co-ordination of economic policy has fluctuated between various bodies during the twentieth century. The following stages can be noted.

(*a*) Before 1914. Responsibility rested with the Treasury with peripheral functions vested in such bodies as the Board of Trade.

(*b*) 1925. Responsibility was vested in a Cabinet Committee on Economic Research.

(*c*) 1930–39. Responsibility was vested in an Economic Advisory Council chaired by the Prime Minister. Despite its high rank the Council was limited by its lack of non-departmental duties.

(*d*) 1939–47. A Central Economic Information Service was set up within the Cabinet secretariat. This was divided in 1941 into the Central Statistical Office and the Economic Section.

(*e*) 1947–64. Economic policy responsibilities were returned to the Treasury in 1947. This period saw a marked reaction against physical control as a means of economic planning (*see* XII) and began a period of more direct Treasury control through monetary and fiscal means. The early 1960s, however, saw an attempt by the Tory Government to reduce the Treasury's absolute control, by establishing economic planning machinery, e.g. the National Economic Development Council and National Incomes Commission.

However, during the whole period the Treasury retained final responsibility for control of economic planning.

(*f*) 1964–70. The Department of Economic Affairs (DEA) was established. Previously various techniques had been tried to control and co-ordinate economic policy. These took the form principally of advisory committees (before 1940), physical controls under non-departmental ministers (1940–47) and Treasury controls (1947–64).

30. Treasury control. This was achieved through the following agencies:

(*a*) the Central Statistical Office, which provided factual information concerning economic growth.

(*b*) the Economic Section of the Treasury, which dealt with the study of economic problems.

(c) the two national economic groups of the Treasury, which undertook responsibility for economic forecasting and development of policies for economic growth.

NOTE: The economic planning and co-ordinating functions were directly aided by the Treasury's direct responsibility for the budget and supervision of government expenditure.

31. Disadvantages of Treasury Control. Advocates of the DEA pointed to the following defects in Treasury control.

(a) The Treasury was essentially economy-minded and consequently lacked the necessary approach for a planning department.

(b) Fiscal and monetary control were inadequate, and a more positive approach was needed which could only be achieved through the creation of a new department.

(c) The Treasury was overworked and lacked the necessary staff.

(d) The Chancellor of the Exchequer tended to leave too much influence over economic planning in the hands of the Treasury.

(e) There was a need to plan with regional disparities in mind and the Treasury was not suitable for this purpose.

32. Structure of the DEA. The DEA had no executive responsibilities, being concerned principally with short- and long-term economic policy. It was staffed with a high concentration of economists, statisticians and industrialists, and headed by a Cabinet minister. It operated through five divisions, two for economic co-ordination, one for long-term economic planning, one for industrial policy and one for regional development. The divisions sought to co-ordinate the activities of the various economic departments, in particular the Treasury, the Board of Trade, the Ministries of Labour, Technology, Power, and Transport.

In addition it was responsible for the National Plan of 1965, and attempted to develop a prices and incomes policy through the National Board for Prices and Incomes. It also encouraged regional development through the creation of Development Councils in the regions.

33. Return to Treasury control. The Department of Economic Affairs was abolished in 1970 and the economic planning and co-ordination functions returned to the Treasury. The principal arguments in favour of the return to Treasury control were as follows.

(*a*) The Treasury's main concern is with financial policy and the Budget. As the Budget is a major economic weapon the Treasury should have responsibility for economic policy in general.

(*b*) As the Chancellor of the Exchequer raises revenue for the government, he should take the central place in the economic planning machinery.

(*c*) The absence of Treasury control would lead to irresponsible and financially unwise policies, and would result in friction between the DEA and the Treasury.

(*d*) The Treasury has a special place in the machinery of government, with its power of direct influence over all departments. This position could not be matched by the DEA.

34. Volume and cash planning. All governments have problems controlling the volume of public expenditure and eliminating waste. Inflation has led planning to be carried out in volume terms, that is determining what is required in manpower and other resources and then determining the finance necessary to meet the requirements afterwards. The contribution of such a technique to the inflationary process governments are committed to controlling has led to the imposition of *cash limits*. These are given to departments, nationalised industries and local authorities who then have to determine their programmes within the cash limits, a process usually involving cuts in *real* programmes.

35. The Rayner exercise. The Conservative government in 1979 appointed Sir Derek Rayner, joint managing director of Marks and Spencer, as an adviser commissioned to examine administrative practices in various departments with a view to effecting economies. The adviser has a small team which reports directly to the Prime Minister. The method of working is to direct two officials (usually principals) within the department concerned to conduct an investigation into an aspect of the department's work. One report produced advocated the fortnightly payment by credit transfer of social security benefits instead of weekly cash payment. This produced political opposition and was not implemented as happened in other instances. This can be seen as an example of the problems of trying to apply the criteria of private sector efficiency to the operation of the public sector.

36. Other areas of Treasury control. These are as follows:

(*a*) *Nationalised industries.* The Treasury has involvement with the nationalised industries in so far as these depend on the Treasury for investment capital. In 1956 the government placed a restriction on the open market borrowing of the industries, with the result that the industries have become dependent on the Treasury for their capital projects. Currently the government has imposed on the nationalised industries External Financing Limits (EFLs)—a form of cash limit on the borrowing powers of the industries (*see* XIII).

(*b*) *Civil service.* (*See* VI.)

PROGRESS TEST 8

1. What is Parliament's role in public expenditure? (**2**)

2. Explain the functions and importance of the Public Accounts Committee. (**4–6**)

3. Explain the development of control through Parliamentary committees (**3–10**)

4. What is the case for a select committee on taxation? (**11–12**)

5. Explain the nature of the Public Expenditure White Papers. (**13–16**)

6. Explain the relationship on the official side of the control and the spending departments. (**17–19**)

7. What is meant by Treasury control? (**25**)

8. How does the Treasury exercise its responsibility for the co-ordination of financial policy? What is the importance of Treasury control? (**26, 27**)

9. An experiment was made in setting up a Department of Economic Affairs. Explain the disadvantages and advantages of the DEA as compared with Treasury control. (**30–33**)

10. Distinguish between cash and volume planning and outline the merits of each. (**34**)

CHAPTER IX

Financial Administration in Local Government

INTRODUCTION

1. Aim of the chapter. It is not the purpose of this chapter to present a critique of the various forms of local government income, nor to examine the financial relationship between central and local government (*see* XII), but to examine the administrative aspects of the local government financial system (i.e. the internal aspects) for the following reasons:

(*a*) to complete the overall picture of public expenditure procedures by dealing with local matters, central financial procedure having been dealt with in VIII;

(*b*) to present a comparative view of local government and central government financial procedures;

(*c*) to consider the administrative structure of local government finance and its attendant problems, e.g. amateur/professional relationships, the divorce of spending functions and financial control functions.

2. Matters involved in local financial administration. These include the following:

(*a*) planning;

(*b*) routine control functions;

(*c*) the provision of financial information in support of the management function of local authorities;

(*d*) control through integration of finance with policy objectives and their achievement, e.g. PPB (*see* XVI, **11**);

(*e*) measurement of performance in financial terms.

3. Problems of traditional organisation. Finance being an integral, if not the central, factor in local administration, it is necessary to isolate those factors which are characteristic of local administration and which have a bearing on problems of financial administration. These may be stated in general terms as follows.

(a) The frequent failure of local administration to establish a clear division of respective responsibilities and authority between elected members and officials.

(b) The absence of central objectives in local administration and consequent diffuseness of purpose between the various individual factors constituting the administrative whole.

(c) The problem of measuring the effective performance of functions as a result of the interplay of social and economic factors in local administration. This factor, however, is often misused when utilised as a defence against allegations of inefficiency in local administration, and techniques and practices now exist which moderate this disadvantage, e.g. management by objectives.

(d) The existence, in the typical local government organisation, of an absence of effort towards a corporate whole together with absence of overall objectives.

(e) The lack of such checks as exist in business management to prevent individuals hiding their responsibilities behind various group entities, e.g. committees and departments.

(f) Departmentalism and its disadvantageous effects on establishing overall objectives, co-ordination, etc. (see VII).

(g) Lack of independent criticism from within as a result of the tendency to merge policy and administrative functions in the elected members and consequently to reduce the status of officers to mere agents without individual initiative.

INTEGRATION OF FINANCIAL ADMINISTRATION

4. Principles of integration. A. H. Marshall (in *Financial Administration in Local Government*, Allen and Unwin, 1976) maintained that integration should be the guiding principle in local government financial organisation. In particular he stressed the following points.

(a) Financial administration should not be independent and an end in itself, but should be interwoven with the overall local authority administrative structure.

(b) Financial responsibility should not only be a function of the Treasurer's department and the Finance Committee but should be diffused throughout the whole authority.

(c) A single officer should be responsible for financial work. Such work should be conceived of as machinery for servicing the whole of the authority and not merely a number of uncoordinated units varying in aim and under different control.

NOTE: This principle, of course, goes to the root of local government and transcends mere financial administration, revealing the need in local authorities as a whole for a spirit of corporate responsibility to be evolved, and for overall objectives to be established.

(*d*) At policy formulation level, finance should be conceived as one of a number of aspects, each of which must have proper consideration and not as a separate isolated factor.

5. Difficulties in achieving integration. Integration as a concept of organisation and procedure is made difficult in local government as a result of the following.

(*a*) The existence of departmentalism and inter-committee rivalry. This has resulted from local administration taking the attitude in the past that it is a form of federation of loosely related services, rather than one of subsidiaries working towards a collective whole.

(*b*) The concept of the relationship between member and officer and the domination of the professional by the amateur.

(*c*) The treatment of finance as a control function rather than as an administrative function. Although the control function is still of great importance in securing accountability for public funds, the underlying administrative aspects and contribution of finance to policy formation cannot be overrated.

(*d*) The absence of central policy units in many authorities responsible for co-ordinating otherwise effectively independent departments and establishing overall policy objectives towards which the functional departments should work.

6. The purposes of integration. The objects of integrating financial administration with the overall administrative context of local government are as follows:

(*a*) to diffuse financial responsibility throughout the authority;

(*b*) to enable effective setting of objectives and the measurement of the performance of such objectives;

(*c*) to exert a direct influence towards rationalisation in a local authority's structure by highlighting deficiencies in organisation and procedure;

(*d*) to engender the habit of co-operation, both in financial and non-financial fields.

BUDGETARY PROCEDURES

7. Introduction. A local authority budget differs from the central government Budget in the following ways.

(*a*) It is essentially a revenue-raising exercise, whereas the national Budget is both a revenue-raising exercise, and the operation of techniques of monetary and fiscal control. The latter thus goes well beyond the normal meaning attributed to budget.

(*b*) Although not always successful, a local authority is effectively required to balance its budget by equating income with expenditure. Balancing the budget has long since ceased to be a national requirement.

Local authority spending now accounts for approximately 30 per cent of all public sector spending and thus has a considerable impact on the national economy. National government has therefore in recent years taken various new measures of control. The *Consultative Council*, chaired by the Secretary of State for the Environment, aims to co-ordinate major economic and financial measures with an eye to keeping local authority finance in accord with government macro-economic policy. *The Joint Manpower Watch* has a longer-term aim to monitor manning levels.

8. Local Government Planning and Land Act 1980. Local authorities determine the *rate* they are going to charge having deducted the amount of grant they are to receive from central government from their estimated expenditure. The determination of the amount of grant and its distribution is always contentious—the local authority associations pressing for more, and the government looking for economies. The 1980 Act revised the allocation system and introduced a method whereby allocations are based on a concept of *grant-related poundage* (GRP) and *grant-related expenditure* (GRE). GRP is the revenue that could be derived from a set national rate poundage. GRE is what the government believes it would cost an authority to provide a national level of service. Grants will be equal to the difference between the two. "Overspending" authorities will be penalised and have to increase their rates further to cover their expenses.

The method has been criticised as increasing central control and reducing the freedom of local authorities to determine their own needs.

9. Capital and revenue expenditures. At the basis of local government financial procedure is the distinction between "capital" and "revenue" expenditure. These terms are difficult to define precisely, particularly as they may vary according to the size of the local authority, but in general the distinction may be taken as relating to the nature of the assets produced by the expenditure; i.e. capital expenditure results in permanent, long-term benefits, whereas revenue expenditure deals with matters of a temporary or recurrent nature. In practice, capital expenditure must be raised by borrowing, whereas revenue expenditure must be raised annually. Thus the distinction raises questions of incidence, interest rates, effect of capital charges on revenue expenditure, etc.

NOTE: This chapter is principally concerned with revenue expenditure and capital expenditure will be only generally approached (*see* **23–24**).

10. Functions of the revenue budget. The revenue budget has the following functions.

(*a*) It fixes the local rate and the purposes to which the income shall be applied.

(*b*) It assists policy-making functions by requiring annual review of services and an overall examination of the development of local functions. In practice, it is the only time the operation of the local authority is looked at as a whole.

(*c*) It represents a plan of action.

(*d*) It illustrates in financial terms the effect of policy options and changes.

(*e*) It provides a medium for ensuring that revenue is spent for the purposes provided (subject of course to "supplementaries", etc.).

(*f*) It provides a yardstick against which administrative performance can be judged, and encourages a methodical and responsible approach.

(*g*) It compels officers annually to review departmental aims and the means adopted for their fulfilment.

NOTE: Revenue budgets alter in form between local authorities and no statutory requirements as to form is established. However, the Institute of Municipal Treasurers and Accountants have introduced a standard form of accounts (*The Form of Published Accounts of Local Authorities*).

11. Preparation. Between April and August central government decides the allocation of public expenditure for the next year, then by negotiation with the local authority associations and senior local authority staff the GRE and GRP (*see* **8**) are determined and following a formal meeting between the Secretary of State and association representatives the levels of grant are announced in November. (For 1981–82 central government provided 59.1 per cent of total relevant expenditure.)

During the same period local government, staff and councillors plan and estimate spending needs, estimates based on previous expenditure, plans, changing circumstances, new legislation etc. Departmental estimates will be submitted and the overall position determined following corporate planning meetings of senior staff and the Policy and Resources Committee. The budget will be finalised.

12. Determination of the rate poundage. The Rate Support Grant order will pass through Parliament around Christmas and local authorities will thus find out exactly how much grant they will receive. The government publishes a White Paper outlining plans for the future and local authorities determine the rate-in-the-pound necessary to provide sufficient revenue.

13. Rate capping. The 1980 Act (*see* IX, **8**) led to many authorities increasing rates substantially. Thus in 1984 central government imposed limits on the amount local authorities might increase their rates.

THE POLICY AND RESOURCES COMMITTEE

14. Traditional position. Prior to the reorganisation effected in most authorities as a result of the Bains Report (*see* V, **20** and XVII, **19–25**), the major horizontal committee was the finance committee, particularly where no other formal means of co-ordination had been adopted. Its advantageous position resulted from two factors.

(*a*) It had knowledge of the overall financial position and requirements of the local authority.

(*b*) Being non-functional, it was better placed to take an overall and detached view of the authority's spending activities.

In addition where an authority was politically organised the council was in a position which made it difficult to override the views of the committee. On the other hand difficulty was caused by the inability to demarcate adequately between matters of policy and matters of finance, e.g. where the finance committee was required to consider the financial implications of a new service or the extension of an existing service.

15. The post-Bains position. The establishment of a central policy and resources committee, supported by resource sub-committees in respect of finance, land, and personnel, often together with a performance review committee, now means that a corporate approach may be established in respect of policy and finance matters. This position is achieved as:

(*a*) the policy and resources committee is a key structure in recommending policy;

(*b*) the reports of committees on the financial implications of the overall council strategy and their capital and revenue programme proposals are filtered through the policy and resources committee before submission to the council;

(*c*) the traditional function of routine financial control is exercised by the finance and other resource sub-committees and is only brought together with policy implications at policy and resources committee level;

(*d*) the composition of the policy and resources committee, invariably comprising the major committee chairmen, enables effective control and co-ordination to be exercised at this level.

16. Its similarity with Treasury control. The functions of the finance committee have been compared with those of Treasury control as defined by the Select Committee on Estimates, 1957–58, which are as follows:

(*a*) deciding on total expenditure;

(*b*) securing a proper balance between services;

(*c*) securing a proper balance of expenditure within services;

(*d*) helping determine expenditure on individual policies and services.

NOTE: Treasury control in fact goes beyond these functions and is facilitated by the hierarchical position occupied by the Treasury in the central government structure, a position not likely to be equalled by a finance committee.

THE FINANCE DEPARTMENT

17. Importance. The finance (or treasurer's) department of a local authority occupies a central position in the departmental structure for the following reasons.

(*a*) It is a unique position to counteract the forces of departmentalism.

(*b*) It can be organised in such a way as to avoid the obsession with detail which is such a characteristic of committee level operations.

18. Its relationship with the spending departments. It is usual for there to be regular collaboration and consultation between the finance department and the individual operational departments. This manifests itself particularly in the drawing up of the estimates, with discussions taking place on new items of expenditure and alterations to existing items between departmental and finance department officials. In addition, it will be the responsibility of the finance department to interpret the implications of the finance committee's views to the departments.

NOTE: The influence of the finance department on the spending committees and departments is difficult to quantify owing to the interplay of such factors as relative strengths of committees and departments, the political structure of the authority, tradition, personalities of chairmen, etc.

One vital factor in the finance department's role is the annual *Report* of the treasurer to the finance committee, though again its importance varies among local authorities according to the importance of various intangible factors. The *Report* itself is of considerable significance in that it sets out such matters as the state of the local authority's working balances, its reserves, renewals and capital funds, changes expected in the future operations of the authority and such matters as trends in costs, etc.

BUDGETARY CONTROL

19. Nature of budgetary control. Traditionally, the finance department exercises routine "after the event" control, the more rigorous checking being a function of the spending departments. Its function will also be affected by standing orders which may permit the treasurer to authorise variations due to unexpected factors, e.g. pay awards, and which may restrict "virement", i.e. changes of expenditure between items. This latter may be permitted where a saving on one item is due to economy, as opposed to representing a mere fortuitous gain.

NOTE: The increase of computerisation both facilitates budgetary control in local authorities and enables the use of new forms of such control; e.g. it permits an accounting system based on control of commitments rather than of expenditures.

20. Planning, Programming and Budgeting (PPB). (*see* XVI, 11). The importance of the development of the use of PPB in local government is as follows.

(*a*) It facilitates the establishment of a system of overall objectives with subsidiary departmental and committee objectives. It consequently cuts across departmental factors and subordinates these to the goals of the authority as a whole.

(*b*) It requires, of necessity, long-term policy formulation and consideration on an overall basis of related services.

(*c*) It requires supplementation of the programmed budget by sub-objectives, and techniques for the measurement of performance.

(*d*) It may contribute accordingly to the establishment of central research and statistical units, e.g., as in the GLC.

(*e*) It avoids the traditional conceptual difference between capital and revenue proposals.

(*f*) It places emphasis on long-term financial strategy rather than the present annual approach.

CAPITAL EXPENDITURE

21. Capital expenditure programmes. Because of their large and long-term effects, it is vital that a local authority has adequate machinery for the review of capital expenditure proposals. In general, the procedure for approval of capital commitments is as follows.

(*a*) The project is scrutinised when it is included in the long-term capital programme. The programme is of great importance, as it enables decisions to be taken on such matters as priorities, effects on the revenue budget, forward planning, etc.

(*b*) The programme is submitted to the council.

(*c*) Central government sanction must be sought (*see* XII).

22. Form of the long-term programme. This is a matter which has been facilitated in certain authorities by the use of OR techniques (*see* XVI). Essentially the programme must contain a long-term projection (three to five years), classification of schemes put forward, annual charges and running costs, as these will affect future revenue budgets, and reports of the officers concerned pointing out the effects of the capital programme on the overall finances and objectives of the authority.

CONCLUSIONS

23. Views of the Maud Committee on Management. The Committee favoured the establishment of a centralised management board (*see* XVII) which, amongst other matters, would assume financial responsibilities. This proposal was opposed by the Institute of Municipal Treasurers and Accountants, which not only felt that financial control would be effectively reduced, but also mentioned the following points.

(*a*) Financial administration and control should be independent of the main spending elements in the local authority.

(*b*) Financial administration and control should be the responsibility of the treasurer, who should have a direct right of communication to all management levels.

(*c*) The treasurer, should continue to be under a public obligation to maintain the integrity and openness of the control system.

PROGRESS TEST 9

1. What problems were commonly involved in traditional local authority financial organisation? **(3)**

2. What are the "principles of integration" laid down by A. H. Marshall? What are the objects of such integration? **(4, 6)**

3. Describe the difficulties in achieving integration. **(5)**

4. Compare the budgetary procedure of a local authority with that of the central government. **(7)**

5. Distinguish between capital and revenue expenditure. What are the functions of the revenue budget? **(9)**

6. Outline the budgetary process in local authorities. **(11–13)**

7. What are the functions and relations of the policy and resources committee? **(14–15)**

8. How do the functions of the policy and resources committee resemble Treasury control? **(16)**

9. What are the functions and relations of the Finance Department? **(17–18)**

10. What is involved in budgetary control in a local authority? **(19–20)**

CHAPTER X

Planning

INTRODUCTION

1. A definition of planning. There has always been a tendency to give planning emotive connotations, particularly in the context of the controversy between individualism and collectivism. This approach tends to obscure the true meaning and purpose of the planning process. It is thus necessary objectively to define planning, and to determine the goals criteria obtaining therein.

Planning has been defined as "that activity that concerns itself with proposals for the future, with the evaluation of alternative proposals, and with the methods by which these proposals may be achieved" (H. A. Simon, D. W. Smithburg and V. A. Thompson, *Public Administration*, Alfred Knopf, 1967). Planning is thus concerned with the future human behaviour and involves both the following.

(*a*) *Ultimate activities.* Those anticipated if a plan is carried out.

(*b*) *Intermediate activities.* Those required to carry out the plan.

2. The reasons for planning. Planning is indispensable to the administrative process as any decision and consequent activities carried out to achieve the objectives of that decision will limit the range of choices available to the administrator in the future owing to the limited nature of resources. It is thus necessary whenever the execution of policy involves "sunk costs".

3. Planning goals. The traditional administrative theory of the distinction between policy and administration, i.e. between the formation of the plan and its execution, is not practicable in planning for the following reasons.

(*a*) By their political connections and involvement, planning bodies can rarely be neutral and therefore underlying any long-range planning objectives of a government will be assumptions as to what are the desirable goals to be achieved.

(*b*) Short-term goals are probably less overtly political, though they must of course work within the framework of the long-term plan.

(c) The executive organs are involved in planning in both their function as supplier of the basic material upon which the plan is based and in their function of "planning for planning", i.e. establishing the organisational framework necessary for implementation of a plan.

A basic requirement in planning is that of co-ordination in order that contradiction of goals between various groups involved in the plan is avoided. Rational co-ordination in turn can only be achieved if there is some overriding goal to which all the groups are working. In a democracy the process of co-ordination is made more difficult, and of necessity becomes a political function which must be set against dominant social goals.

4. Implementation of goals. In order to be effective, planning must be concerned not only with materialistic ends but also with human behaviour which may inhibit the achievement of the goals. Such planning goals must therefore attempt to rationalise and account for the following.

(a) *Resistance to goals.* Resistance may be expressed overtly or, more commonly, implicitly, and may be effected by inertia, community or personal values, self-interest or dislike of subordination.

(b) *Dynamics of planning.* An operable plan must account for elements which are not directly under the influence of the plan and how these external factors may affect achievement of the plan's goals. This necessity arises as no plan can be comprehensive and must therefore seek some form of evaluation of non-planned factors.

5. Organisation for planning. In general terms, planning may take place through specialised planning units or through units of government which at the same time perform other functions. In the first place, however, whichever type of unit is utilised, it is necessary that planning should take place at a level where there is responsibility for the achievement of some overriding and unitary social policy, and thus there is a natural tendency, as government activities become more complex, for the level of integration of planning to rise in the administrative structure.

The advantages of non-functional planning units are as follows:

(a) they secure proper attention to research;

(*b*) they are not dominated by political objectives and controversies outside the scope of the plan;

(*c*) they will generally be concerned with long-range aspects of a plan with shorter-range planning taking place through the administrative process;

(*d*) pressure of day-to-day administration will not be present to divert attention from long-range problems. When a planning unit is contained in a functional organisation there is a tendency for resistance to the planning unit to occur, and such resistance may be in fact encouraged as the planning unit relieves the rest of the organisation from long-term responsibilities.

Macdonald and Fry (*Public Administration*, Winter 1980) were able to identify only thirteen policy planning groups in the civil service. They included the Civil Service Department Planning Branch and the Customs and Excise Departmental Planning Unit. None had access to the Minister, but reported to the Permanent Secretary in a steering/management capacity.

POLITICAL CONSEQUENCES OF ECONOMIC PLANNING

6. Fundamental difficulties. Economic planning, of necessity, requires the granting of considerable executive discretion in order to facilitate immediate response to economic contingencies. Continual reference to political control will thus inhibit the effective implementation of a plan. There thus arises the basic problem of resolving the need for executive discretion with adequate political surveillance. This in turn is made difficult by the following:

(*a*) the inadequacy of annual budgets to achieve such political control;

(*b*) weak control of public expenditure (but *see* VIII).

7. Political problems in planning. Political problems arise as a result of the long-term commitments involved in planning. These problems may be classified as follows.

(*a*) The binding nature of planning on future governments. Although commitments undertaken are not legally binding they may be *de facto* binding owing to a high degree of "sunk costs" and the rigidity or complexity of a plan.

(*b*) The undertaking of commitments over a period of time must be reconciled with the need to make such plans democratically responsive to changes in public opinion.

(*c*) Freedom in operating and modifying the plan accorded to governments, ministers, administrators, etc., decreases proportionately the thoroughgoing nature of a plan.

(*d*) The budgetary process is too cumbersome for short-term policy responsiveness, and too limited in scope for long-term planning.

(*e*) There is a need to develop effective means of financial accountability and to prevent side-stepping of control exercised through the budgetary process.

(*f*) There is a danger that a gap may develop between the controllers of a plan and the operators, and that what are effectively political value judgments may be concealed by technical jargon.

(*g*) There has been a tendency to transfer planning functions to *ad hoc* bodies outside the sphere of ministerial responsibility. This transfer of power gives rise to problems of responsibility. The older institutions tended to be subordinate, peripheral or specialised bodies and within the direct control or influence of a minister. The new bodies present problems owing to the central role of planning in the government process and, as they tend to fall outside direct control, there is a need for the creation of extra-parliamentary safeguards.

(*h*) Promotion of economic growth is one of the prime influences on electoral opinion and therefore is the most political activity of government. There is thus the need to reconcile the role of public opinion with the need to take the unpopular decisions which planning necessarily involves.

MANAGEMENT OF THE BRITISH ECONOMY

8. Reasons for state involvement. Governments have become involved in economic management since the war for two main interconnected reasons:

(*a*) the unregulated, *laissez-faire* economy tended to produce boom and slump associated economic and social problems;

(*b*) the sheer size of the public sector places the government in a central position in the economy where its spending decisions are bound to impact upon the workings of the rest of the economy.

Several key factors may be noted in the development of the *managed economy*.

(*a*) The "Great Depression" of the 1930s provided the impetus for action and research;

(*b*) The ideas of *J. M. Keynes* provided the method of intervention—that the government should no longer act as just another organisation in the economy, but should spend *counter-cyclically*, in other words, against the trend of the trade cycle;

(*c*) The *Beveridge Report* 1944, that laid the foundation for the welfare state, developed the idea of state responsibility for health and welfare.

(*d*) The *Labour Government 1945–51* was committed to an interventionist role in the economy.

9. The machinery for management. No coherent and co-ordinated approach has been made to the machinery of planning and economy co-ordination. There has been recourse to the conferment of new duties on old ministries, e.g. the old Board of Trade; the creation of new ministries, e.g. the short-lived Department of Economic Affairs; and the use of *ad hoc* agencies, e.g. Regional Planning Boards.

10. Early developments. By the end of the War economic planning had become a central political issue, but the problem of establishing permanent machinery had not been solved. The major developments were as follows.

(*a*) *1945–51.* The Labour Government made piecemeal attempts to establish central planning machinery. Initially there was created a Ministry of Economic Affairs and a Central Economic Planning Staff (CEPS) for giving information and advice. In support, both the Central Statistical Office (CSO) and the Economic Section of the Cabinet (ESC) were strengthened. However, this seemingly impressive force was largely concerned with the production of planning documents in the form of surveys. In 1947, the Ministry of Economic Affairs was wound up, and both the CEPS and responsibility for economic affairs were taken into the Treasury, which is not a suitable vehicle for long-term economic planning. In turn the CEPS was abolished in 1951, and in 1953 the Treasury absorbed the ESC.

Thus, in 1951, the only planning mechanism was an Economic Planning Board (EPB) which was largely a toothless institution and, despite its being the major consultative committee on economic policy, it was not a central planning agency.

There were few developments in the planning field during the Conservative administrations of the 1950s. In 1961, however, Selwyn Lloyd made recommendations to Parliament that led to the establishment of the National Economic Development Council (NEDC).

11. The information problem. Economic planning requires accurate information as to the extent of the problems faced and forecasts of future performance and trends. In any "mixed" economy it is the decisions of independent production units that determine the overall pattern, thus government does not control in a direct sense but through policy, and as the largest employer and spender it is very influential.

Basic data about the economy's behaviour is derived from the statistical surveys collated by the Central Statistical Office for example balance of payment and employment figures. This data may enable *diagnosis* of problems, but it is inevitably *historical* as the statistics will relate to events that have already occurred. Before policy can be implemented, *forecasts* must be made—on the basis of computer "models" and economic theory, to determine whether the historical problem remains or is likely to persist without policy action. The "models" are also used to "test" the probable implications of different policy options. University schools and other organisations operate similar models to the Treasury and there is "competition" between them to produce better variations—the best being the one whose forecasts approximate most closely to the actual out-turn.

The NEDC structure was designed to contribute information to the policy-makers—it may be seen as a system of information gathering tentacles—reaching into the economy, extracting, evaluating and transmitting problems and possible solutions to the centre. NEDC itself is a high-powered organisation, chaired by the Prime Minister, and not therefore concerned with details. It consists of representatives from trade unions, employers and the government. It is serviced by the National Economic Development Office (NEDO)—a permanent staff that establishes working parties and committees to deal with particular problems.

The national structure is paralleled by Regional Economic Development committees, also tripartite but operating at regional level, feeding information and ideas to the central structure.

The importance of NEDC lies in the fact that it brings the three most important groups within the economy together—i.e., government, controlling aggregate spending; unions that powerfully influence wage rates; and management with its influence over prices and output. NEDC discussion will persist even when relations between the government and one of the others may have broken down through other channels. The operation of NEDC is thus on a parallel with the French Economic and Social Council which provides a constitutional basis for ensuring continuous dialogue.

12. The need for a planning agency. The Labour government 1964–70 was anxious to establish a stronger and more authoritative form of planning. To this end they established the Department of Economic Affairs (DEA) responsible for "the management of the national economy as a whole". There are several arguments in favour of centralised planning agencies including the following.

(*a*) Planning depends essentially on the effective encouragement of economic growth, and how successful this is politically. These intertwined responsibilities can be more effectively carried out by a single agency.

(*b*) There is a vital need for a central department concerned with projecting and co-ordinating functions.

(*c*) The Treasury is inadequate for the carrying out of such functions (*see* VIII).

Against such an agency are the following points:

(*d*) The difficulty of reconciling the British preference for indicative as opposed to command planning with the creation of a strong authoritative central agency.

(*e*) The difficulty of creating a sufficiently high-ranking department, whilst at the same time giving adequate power to the individual departments.

13. The performance of the DEA. The DEA consisted of three main sections: Economic Planning and Public Expenditure, Regional Planning and Industrial Policies, and Prices and Incomes. The Department was abolished by the Conservative government of 1970 and its failure can be traced to the following defects:

(*a*) poor relations with the Treasury resulting from areas of responsibility that overlapped;

(*b*) recurrent economic crises that reinforced the position of the Treasury in relation to the DEA;

(*c*) the National Plan which it produced that soon proved inadequate and undermined the credibility of the Department's operation.

Following the demise of the DEA in 1970 the whole responsibility for finance and economic affairs returned to the Treasury,
and, in the context of planning, the Chief Economic Adviser's
section is responsible for economic forecasting, while the Domestic
Economy Sector covers such matters as counter-inflation policies,
taxation policy, etc. Other features in economic planning during
this period have been as follows.

(*a*) Working parties were established in 1972, and still operated
in 1978 on an *ad hoc* basis, with representatives from the government, the TUC the CBI and NEDO to draw up outline policies
for pay and prices.

(*b*) In 1973 a Price Commission and a Pay Board were established.

(*c*) The Pay Board was abolished in 1974 on the establishment
of the "Social Contract".

(*d*) The Industry Act 1975 established the National Enterprise
Board (NEB) to act as an agency managing government share-
holdings in private enterprise firms. Originally envisaged as "a
vehicle for the socialist transformation of industry" (Eric Heffer)
it quickly came to operate as a state holding company. Its subsidiaries fall into two categories—the "lame ducks" such as British
Leyland and Rolls-Royce which without aid would have failed,
and companies that it was felt were to the benefit of the economy
generally, yet were having difficulty raising venture capital. These
included companies in the electronics field such as Sinclair Radio-
nics and the "microchip" enterprise INMOS.

(*e*) In 1975 the Government White Paper, *An Approach to
Industrial Strategy* was published, the main effects being to firmly
entrench planning with the Treasury and the Department of Industry, and to create a number of NEDO working parties for
particular industries.

(*f*) In 1981 the government established "Enterprise Zones" in
depressed inner-city areas, within which restrictions on the establishment of new businesses including rates were reduced. This
policy reflects the difficulty of planning and is an attempt to
achieve the desired objective without specific assistance.

PROBLEMS OF PLANNING RESPONSIBILITY

14. Macro and micro-economic policy. Macro-economic policy,
directed at the economy as a whole, through the control of aggre-

gate demand presents governments with an inherent problem. It is generally agreed that there are four primary targets of economic policy: growth, full employment, balanced international payments and a stable price level. In macro-policy terms these objectives tend to be mutually incompatible: expansionary policies tend to improve output and employment but have an *adverse* effect upon the balance of payments and the level of inflation. This dilemma was reflected in the policies of the 1950s which became known as "stop–go", where periods of expansionary policy led to balance-of-payments crisis, which necessitated a reversal of policy.

The particular policy objectives a government pursues is thus a matter of political choice; clearly the Conservative government of 1979 saw as its main target inflation and thus pursued restrictionary policies at the expense of employment and growth.

The need to avoid a repetition of the "stop–go" problem has led to some new policy directions, supplementing the basic process of demand management. Micro-policy refers to specific measures aimed at eliminating particular trouble-spots in the economy, with the idea that the whole system will in turn benefit. The NEDC structure is central to the process, by which problems are identified, quantified and solutions devised. The Industry Act and the NEB represent other measures in this direction.

15. Indicative planning. The essential element of indicative planning is the preparation by the central authorities of a target plan that lays down the expected performance of the economy in the immediate and medium term. The target gives all the other decision-making units in the economy a framework within which to plan their own policies. Success breeds success in indicative planning; if one plan's forecasts are realised, confidence in the predictions is generally increased and the next one may thus be more optimistic. The first serious attempt at a comprehensive indicative plan in the United Kingdom was the "National Plan" produced by the DEA. It failed mainly due to external factors but also because of inherent weaknesses, particularly the delineation of a single growth rate, rather than for various sectors of the economy, and its rather optimistic assumptions about the ability of the economy to achieve such a target growth.

16. Monetarist and Keynesian policies. These represent approaches to macro-economic management. Monetarist thinking suggests that the most important function of government is to control the monetary system, especially the quantity of money; the result will be a stable price system within which the economy will, through the price mechanism, eventually achieve full employment and growth. The revival of interest in this fundamentalist thinking reflects the contemporary political significance of the control of inflation.

Keynesian thinking stems from the Depression era when the need to do something about unemployment was the overriding policy objective and the side-effects of deficit budgeting in terms of inflation and balance of payments seemed less important. The current consensus seems to be that a balance between monetary management and demand stimulation needs to be made in order to achieve a balance between the mutually incompatible aims of the policy process.

It is to be expected therefore that governments must make choices in the policy field that will always have undesirable side-effects, and the direction chosen will reflect the balance of political forces at the time.

17. Constraints on economic policy planning. In a mixed economy it must be remembered that the government does not run the economy, it is simply a significant unit within it and able to influence it through policy measures and controls. Various significant constraints may be identified.

(*a*) *Interest groups.* Through bargaining at government level, groups, especially the representatives of employers and labour, will be able to exert a significant influence upon government.

(*b*) *Electoral considerations.* Unpopular options may effectively be ruled out to governments that are approaching re-election. It is common to observe easing of restrictive policies as elections approach.

(*c*) *International factors.* Policy will be affected by the decisions of other bodies in the world system. For example the impact of the OPEC countries' decisions about oil pricing impacted upon all Western economies. Similarly governments are tied through organisational links, e.g. membership of the EEC, and because of international agreements such as the General Agreement on Tariffs and Trade (GATT).

18. The interrelation of physical and social planning. The following points should be noted.

(*a*) *Physical plans.* The first compulsory and national physical planning policy was embodied in the Town and Country Planning

Act 1947, and the New Towns Act of the preceding year. These established an elaborate apparatus of physical planning controls. These were not, however, related to vital economic questions, such as the economic costs of physical planning in limiting urban growth, accommodation of overspill and construction of new towns. These questions were rarely dealt with in the context of the relation of the cost of economic resources to the benefits accruing. It was not until the later 1950s and the 1960s that it became common to relate physical planning to underlying economic and social data.

(b) *Social planning*. Prior to 1939 there was a growing government responsibility for public welfare. This manifested itself in the growing public social sector after the War and in government involvement in what had hitherto been matters of private, or peripherally public, concern.

(c) *Multi-disciplinary planning*. The first multi-disciplinary planning exercises have now taken place, though generally on a regional basis. This development has been brought about by the following:

(*i*) dissatisfaction with the planning achievements of the 1950s;

(*ii*) the effects of the population explosion and transport revolution;

(*iii*) the development in economic planning and its emphasis on growth;

(*iv*) the political stimulus to regional policy.

REGIONAL PLANNING

19. Introduction. In Great Britain and Western Europe in general, regional planning has primarily been conceived of at national level, e.g. the Distribution of Industry Acts. In general there has been a failure to treat regions as other than spots of localised unemployment, and a reluctance to treat them as "polarised integrated wholes" (J. R. Boudeville, *Problems of Regional Economic Planning*, Edinburgh University Press, 1966). Regions have thus been treated as areas which would spontaneously develop as action was taken to stimulate the economy as a whole. This policy for spontaneous development has been proved inadequate and the necessity of treating regions as independent problems has been highlighted, e.g. by long-term unemployment in the North-East. Consequently, decentralised regional planning becomes necessary and stems either from a federal concept of the state, or from some type of administrative deconcentration.

20. The need for regional policy. The following aspects should be noted.

(*a*) *Political.* Apart from questions of governments' electoral self-interest, questions of separatist movements affecting the cohesion of the state may arise through neglect of regional disparities, e.g. as in Belgium between Walloon and Flemish areas.

(*b*) *Social.* This factor will include such matters as redistribution of income, preservation of cultural backgrounds, equalising of opportunity, etc.

(*c*) *Economic.* This factor has three main parts:

(*i*) a recognition of the inadequacy of economic forces to operate satisfactorily in location of industry matters;

(*ii*) the incompatibility of growth and idle resources;

(*iii*) the fact that inflation avoidance and growth encouragement are only effective if wide regional unemployment disparities are avoided.

21. Regional policy in the 1960s. This may be stated briefly as follows:

(*a*) The Local Employment Act 1960 (as amended and strengthened in 1963) which replaced the old development area concept with a more flexible system of development districts;

(*b*) White Papers of 1963 on Central Scotland and on North-East England which provided the first step towards effective regional planning;

(*c*) The Industrial Development Act 1966 which replaced the development districts with new developing areas;

(*d*) increased use of controls, for example the Control of Office and Industrial Development Act 1965;

(*e*) grants, loans and financial inducements.

22. Regional policy since the 1970s. Regional policy in the 1970s has shown little substantial advance. The main forms of regional policy involve the operation of inducements through the use of allowances and grants, in particular regional development grants introduced by the Industry Act 1972. These are administered through four Regional Development Grant Offices headed by an Assistant Secretary, and are payable only in assisted areas, but are available for buildings as well as new machinery or plant, but subject to central directions given by the Department of Industry.

Backing up the policy of inducements is the compulsive nature of Industrial Development Certificates which have to be obtained for industrial development above certain limits outside the assisted areas.

The introduction of "enterprise zones" as areas free from government influence rather than with government assistance reflects the difficulty of managing local areas.

23. The system and purpose of regional planning. England was divided into eight planning regions by the Labour Government of 1964–70. Within each region there is a Regional Economic Council and a Regional Economic Planning Board. The Councils are representative institutions (though not elected) and the Boards are made up of civil servants.

The purpose of the machinery has been described by the Secretary of State as being "to provide effective machinery for regional economic planning ... (and) for economic development. The Economic Planning Councils will be concerned with broad strategy on regional development and the best use of the region's resources ... the Economic Planning Boards will provide machinery for co-ordinating the work of government departments concerned with regional planning and development, and their creation will not affect the existing powers and responsibilities of local authorities or existing ministerial responsibilities" (*Hansard*, 10th December 1964).

The Councils were abolished in 1979 for reasons of economy.

24. The functions of regional planning. These are as follows:

(*a*) to provide the basic cost and benefit data and analysis upon which regional planning policies may be based;

(*b*) to forecast a region's future pattern of development;

(*c*) to provide a plan for such matters as growth areas, the interrelation of the private sector, the need for investment, social capital, etc.

25. Problems of regional planning machinery. The following points should be noted:

(*a*) the need to establish the appropriate level and degree of democratic control and responsibility;

(*b*) co-ordination between central and regional authorities;

(*c*) the question of what machinery is appropriate.

26. The appropriate machinery. In general terms, regional planning machinery may take one of the following forms.

(a) *Advisory bodies without executive responsibilities such as the present British system.* In this case, the regional machinery merely advises and supplies data and recommendations upon which the central government may or may not act. Although this system has the advantage that reports may be made without the inhibitions which commitment to firm recommendations would have, it suffers from the disadvantage that, in general, reports never receive either the government or public attention which they might otherwise achieve.

(b) *Executive bodies.* The creation of such bodies would, however, pose certain problems:

(i) their effectiveness would depend largely on the provision of an independent source of finance;

(ii) problems of co-ordination both with government and other regional policy would arise;

(iii) such a body would of necessity be required to be democratically elected.

(c) *Mandatory plans without executive capacity.* This would involve the government in being bound by regionally prepared plans without the regional authorities themselves having executive capacity. This would imply, however, a degree of compulsion which governments would generally be unwilling to undertake, as well as giving rise to substantial problems of co-ordination.

PROGRESS TEST 10

1. What is meant by "planning"? What are the reasons for planning? **(1, 2)**

2. Consider the meaning and implementation of "planning goals". **(3, 4)**

3. How may organisation for planning be achieved? **(5)**

4. What are the fundamental *political* difficulties and problems of economic planning? **(6, 7)**

5. What are the reasons for government management of the economy? How was such management organised from 1945 to 1964? **(8, 10)**

6. What is the nature of the "information problem" that must be tackled if governments are going to effectively plan the economy? **(11)**

7. On what grounds might a central economic planning agency be established? **(12)**

8. What are the inherent difficulties involved in macro-economic management? **(14)**

9. Why is it essential if indicative planning is to be successful that the plans do not overestimate the performance of the economy? **(15)**

10. How are physical and social planning interrelated? **(18)**

11. Why is regional planning needed? What was British policy in this field during the 1960s? **(19–23)**

12. What are the functions and problems of regional planning? **(24, 25)**

13. Consider the possible forms of appropriate machinery for regional planning. **(26)**

CHAPTER XI

Devolution and International Administration

INTRODUCTION

1. Definitions. The following definition should be noted.

(*a*) *Decentralisation.* This may be treated as a general term signifying the removal of functions from the centre.

(*b*) *Deconcentration.* This is establishment of provincial but centrally controlled outposts of central government—such as the Driver Vehicle Licensing Centre in Swansea.

(*c*) *Devolution.* This may generally refer to the process of decentralisation, but in the UK context it is usually used in connection with the creation of regional elected authorities having at least some powers that are at present exercised by Whitehall.

(*d*) *Federalism.* This is the creation of a government and administration with powers given by several sovereign states.

(*e*) *International association.* An association of independent sovereign states that does *not* have separate or superior authority to that of the member countries. Its decisions and actions are implemented only through the authority and agreement of the members and it cannot enforce its decisions over that of member governments.

2. The need for decentralisation and federalism. Government administrative structures develop in order to implement the decisions of the state's political institutions, and changing circumstances will demand reform, both of political and administrative structures. Generally the need to devolve decision-making and implementation stems from the politically expressed wish (e.g., through nationalist movements) to have more localised control over decision-making. The motivation to create federal institutions stems from the recognition of mutual problems involving several countries and the need to deal with them collectively. If these problems are of a continuous nature (e.g., associated with trade) then there is a tendency to establish some sort of permanent body with some authority in each of the member states, while if the problems are temporary then a series of meetings, or perhaps a forum within which meetings can take place, is the more likely outcome.

In all cases change of this kind is usually highly contentious, involving conflict between those jealously guarding their power base within the existing system and those seeking it within a new structure.

DECENTRALISATION

3. The need for decentralisation. Some measure of decentralisation becomes necessary for the following reasons:

(*a*) the increasing complexity of government functions;

(*b*) the need to delegate information-collecting functions and decision-taking responsibilities in order to achieve greater efficiency;

(*c*) applying general policies and standards to local situations where the size of area and population served by an administrative system is large constitutes a major problem.

(*d*) political demands for increased local autonomy.

4. Regional authorities. In determining the structure of regional decentralised authorities four main problems arise, namely:

(*a*) definition of the areas of the authorities;

(*b*) the amount of decision-making authority to be delegated;

(*c*) the machinery for the co-ordination of the various authorities.

(*d*) delineation of power between central and regional bodies and procedures for resolving disputes on this matter.

5. Types of regional authority. Various regional administrative structures have already been established, e.g. planning regions, regional health and water authorities and the concept explored by Derek Senior in his dissenting memorandum to the Redcliffe-Maud Report.

During the 1939–45 war the country was divided into ten regions, each under a commissioner, and following the war ministries maintained a network of regional agencies based on the standard regions defined by the Treasury in 1946.

POLICY CHANGES

6. Changing trends. During the 1950s there was a reaction against regional machinery in most areas of planning and co-ordination. In the 1960s, however, the Labour government of 1964 reversed the trend. This was partly as a reaction to a growth in grass-roots regional consciousness and as a part of the renewed interest in economic planning.

7. The continuance of regionalism. Two factors have been identified by Sharpe as ensuring that some form of regional organisation will survive changing trends.

(*a*) *Functional.* "The interposition of an agent of the central government responsible for the oversight of central government services for an area wider than individual local authorities is necessary if the planning and co-ordination functions are to take the burden from Whitehall, whilst being able to reflect back to the centre the particular interests and problems of the area" (*British Politics and Two Regionalisms*).

(*b*) *Political.* A measure of devolution will satisfy political demands for autonomy that cannot be met by a centralised administrative system. The extent of decentralisation will depend at least to some extent on the strength and organisation of regionalist or nationalist groups.

8. Developments during the 1970s. The implementation of local government reform in 1974 and the proposals for devolution made in the Kilbrandon report (Cmnd. 5460, 1973) are the main developments impinging on the question of regionalism.

9. The reform of local government. Although the new local government system is not a regional system it involved the creation of authorities that are, on average, substantially larger than those they replaced. The Redcliffe-Maud report that preceded the reform was also concerned with regionalism and recommended the creation of larger single-tier authorities rather than the two or three-tier system that was introduced. Derek Senior, a member of the commission, produced a dissenting memorandum to the report in which he advocated the creation of thirty-five regional authorities and 148 second-tier authorities. His ideas were based on the belief that reorganisation should reflect social geographical considerations, i.e. where people live and work and in which areas they function. Senior classified each *city region* into *mature* (e.g.,

Leeds, London, Birmingham), *emergent* (e.g., Hull, Middles-brough, Norwich), *embryonic* (e.g., Leicester, Coventry, Exeter) or *potential* (e.g., Ashford, Ipswich, Plymouth), each with a minimum population of 250,000.

10. The Kilbrandon Report. The Royal Commission on the Constitution considered the question of separate legislative assemblies for Scotland and Wales.

It identified the arguments in favour of such a reform as being political and administrative, considering that there were advantages of efficiency to be gained from more localised control of administration and decision-making. However, it noted that EEC membership curtailed the scope for regional variation of policy and the danger of incompatible policies being developed.

11. Subsequent policy. The White Paper *Our Changing Democracy: Devolution to Scotland and Wales* (Cmnd. 6348, 1975) favoured devolution of powers to elected assemblies, a policy based partly on the arguments of the Commission, but mainly upon political events—the Scottish National Party had polled 11.4 per cent of the Scottish vote in the 1970 election, 22 per cent in February 1974 and 30 per cent in October 1974.

However, the Labour party because of dissidents within Parliament failed to secure the passage of the Scotland and Wales Bill in 1977, but managed to pass devolution bills for Scotland and Wales in 1978—these however were dependent upon referenda approving the measures.

12. The devolution referenda. Held in March 1979, the Welsh electors rejected the proposal heavily by nearly 4 to 1, while in Scotland there was a majority in favour (51.6 per cent to 48.4 per cent). There was, however, a requirement of 40 per cent of electors approving for the measure to go through and the 51.6 per cent of those actually voting only amounted to 32.5 per cent of those entitled to vote. The government's setback in these referenda led indirectly to its defeat in a vote of confidence and to the 1979 election. The present Conservative government is committed only to convening all party talks on the question and the fall in the share of the vote of the SNP (to 21.9 per cent) has meant that for the time being the pressure for devolution is off.

FOR AND AGAINST REGIONALISM

13. General advantages of regionalism. These may be seen as follows.

(*a*) Economic planning is more effective where larger regional authorities exist, having sufficient resources and powers to enable them to exert an influence on central policy.

(*b*) Regional authorities would constitute a more effective democratic counterbalance to the power of central government than is provided by the present local authorities.

(*c*) Environmental planning can only be effective over wider areas than those at present existing. Regional authorities would be able to achieve an overall rather than a piecemeal approach, and thus could justify the devolution of "real" powers.

(*d*) The economies of large-scale organisation could be reaped, both in the spheres of capital use and in elected and official manpower.

(*e*) The inadequacy of present local boundaries in regard to such matters as roads, further education, etc., could be overcome.

(*f*) Regional authorities would be in a stronger position to raise capital on the open market.

14. Arguments against regionalism. These are as follows.

(*a*) It is suggested that certain almost insoluble questions are basic to the whole concept of regionalism, namely:

(*i*) at what level should the authorities operate?

(*ii*) what should be their relations with the central government in order to achieve an adequate balance of power?

(*iii*) how should they be organised to achieve their objectives?

(*b*) Certain functions go beyond regional boundaries, e.g. location of industry, investment programmes and priorities, and would thus operate to reduce regional authorities to a mere advisory status in many important fields.

(*c*) It is constantly argued that regional authorities would be too remote from the electorate to be effective democratic organisations. However, against this should be noted the following points:

(*i*) the increase in spatial mobility has expanded the concept of the locality;

(*ii*) there is no necessary connection between size and democracy;

(*iii*) provisions for second-tier authorities within the regions are constantly advanced by most proponents of regionalism.

(*d*) There is likely to be an internal lack of unity of purpose between representatives of areas within the regions which will detract from an overall objectivity in decision-making, e.g. in such matters as slum clearance priorities.

EUROPEAN ADMINISTRATION

15. The European Economic Community. It is necessary when studying the system of public administration in any one of the ten member countries of the EEC to consider the institutions of the Community. As the Community is a body possessing a measure of sovereign power that it uses to make and implement decisions, its institutions are a part of the system of administration in each member state. For students of public administration the case of the EEC is particularly interesting as an example of how a political administration has to adapt itself to the political system and institutions it is designed to serve (*see* **19** below).

16. The nature of the EEC. The EEC has been described as a *hybrid* organisation (R. Stacey and J. C. Oliver, *Public Administration, The Political Environment*, Macdonald and Evans, 1980), in as much as it contains elements of a *federal structure* (having some autonomous power over member states) and elements of a simple *international association* in that its supreme decision-making body (the Council of Ministers), consists of delegates from each of the member states.

17. The structure of the Community. *The Treaty of Rome*, signed in 1957, effectively represents the Community constitution. It is a long and complex document dealing with two fundamental issues. Firstly, it is concerned with the key question in any federal arrangement—how much power is handed over. In Europe this difficulty was compounded by the long-established independent legal, social, economic and political systems operating within each member state. Thus the second concern of the Treaty was to provide a framework for the *gradual development* of a supranational authority—a more complex task than setting up a system where before there had been none.

The Treaty declares that *eventually* an *Economic Union* is to be established and that it is the duty of the signatories and the Community institutions to work towards this end. If achieved, union would imply the same freedom of economic activity anywhere within the Community as at present enjoyed by citizens within their nation-states.

18. The administrative structure and its political leadership. All political systems are concerned with the resolution of conflict, the making of authoritative decisions and their subsequent implementation. Where political differences between groups of people, organisations and political parties are particularly wide, the political system is always under greater strain. In the case of Europe the differences to be resolved *within* countries are compounded by those *between* countries, which makes reaching a decision particularly difficult. This difficulty is regularly evidenced by reports of talks in Brussels (the Community headquarters) "breaking down". The institutional structure of the Community recognises the likelihood of this difficulty and is designed to ensure that efforts towards agreement are sustained rather than abandoned as would probably be the case if it were simply an international association and not a hybrid federation.

THE COMMUNITY INSTITUTIONS

19. The Commission. The Commission represents the force for *unity* within the system. It comprises fourteen Commissioners (two each from the four largest member states and one each from the other six). The Commissioners have a staff of about 6,000, which is much smaller than the impression given in the press when describing the "Eurocrats" of Brussels.

20. The independence of the Commission. Commissioners, although appointed by member governments, are all committed "pro-Europeans" and when in office operate independently of their country of origin and act in the interests of the Community as a whole.

21. The role of the Commission. The Commission represents the civil service of the Community and as such *executes* the policies decided upon. The Common Agricultural Policy (CAP) accounts for the bulk of its work at present as this is the only large-scale developed policy so far. The Commission also has a *policy* role, being responsible for the initial formulation of proposals that the Council of Ministers will discuss. It is in this work that the Commission has to be especially sensitive to political feeling within and between the member states. To achieve this the Commission is constantly engaged in a massive consultation exercise—taking opinion and evidence from governments, organisations and individuals before formulating proposals. Revision of proposals may take place during Council meetings in order to take account of difficulties encountered there.

22. The Council of Ministers. The Council does not have a fixed membership, it consists of ministers from the member governments, which depending upon the subject under discussion; for example, at a Council considering agricultural matters the ten agriculture ministers will attend. Although pledged through the Treaty to seek unity, the Council reflects *disunity* within the system, with ministers arguing strongly to maximise their country's benefits and minimise their contributions. Thus the Council and Commission must act together to progress.

European summit meetings between the heads of state are now a regular part of the Council process and they may be regarded as Council meetings considering policy at the highest, most general, level.

23. Committees of permanent representatives. Each country sends an ambassador and staff to the Community to liaise and brief ministers attending Council meetings. These civil servants provide a link between the administrations of the member countries, ministers and the Commission. Very often the "Corepers" are able to agree a considerable part of the agenda of Council meetings in advance enabling ministers to simply give formal approval.

24. The European Parliament. The Parliament does not represent the legislative power of the community; this is held by the Council. It is a consultative body, and an examination of Fig. 5 will show that it does not occupy a central position in the Community decision-making system. Since 1979 the Parliament has been directly elected and it can be expected that its members, being able to claim that they directly represent the citizens of the community, may politically manoeuvre to gain more power.

25. The European Court of Justice. The Court interprets the law of the Community and is the supreme arbiter on questions involving Community law—again illustrating the federal element in the system. The Court also has review powers, in that it may question the actions of the Council or Commission if they act outside the

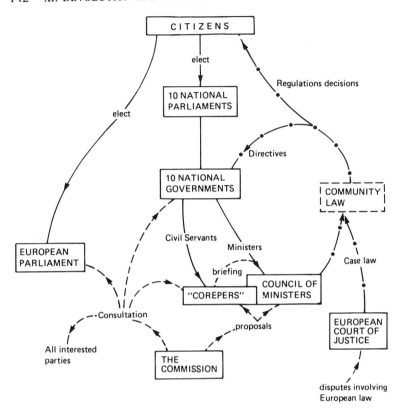

FIG. 4   *Operational relationships between European and national institutions.*

powers given to them in the Treaty, so it is thus a *Constitutional Court.*

26. The authority of the Community. Legally this stems from the Treaty, however, politically it is derived from the fact that the Council has agreed decisions, and Council members represent the citizens of their own countries and thus the whole Council represents the whole Community. The importance of this is recognised by the convention that has developed whereby decisions are taken unanimously rather than by vote even though voting provision is laid down in the Treaty.

27. Growth of international organisations. International organisations are a permanent and growing aspect of political life; this is inevitable with the development of issues that have cross-national implications such as war, population, economic growth and its consequences, the resource question, etc. Frankel in *International Politics* (Pelican, 1973) considers that "clearly the State is only a segment of a larger whole, of mankind; for many essential purposes, only the whole world is a significant area of activity."

PROGRESS TEST 11

1. Define and distinguish the terms decentralisation, deconcentration and devolution.   **(1)**

2. Why is decentralisation necessary?   **(2)**

3. Explain why, despite the evidence of the Kilbrandon Report and acceptance by the government, that Scottish and Welsh devolution did not come about.   **(11–12)**

4. Outline a general case for and against regionalism.   **(13–14)**

5. Explain why the EEC has been described as a hybrid organisation.   **(16)**

6. Explain the way that the institutions of the EEC work together to bring about common policies.   **(18–25)**

7. Why must the Commission be aware of political differences between various elements in the EEC?   **(18–21)**

8. By reference to examples explain why international political institutions are likely to increase in number in the future.   **(27)**

CHAPTER XII

The Relationship of Central and Local Government

INTRODUCTION

1. Basic features of the relationship. As a unitary state local government organisation is created by act of the national Parliament. Although formally Parliament may repeal, amend or revise local government through legislation, in practice local authorities, being elected and having been established in various forms for a long time have power and the established right to be influential in determining their own structure and affairs.

It was intended in the legislation establishing the pattern of local authorities that they should have a measure of independence from central government. How *much* independence is a matter of controversy. Generally the trend of argument has suggested that local government should be more independent on democratic grounds—the reforms of 1974 were justified in terms of creating more effective self-sufficient units. Most administrations have paid lip-service to the idea of giving local government more independence; for example in a 1979 White Paper 300 controls over local authorities were relinquished, though in practice none were really significant.

The Layfield Report 1976 on finance stated that for effective decisions to be made concerning reform of finance a fundamental decision must first be made as to whether it was intended that the authorities should be independent. Given that the most important controls are financial it may be argued that in the light of developments since 1976 central government has exerted more control (*see* IX, **8**)

2. Central government control. The relationship between central and local government hinges on the degree of control exerted by Whitehall. There is no system of control as such, various departments are involved in a complex two-way relationship in which central government is the ultimate arbiter. The following aspects of the relationship are important.

(a) *Absence of unified control*, by contrast with the French system whereby the *Maire* and the *Préfet*, senior officials of the local units of government are Interior Ministry employees.

(b) *Some independent finance* from the rates and charges for services. However the proportion of finance from rates continues to decline.

(c) *Consultation* directly with authorities and with their associations is normal practice and may be regarded as having the force of a constitutional convention.

(d) *The concept of national minima* is one of the key reasons for central control, which is designed to ensure that authorities at least maintain an acceptable level of service provision.

(e) *Party politics* may heighten central–local conflict, thus difficulties will be greater between authorities where a party other than the governing party has control. This applies to relationships between the government and individual authorities and between government and the local authority associations, e.g. the GLC and Metropolitan counties clearly saw the Conservative Government's proposals for their abolition as at least partly stemming from the fact that they were largely Labour controlled.

3. The effects of economic planning. Local authorities are in principle required to conform to the broad economic and social patterns established by the central government. Consequently, elements in the relationship which might have a liberalising effect are suppressed by the exigencies of national planning. Features of such planning over the last twenty years have included the following:

(a) the adoption of patterns of economic development;

(b) the projection of economic trends and the requirement that short-term policy should fall within the boundaries of such projections;

(c) the establishment as a result of the *Plowden Report* of 1961 of long-term surveys of public expenditure and probable resources, and the need to make long-term decisions in the light of such surveys.

4. The inflexibility of planning. The effect of systematic national expenditure planning is emphasis on its relative inflexibility, and consequently to render local authority expenditure and programmes subordinate to this overall picture. Planning is inflexible in the following ways:

(*a*) priorities determinable at any particular point in time are marginal and do not permit of excessive policy changes;

(*b*) major policy decisions involve long-term sunk costs;

(*c*) any expenditure decision must be taken in the context of limited public financial resources.

5. The financial aspect of the relationship. Since 1945 grants to local authorities have increased at a faster rate than local expenditure, and now constitute approximately 60 per cent of combined grant and rate income.

During the 1974–79 Labour government the Rate Support Grant (RSG) was used as a means of enforcing economy, this power was greatly extended in the Local Government Planning and Land Act 1980 and the Rates Act 1984.

THE CENTRAL DEPARTMENTS INVOLVED

6. The departments. The principal departments involved with local authorities are the Department of the Environment, incorporating the very important local government ministries of Housing and Local Government, the Ministry of Transport, and the Department of Education and Science. Relationships with local authorities vary between the departments, and this consideration will probably continue to apply despite merging of departments.

The Environment department has traditionally left the local authorities considerable initiative in public health, housing and planning. It did not operate an inspectorial system and constantly rejected a supervisory role. It exercised informal influence in the field of local organisation, but elsewhere was principally concerned with the approval of schemes (*see* **19**(*b*)) and in the application of legislation to local authorities. Recently, however, in the light of social and economic policy, the role of the ministry as adviser and provider of tools has changed towards interventionism through the use of such forces as loan sanction.

7. Transport. The relationship is affected and modified by the fact that both central and local authorities are providers of services in their own rights. In fact, even in the ministry field of major roads, a considerable impetus has sprung from local authorities. However, cost control through the grant system has proved important, as has the increasing role of highways in national planning.

8. Social services. In a historical context the role of the Home

Office with regard to social services, subsequently transferred to the Department of Health and Social Security, provides an interesting example of the development of control, although this control is at the present day much less significant due to the strengthening of local administration by the concentration of social services at county levels as a result of the Local Authorities Social Services Act. The control developed as a result of the concentration originally of skilled manpower at the centre, and led the Home Office to see its role in relation to local authorities as that of maintaining material standards; disseminating information and advice; and supervising services in the general context of government policy.

9. The Department of Education and Science (DES). Section 1 of the Education Act 1944, *prima facie* gives the Department of Education and Science powerful control powers, and other powers of considerable importance are detailed in specific sections of the Act; e.g. the prescribing of standards for school premises, the role of the inspectorate and indication of education plans by the local authority in a Development Plan.

Table I summarises some aspects of the relationship between the DES and Local Education Authorities (LEAs).

CONCEPTS OF CONTROL

10. *Laissez-faire* approach. This attitude is typified by the old Ministry of Health, which adopted a comparatively less interventionist attitude in relation to such matters as collection, analysis and dissemination of information, research and insistence on compliance with departmental policies. It is possible that this attitude was a result of the small proportion of grant-aided welfare expenditure. This view, however, probably places too great a correlation on finance and control, and tends to mask the ultimate arbiter, which is national interest in the level and nature of services provided.

NOTE: Unfortunately the *laissez-faire* approach is often justified on the fallacious ground that local authorities will only progress if left to learn by their own mistakes, and the reliance on the electorate as the final judge of local authority standards.

11. Hybrid approach. The approach of the old Ministry of Housing and local government was *laissez-faire* to the extent that it

TABLE I. THE RELATIONSHIP OF THE DEPARTMENT OF EDUCATION AND SCIENCE TO LOCAL AUTHORITIES

Tasks	DES decisions	LEA decisions
1. Decisions on structure of education—age of entry, age of compulsory retention.	1. DES proposes laws and controls major resources through building programmes, etc.	1. Able to vary age of transfer between primary and secondary, lower and upper secondary and further education institutions.
2. Decisions on finance of education.	2. DES negotiates elements of rate support grants through Department of Environment.	2. LEA decides proportion of income (grants, rates, etc.) to devote to education generally. And decides all individual projects and rates of capitation funds for books and equipment.
3. Building.	3. DES decides, within Treasury constraints, total amount of major and minor building projects. DES decides lists of major projects.	3. LEA decides which major projects to propose, and which minor projects to build.
4. Teaching and learning processes.	4. (a) Statutory controls over length and number of school days,	4. (a) Decides style of education through appointments of heads,

	(b) statutory controls over prayers and religious education, (c) control of patterns of secondary school and further education examinations. (Plus: gains advice from inspectors.)	(b) advisory services, (c) in-service training, (d) decides overall organisational patterns, (e) local inspectors may make quality judgments affecting, for example, teachers' promotions.

5. Provision of teachers.

5. (a) Control of total numbers reaching and leaving colleges, (b) party to salary and conditions-of-service negotiations, (c) operates "voluntary" quota system.

5. (a) Settles establishments for each institution, (b) controls appointments of heads and deputies, (c) runs promotion system, (d) in-service education.

6. Development of system.

6. (a) Establishment of objectives (but not explicit), (b) decisions on length of school and training life.

6. Make decisions on general response of education service in area to the needs, by providing institutional framework, methods improving service, nature of relationships with community, other services and parents.

Source: *The Economist*, 1 December 1976

permitted local authorities to determine their broad needs and how these are to be met. In the field of housing provision, however, a hybrid or intermixed approach was noticeable in that central officials would not question local housing decisions unless they appeared to be clearly beyond the capacities of the local authorities and local building industries; it was regulatory in the control of standards, layout and design, and it was promotional in the large extent of advisory material issued and in the sponsoring of consortia and industrialised building.

12. Regulatory approach. The Home Office typified this approach in respect of the children's services which are now under the control of the DHSS. Emphasis was placed on the inspectorate for the following reasons:

(*a*) the service was comparatively new and standards uncertain;

(*b*) local authority departments were too weak to admit of great independence;

(*c*) central help was necessary in order to promote minimum standards.

13. Concepts of central control. The relationship of central government and local authorities may be conceptualised as follows.

(*a*) *Constitutional.* Its existence is between two groups of government institutions, each having separate legal existence.

(*b*) *Political.* The powers of one group complement and conflict with the powers of the other. Basically this dichotomy must be resolved in the democratic context by co-operation rather than coercion. However, the departments are in a stronger position and make far more of the important decisions.

NOTE: Any consideration of the reform of the relationship is unreal to the extent that it fails to accept that the government will reject any reform which makes more difficult the execution of government policies.

(*c*) *Administrative.* The relationship concerns the actual execution of policies. However, the assumption that local authorities are merely agents for the execution of policy decided by government departments is incorrect in that it ignores both that local authorities make and influence the making of policy, and that departments themselves are deeply involved in the administrative process at the local level.

(*d*) *Financial.* In any organisational relationship the body providing or having control over finance will be in a superior position and thus able to exert control. The degree of control may be directly related to the amount of finance it provides.

14. The necessary functions of central government. The government has the following responsibilities.

(*a*) *Promotion of the national interest.* The government is basically responsible for defining and promoting the national interest, for ensuring that local and factional interests do not impede the promotion of the general interest. This recognition of national importance necessarily subordinates local authorities politically to the central government, although legally they retain independence.

(*b*) *Fixing of standards.* Professor Griffiths (in *Central Departments and Local Authorities*, Allen and Unwin, 1966) considered that the basic reason that central departments retain control over local authorities is that they cannot trust all local authorities not to economise to such an extent that the quality of services would be inadequate; e.g. it is the universal practice of all government departments to insist on minimum constructional standards. This control over the adequacy of services provided is at the heart of the whole relationship. Adequacy itself involves two separate factors namely:

(*i*) services are inadequate if less than the requirements of national policy;

(*ii*) they are unacceptable if provision exceeds the allotted share of resources, or if they seek to achieve ends other than those laid down as national policy.

NOTE: Where a service complies with national standards but varies in adequacy the right of intervention arises and provides a basic dilemma between local democracy and efficiency. Although perhaps an overriding principle of control it would seem that in view of the economies imposed by central government in recent years it may be suggested that in times of financial stringency the criteria becomes that of preventing overspending.

15. The position of local authorities. Factors influencing the relationship of individual local authorities with the central government include the following.

(*a*) *Size.* Size differences create differences in relationships with the central government. Large authorities (500,000 plus) are able to employ larger staffs, operate larger programmes and are so well known in the departments that their wishes carry a great weight. In particular, their chief officers, committee chairmen, etc., have national political importance. These authorities, being in a better position to persuade and influence, are consequently allowed greater freedom and flexibility of action than the smaller, weaker authorities, which are sometimes adversely treated because of their comparative inexperience and paucity of resources.

(b) *Party political influence.* The degree of coincidence and influence with the central political organisation.

(c) *Physical closeness to London.* This is more effective in maintaining the two-way relationship with the central government.

NOTE: Attitudes may have developed over a period of time, independent of any of the above grounds. In addition, external pressure is more noticeable in popular functions, such as education and traffic, rather than in the more altruistic functions such as mental health.

16. Role of the local authority associations. These are important as collective voices of local authorities in influencing legislation, government policies and administration, and as channels of local authority opinion. Their activities fall into the following three main categories.

(a) *In relation to central departments.* Government departments operate in close connection with the associations, with frequent consultations. However, the associations complain that on occasions they are not consulted in advance on technical publications containing policy statements. In general, however, secretaries of the associations are consulted about changes in government policy affecting local authorities, whether involving legislative or administrative introduction.

(b) *In relation to Parliament.* They operate here to seek amendment of bills affecting local authorities and the sponsoring and promotion of measures affecting local authorities. In this respect they employ parliamentary vice-presidents.

(c) *In relation to members.* In this respect they are principally concerned with advice on legal matters and on administrative and policy questions.

The associations are party controlled—if the majority of county councils are Conservative (which is usually the case) then the Association of County Councils (ACC) will be Conservative controlled. This affects the relationship between the associations and the government. When they are of the same party, as for example in 1979 after the election of the Conservative government, discord tends to be low key and is channelled through other organisations —such as the public sector unions and individual authorities that are aligned with the opposition.

METHODS OF CONTROL

17. Informal central control. Methods of control exist outside the statutory field and are exercised through various conventional forms. Such control is exercised in the following three main ways.

(*a*) Circulars are issued, consisting of letters drawing attention to suggested desirable procedures. They take the form also of practice codes, memoranda, etc., designed both to raise efficiency standards and to explain or reinforce ministerial policy. The tone of circulars indicates the degree of compulsion, Ministers may "require" or simply "request".

(*b*) Departments and ministeries act as "clearing houses" for the dissemination of information, and for guidance of local authorities in respect of administrative problems.

(*c*) Informal advice is given to local authorities through the inspectorial system.

18. Why informal control is effective. Although not based on any statutory foundation, informal influence upon authorities tends to achieve directive status. The acceptance of this non-mandatory control by local authorities rests upon the following factors.

(*a*) *Partnership.* The functional overlapping between central and local government creates a relationship dependent on the development of a partnership approach to various rights and duties.

(*b*) *Informal consultations.* The practice of consultations prior to the introduction of legislation tightens the relationship between central and local authorities and enables the setting of standards which may be clarified by ministerial advice.

(*c*) *Sharing of knowledge.* Administrative and technical knowledge acquired by central departments is made available to local authorities.

(*d*) *Conformity.* The background of central control is the necessity of ensuring conformity with centrally established standards, particularly where the central authority is able to back up such conformity with financial sanctions. Thus in order to secure vital financial aid, local authorities must conform with ministerial policy, expressed in informal means of control.

(*e*) *Ultimate sanction.* In the final analysis, conformity with informal control is reinforced by the possibility of the central authority seeking recourse to additional or existing statutory powers.

19. Statutory powers. Central departments generally seek to rely on specific powers when exercising formal control, rather than on the general powers expressed in certain statutes, e.g. the Education Act 1944. For the purpose of this section it is proposed to deal only with the principal forms of statutory control, namely, financial control and control through the approval of schemes.

(*a*) *Financial control.* This is exercised through the following.

(*i*) Control through grants, which was achieved historically through the medium of specific grants, has now been altered in emphasis, as the greater part of grant aid to local authorities is given through the Rate Support Grant which is of course a general grant. However both the global amount of the grant and its method of allocation are controlled by the central government and the grant is thus a broad-edged tool for influencing local authority expenditure decisions. Its importance has been particularly illustrated over recent years when by a culmination of exhortation and grant control the expenditure of local authorities has been prescribed by the overall national economic strategy and has involved limited growth programmes and capital investment by local authorities (*see* IX, **8**).

Increasing use is being made by central government of "cash limits" as a means of controlling expenditure. The 1979 Conservative administration has moved towards cash-based (rather than volume) planning which represents a further control.

(*ii*) Loan sanction is effected under the provisions of the Local Government Act 1972, which requires ministerial sanction before loan-raising powers are used. As local authorities are forced to borrow for all major projects, a potent form of control is placed in the hands of the minister, such control being enhanced in times of national stringency.

NOTE: A limited measure of freedom in respect of loans was implemented during 1971, but is not sufficient to invalidate the general premise of loans as a potent form of control.

(*b*) *Approval of schemes.* This technique requires local authorities to submit schemes for carrying out particular services to the appropriate central government department. This system is justified on the grounds of taking account of local variations, the devolution of administrative responsibilities and the exercise of local initiative. In practice, however, it necessitates conformity with central policy and standards before a scheme is accepted. Important examples exist under the Education Act 1944, in regard to local educational needs, and under the Town and Country Planning Act 1971, in regard to development plans.

20. Recent developments. New controls have developed as a part of the policy of central government to control public expenditure generally. In 1975 the *Consultative Council on Local Government Finance* (CCLGF) (*see* IX, 8), provides a forum within which economies are discussed centrally. Thus for example the July 1979 CCLGF meeting was concerned with determining those services which were "dispensable" as far as cuts were concerned.

The *Joint Manpower Watch* monitors developments in manpower levels in local authorities with the object of identifying those authorities whose productivity is comparatively poor. Although central government has no power to "hire and fire" locally, those authorities whose manpower levels compare unfavourably will be placed in a weaker bargaining position in the competition for scarce resources.

The *Local Government Planning and Land Act* 1980 and the controls it introduced must also be seen as a significant increase in central government control, far outweighing the relaxation of specific detailed controls of the 1979 White Paper.

CONCLUSIONS

21. Cumulative effect of controls. Central control falls short of dictatorship over local authorities, but the various powers do have a marked cumulative effect. The result of such cumulative effect is that, whilst local authorities exercise a degree of autonomy, they are in general forced to comply with overall central policy. As a result, also, local authorities tend to look to the centre for guidance even when this is not legally or practically required. This attitude of dependence and the wide powers of central influence tend to make local authorities act as local administrative bodies responsible for considering local variations, but basically agents of central policy.

22. Justification of central control. The following points should be noted.

(*a*) *Role of the state*. The increase in state functions, which now range from social welfare to the promotion of economic prosperity, have a notable centralising tendency and can only be effectively operated from the centre.

(*b*) *Defects of local authorities*. The incapability of local authorities, through structural inadequacy and resource disparities, to maintain common standards.

(*c*) *Financial assistance*. Increasing financial dependence of local authorities on central grants, and the inelasticity and inadequacy of the rating system.

(*d*) *Uniformity*. The need to achieve common standards can only be achieved through government direction.

(*e*) *Greater resources*. The larger resources of the central government both financially and on the technical and administrative sides.

(*f*) *National interest*. The requirement that sectional interests be subordinated to those of the nation as a whole and the necessity of central control for the implementation of such domination.

(*g*) *Economic policy*. Most recent controls have been directed towards limiting public expenditure.

23. Disadvantages of central control. In modern social and economic conditions a measure of central control is probably both inevitable and desirable. Disadvantages stem, however, from excessive control, in particular the following:

(*a*) local variations are often ignored as a result of the remoteness and size of the central machine;

(*b*) local initiative may be destroyed;

(*c*) loss of interest may be attributed to a lack of local power, and the accompanying feelings of impotence and lack of importance.

24. The outlook and suggested principles. The following points have been made.

(*a*) The Local Government Manpower Committee, 1948, suggested that the relationship should be one where "local authorities are responsible bodies competent to discharge their own functions ... they exercise their responsibilities in their own right ... the objective (of central control) should be to leave as much as possible of the detailed management of a scheme or service to the local authority and to concentrate the department's control at key points where it can most effectively discharge its respon-sibilities for government policy and financial administration".

(b) The Maud Committee on Management considered that there was a need to check the steady reduction of discretion allowed to local authorities and to prevent their conversion into mere agencies of the central government. In particular, the Com-mittee thought that though Whitehall should in the national interest control investment policy it ought not to exend this control to details of local building and expenditure. In consequence it recommended a strengthening of local taxing powers and a greater realism in respect of loan sanction.

(c) The Redcliffe-Maud Commission considered that imple-mentation of its proposals would result in a shift of power and responsibility from the central government to the strengthened local councils, and would involve a more meaningful dialogue be-tween the two. Lord Redcliffe-Maud himself subesquently asserted that the central government would be happy to transfer such authority. The Commission considered that the key factor in lack of local autonomy was the size and ability of local units to meet their enhanced responsibilities.

25. The dynamics of the relationship. Although attention has been drawn to the formal and informal methods of control it is impor-tant to consider the nature of the central–local relationship as a dynamic process. In this respect the following basic assumptions may be suggested.

(a) Each local authority and each central department is an individual decision-making unit with its own values.

(b) Each individual authority has different strategies open to it in the pursuit of these values.

(c) The two-way process may be viewed as one of *control* flowing from the centre which is reciprocated by *influence* flowing inwards from the localities.

(d) The overall pattern is in turn largely structured by the financial system in which the system operates.

A pattern may thus be built up describing in general terms the relationship. Bearing in mind that the centre is internally differen-tiated and that this produces a fragmentation of central–local relationships, the central influence may be seen as a two part process, viz. conflicts leading to the use of regulations, schemes, etc., resolving into the local authority decision (*control function*) and on the other hand the objective of influencing local values and dispositions through the use of grants and informal methods of control and resulting in the ultimate local authority decision (*influence function*).

For its own part the local authorities exercise influence through local political parties, MPs, petitions, deputations, and act collectively as pressure groups (*counterbalancing function*).

26. The future. It is suggested that the most important factor in the future of local government is that of enabling the system to adapt sufficiently to undertake all it should and could perform. Since 1945 there have been appreciable changes in the factors affecting the role of local government, each tending to reinforce central concentration, as follows:

(*a*) the development and acceptance of the ideal of national physical, financial and economic planning;

(*b*) the demand for more and better public servants and the political response of such demand (particularly with regard to schools, roads and urban renewal);

(*c*) the demographic and other movements which have made regional movements more apparent and which have resulted in increased political activity.

These factors must be considered when examining local autonomy and although the reforms of 1963 (London) and 1974 increased the potential power of local government the 1980 and 1984 Acts together with the planned abolition of the GLC and Metropolitan counties can be seen as re-establishing central control.

PROGRESS TEST 12

1. What basic features may be discerned in central and local government relations? (**1**)

2. How does economic planning affect the relationship? (**3**)

3. What central departments are mainly concerned with local government? (**5–9**)

4. What different approaches and concepts of control exist? (**10–13**)

5. What are the necessary functions of central government? (**14**)

6. What factors influence the position of local authorities? (**15**)

7. What is the role of the local authority associations? (**16**)

8. What are the principal methods of informal control? Why is such control effective? **(17, 18)**

9. What are the principal forms of statutory control? **(19, 20)**

10. What are the justifications of central control? **(22)**

11. What are the disadvantages of central control? **(23)**

12. What principles of central control have been suggested? **(24)**

CHAPTER XIII

Administration of the Public Sector

INTRODUCTION

1. The extent of public ownership. Public expenditure now accounts for more than half of the Gross Domestic Product. A considerable part of this stems from the spending of the departments of central government and local authorities. However, the so-called "public sector" covers a wider area and includes the activities of public corporations, including the nationalised industries and quangos.

2. Reasons for public ownership. These may be conveniently grouped under three headings: economic, social and political.

(*a*) *Economic*

(*i*) The "commanding heights" argument postulates that certain key industries are so vital to the operation of the whole economy that to leave them in private hands might jeopardise the system.

(*ii*) Control of monopoly power—it is accepted that monopoly firms are able to exert undesirable pressure and that they need to be controlled, so ownership may be considered as the ultimate form of control.

(*iii*) Controlling the economy—through controlling the policies, particularly the investment of state industries, the government may exert influence on the whole economy. Although such control has been criticised as interfering with the commercial freedom of nationalised industries it would appear that the 1979 Conservative government has revived the practice.

(*b*) *Social*

Consideration of social cost benefits rather than simply private cost/profitability is possible. For example, a state rail company may operate "uneconomic" branch lines on government direction because closure would impose too many other "social costs" on the communities affected—costs that would impose burdens upon other state agencies and individuals such as road congestion, accidents, etc.

(*c*) *Political*

(*i*) Strategic activities—some enterprises, for example communications, are so central to the power of the state that governments cannot conceive allowing them to be in private hands. Certain industries such as steel, atomic energy, vehicles and defence goods are so basic to defence that few governments allow them to be in completely private control.

(*ii*) Socialist party policy favours the extension of public ownership, thus Labour governments have been more inclined than Conservative ones to view the above arguments as requiring nationalisation measures.

3. Arguments against public ownership. These can be stated as follows.

(*a*) The advantages of the free working of economic forces are lost.

(*b*) Public bodies do not provide suitable means of running public concerns.

(*c*) It is difficult to establish suitable working relationships, e.g. between the industries and Parliament.

NOTE: The above arguments (*a*) and (*b*) only apply where the whole of an industry is nationalised and cannot justify piecemeal public control.

4. Main forms of public ownership. The following can be distinguished.

(*a*) *Departmental method.* In this case a minister is directly responsible for all aspects of policy and administration, employees are civil servants and the Treasury has direct financial control; i.e. the acquired industry is on the same status as any other government department. The Post Office was the principal example of this form of organisation until it became a public corporation.

(*b*) *Public corporation method.* The industry is run by an administrative board with a minister responsible for overall policy, but not for day-to-day administration. The board has a self-contained financial structure. The method is based on the desirability of combining commercial freedom with public accountability, the underlying assumption being that such freedom is inhibited by an excessive degree of centralised ministerial control.

5. Other forms of public ownership. As in the private sector there exist in the public sector many different organisational forms.

This is partly a result of the *ad hoc* development of state involvement in a wide range of activities and partly due to conscious attempts to devise structure appropriate to the functions they are to perform.

Many of the semi-autonomous bodies created recently have been dubbed *quangos*, i.e. quasi-autonomous national government organisations. The term covers a wide range of organisations from the Police Complaints Board to the Manpower Services Commission.

The original US definition of the term "quango" referred to *non-governmental* rather than *national* government organisations; this definition is more exclusive, and would not, for example, include the Manpower Services Commission with its staff of civil servants. Such a definition emphasises the patronage power of ministers in appointments to quango boards. The Civil Service Department has established a Public Appointments Unit with a view to monitoring appointments to quangos, and the 1979 Conservative government, anxious to curtail their proliferation, appointed Sir Leo Pliatzky, a former Trade Permanent Secretary, to review this area of government.

Regulatory agencies such as the Monopolies Commission, and marketing boards such as the Milk Marketing Board and the services provided by local authorities controlled by committees, must all be taken into account when reviewing the administration of the public sector.

THE PUBLIC CORPORATION

6. Significance. The public corporation is an important area of study in public administration as it represents a conscious attempt to unite the advantages of public and private administration in one enterprise. Inevitably such a union provokes valid criticisms from both standpoints.

7. Characteristics of public corporations. Professor A. H. Hanson (*Nationalisation*, Allen and Unwin, 1963) identified public corporations as having six principal characteristics.

(*a*) They are wholly state-owned.

(*b*) They are not subject to parliamentary financial scrutiny such as that to which departments are submitted.

(*c*) They are statutorily created and outside the ambit of ordinary company law.

(*d*) They have corporate status and thus can be sued, hold property, enter into contracts, etc.

(*e*) In theory at least they are independently financed through their revenue and through capital borrowing.

(*f*) Employees of public corporations are not civil servants but are employed directly by, and subject to conditions of, the corporations.

8. Their significance in public administration. This results from the following:

(*a*) the nature of the relationships between the corporations, ministers and Parliament;

(*b*) the role of the public corporations in the general sphere of government economic control;

(*c*) the organisational structure of corporations in so far as it represents management organisations and problems in the public sector;

(*d*) their basic nature as instruments of government, i.e. their status as social, economic, or hybrid organisations.

9. Administrative structure. In general, the corporations are governed by boards of ten to twelve people. Problems have arisen with regard to the attraction of suitable membership due to such matters as image, salaries, etc. This has in turn resulted in key significance being placed on a board's chairman. The commercial freedom or otherwise of a corporation may thus largely turn on the formal and informal relations worked out between a minister and individual chairmen.

An early feature of the post-1945 corporations was an emphasis on centralised government control and administrative structure. This was considered desirable for the following reasons:

(*a*) to facilitate large-scale planning;

(*b*) to achieve co-ordination and co-operation between the industries;

(*c*) to involve the industries effectively in the national economic development;

(*d*) to ensure public accountability.

NOTE: This approach was criticised as leading to remote and bureaucratic control, excessive middle management and duplication of functions between the boards and associated departments.

10. Parliamentary supervision. Parliamentary supervision is effectively constrained by such matters as time, the technical nature of the issues involved, and the failure to determine the proper areas of control. The following bodies are involved.

(a) *The finance committees.* The old Select Committee on Estimates, the Public Accounts Committee and the Comptroller and Auditor General do not carry out examinations of the estimates or account of the public corporations, though the Public Accounts Committee retains the power to look at accounts and reports in general terms.

NOTE: However, in so far as the industries rely on the Treasury for capital, Parliament and the Comptroller and Auditor General do have direct involvement with the financial affairs of the corporations.

(b) *Departmental select committees.* A consequence of the new system of departmental select committees (*see* II, **29**) was the winding up of the Select Committee on Nationalised Industries. The industries are now monitored by the relevant departmental committee—they are empowered to establish joint subcommittees to consider matters affecting two or more industries.

11. Some proposals for reform. Proposals to increase parliamentary supervision and ministerial control have included the following:

(a) the attachment of Comptroller and Auditor General functions to the Select Committee;

(b) the creation of ministers as board chairmen;

(c) the creation of a Ministry for Nationalised Industries;

(d) the appointment of a specialised committee (as in France) to examine the efficiency of the industries;

(e) the securing of greater consideration of annual capital expenditure programmes of the industries by the introduction of a Nationalised Industries Investment Bill, or by the creation of a National Advisory Council for Capital Spending.

12. Ministerial responsibility. The main problem is the reconciliation of ministerial responsibility and its attendant control with that of managerial autonomy. The two basic principles of ministerial responsibility are as follows:

(a) securing the public interest;

(b) overseeing the efficiency of the industry.

The minister's powers can be divided as follows.

(*a*) *Statutory powers.* These are probably in many cases of less significance than informal extra-statutory powers, though they of course form the basis of these. The principal statutory powers are concerned with the appointment of boards, giving directions in the national interest, approval of investment programmes, control of borrowing, education and training policy, approval of form of accounts and control of research and development.

(*b*) *Extra-statutory powers.* The minister has important informal powers and influence, operating in such basic fields as broad policy, pricing, etc. The Select Committee on Nationalised Industries considered that a feature of the constituting legislation was that "vital administrative questions, such as the relationship between the managing boards and ministers and Parliament, remains subject for disagreement and negotiation". This results in ministers and industries arriving at informal arrangements concerning such matters as balance of powers, duties of the industries and the nature of ministerial control.

13. Interpretations of control. As a broad division, ministerial control has been concerned with financial and economic matters. Views on the proper extent of ministerial control have ranged as follows.

(*a*) *The commercial view.* The board's autonomy is emphasised.

(*b*) *The middle view.* Balancing of commercial motives and the public interest.

(*c*) *The departmental view.* Boards treated in practice as ministerial departments, with full and detailed control.

The degree of control actually exercised by ministers over nationalised industries within their purview varies considerably; it will depend on, amongst other factors, the personality of the Minister and board chairman involved, political and economic pressures upon the minister and public opinion. In practice these are hard to evaluate and the single most important question is probably that of finance—is the industry self-financing, profitable or loss-making? It could well be argued that the degree of ministerial intervention is in direct proportion to the subsidy the minister has to justify before party and Parliament.

14. Three basic questions. These three diverging views point to three basic questions of control which have to be resolved, namely:

(*a*) to what extent should the boards be commercial bodies?

(*b*) to what extent should ministers be concerned with policy, public interest and operational efficiency questions?

(*c*) should control be intimate or exercised at arm's length?

15. Recent trends. Trends such as decentralisation have been observed within the development of nationalised industries in the United Kingdom but it is difficult to establish a general pattern. For example, the railways in 1955 established six regional boards, while in the same year the Fleck committee considered the National Coal Board to be too decentralised and consequently control over local areas was increased.

Labour governments between 1964 and 1979 marginally increased the extent of nationalisation, taking into public ownership steel, aircraft and shipbuilding firms. The Conservative govern government took over Rolls Royce as an NEB subsidiary emphasising the pragmatic rather than doctrinaire approach to state ownership in the United Kingdom and the importance of reasons other than party programme behind the bulk of state purchasing.

The Conservative government of 1979 was more committed to "privatisation" than most of its postwar predecessors and introduced measures turning British Aerospace, British Airways and the National Freight Corporation into Companies Act companies. Parts of the holding in BP and the NEB holding in ICL were sold and the revenue derived helped finance public expenditure and tax cuts.

The shift towards denationalisation by the Conservative party, and at the same time a more doctrinaire attitude in its favour by the Labour party, effectively illustrates the circumstances under which the Social Democratic Party emerged during the same period.

PROPOSALS FOR REFORM

16. Introduction. Numerous proposals have been made concerning the operation of the public corporation, particularly in the case of the nationalised industries. The difficulties involved in making improvements do not stem so much from the problems of administrating large organisations but from the definition of the aims of the organisation (*see* **5**, **13** and **14**). Reform proposals taking the *commercial* view tend to take the form of defining performance criteria, e.g. rates of return on capital employed; while those taking the *departmental* view tend to concentrate on improving the working relationship between the minister and board. Examples of both situations follow.

17. Select Committee on Nationalised Industries Report, 1968. The Committee concentrated on the relationship between the minister and the industry and the nature of the control exerted by the former.

The Committee considered that the twin basic responsibilities of the minister *vis-à-vis* the industries were the securing of the public interest and the securing of industrial efficiency. Allied were two subsidiary functions, namely acting as spokesman for the industries in Parliament and the Cabinet, and representing parliamentary and Cabinet views to the boards.

Existing methods of control were criticised as follows.

(*a*) Imprecise definition of extent has led to criticism in both the statutory field of investment control and the informal field of price control.

(*b*) Lack of clarity contributes to confusion of purposes, policies, methods and responsibilities; e.g. British Airways have consistently sought to obtain clear policy guidance on the allocation of overseas routes, particularly with the development of independent airlines such as British Caledonian.

(*c*) Confusion of responsibilities between board and minister tends to reflect in two resultant controversies, namely:

(*i*) the responsibilities of the Treasury;

(*ii*) the staffing of the sponsoring departments.

18. Conclusions of the Select Committee. These are as follows.

(*a*) *Advantages of control.*

(*i*) The positive influence of the minister, particularly in the fields of economic thinking and methods.

(*ii*) The importance of control with regard to resolution of conflict between social obligations and efficiency.

(*b*) *Disadvantages of control.*

(*i*) The fact that the advantages would take too long to come to fruition.

(*ii*) The existence of strained relationships.

(*iii*) The danger of an increase in government involvement in detailed management.

(*iv*) The ineffectiveness of ministerial control in policy and operations co-ordination.

(*v*) The lack of clarity of purpose and responsibilities.

19. Principles of control. These are as follows.

(*a*) Control and management cannot be divorced.

(*b*) The overall efficiency of the industries has suffered from a lack of accepted principles.

(*c*) A feature of the statutory basis has been the absence of a definition of relationships.

(*d*) Responsiveness to public interest is really only obtainable through ministerial control.

(*e*) Conclusions as to Parliament's intentions may be drawn from the particular form of nationalisation used.

20. Strategic or tactical control. The former consists of laying down broad economic guidelines, including financial objectives, broad pricing and investment criteria, investment reviews, and overall policy requirements. This form of control is associated with the Department of Trade.

Tactical control involves the application of detailed duties and responsibilities in specific areas of management the use of detailed financial control, close investment scrutiny and the issue of specific directions. This form is associated with the Ministry of Transport. The Committee was broadly in favour of the trend to strategic control, though it felt that tactical control may be appropriate in the case of industries in deficit.

21. Parliamentary accountability. The Committee considered that all ministerial control should be seen against the background of responsibility to Parliament. This Parliamentary concern about accountability together with government concern about efficiency led to the Competition Act 1980 providing the Monopolies and Mergers Commission with powers to investigate efficiency and costs for services provided and any abuse of monopoly power.

22. Conclusions on ministerial responsibility. "The aim should be to allow the boards of the industries to operate within a more certain framework of social and economic requirements, and then to leave them free to attain the best results they can within that framework. Their results should be subject to examination by various devices of accountability" (W. Thornhill, *The Nationalised Industries*, Nelson, 1968).

The Committee established the following ten principles.

(*a*) Ministers must be primarily concerned with the public interest.

(*b*) Economic efficiency should be the responsibility of the minister through broad oversight, but not through involvement in management.

(*c*) Within the above limits the industries should be left as free as possible.

(*d*) Clear demarcation of responsibilities should be established.

(*e*) Strategic control rather than tactical control should be applied.

(*f*) Control should not be wholly formal.

(*g*) Ministers and industries should be publicly accountable.

(*h*) The measure of management success should be the efficiency with which its joint social-economic functions are carried out.

(*i*) Improvement in management should be the objective of the minister.

(*j*) Fruitful control depends on the attitudes of boards and ministers.

23. Social obligations. The Select Committee made the following observations.

(*a*) Social obligations should not be equated with unremunerative operations.

(*b*) Social obligations cover goods, services and methods of production.

(*c*) Such obligations may involve not doing something profitable, as well as carrying out unprofitable tasks.

(*d*) Pricing may take into account social obligations.

(*e*) Social obligations may be imposed by statute.

24. Responsibility. In determining social obligations, two relevant questions are involved.

(*a*) Who should be responsible for determining the nature and extent of social obligations?

(*b*) Who should pay for social obligations?

The Committee took the view that ministers and boards should be commonly motivated, except where variations were necessary to promote social welfare. The minister should interpret public interest in meeting such obligations, and the boards should be compensated for carrying out such tasks.

25. Selection and definition. The minister should be responsible for precise definition of social obligations to be imposed upon the boards for the following reasons:

(*a*) he carries wider responsibility for the social, economic and public interest;

(*b*) value judgments are his province;

(*c*) relevant figures for wider costs come from outside the industries;

(*d*) there is a likelihood of bias in the industries;

(*e*) the minister is responsible for handling public funds.

The Select Committee report is still widely regarded as a reference point against which performance is still judged. Other reform proposals on particular aspects of the industries activities are dealt with in each of the following sections. It is interesting to distinguish the proposals made by select committees and "outside" bodies such as the NEDC (*see* **40**) from the intentions of governments as defined by their White Papers on the subject . Here the more persistent theme of Labour (intervention), Conservative (defining performance criteria) may be seen. Governments tend to take an expedient rather than theoretical view of the question.

ECONOMIC AND FINANCIAL FRAMEWORK OF PUBLIC CORPORATIONS

26. Basic features. These are as follows.

(*a*) The economic obligations of the industries are the main determinants of their activities.

(*b*) The constituting statutes are inadequate in regard to financial obligations.

(*c*) The choice of instruments for economic control has varied over the years.

27. Recommendations of the 1961 White Paper. The White Paper *Financial and Economic Obligations of the Nationalised Industries* (Cmnd. 1337) laid down the principle that "although the industries have obligations of a national and non-commercial kind, they are not ... to be regarded as social services absolved from economic and social justification".

The industries had been criticised because of their inadequate reserves position, their heavy reliance on Treasury borrowings and their low returns. The White Paper in consequence recommended the following.

(*a*) The duty of the industries to pay their way should be applied over five-year periods.

(*b*) Provision should be made from revenue for capital development.

(*c*) Investment review procedures should be codified.

(*d*) Ministers should take an interest in pricing policies.

(*e*) Boards should be compensated in respect of unprofitable "social" activities carried out at the government's request.

28. Criticisms of the White Paper. The 1961 White Paper was criticised on the following grounds.

(*a*) The concepts of financial objectives were equivocal and could be interpreted either positively, as the achievement of profits, or negatively, as the mere preservation of capital.

(*b*) Whilst concentrating on end results it gave little guidance as to the means for achieving these ends.

(*c*) Financial objectives gave inadequate guidance as to investment policies.

29. Recommendations of the 1967 White Paper. The White Paper *A Review of Economic and Financial Objectives* stated the following.

(*a*) Emphasis should be placed on "laying down criteria which will have a regulatory effect" rather than the exercise of ministerial control by "end result" objectives. Financial objectives are only "economically justifiable to the extent that they reflect sound investment and pricing policies".

(*b*) Emphasis should be placed on optimising the allocation of resources and the need for developing the economic thinking of the industries.

(*c*) Emphasis should be placed on "strategic control" (*see* **18**).

THE RELATIONSHIP BETWEEN GOVERNMENT AND PUBLIC CORPORATIONS

30. The developing relationship. The relationship of ministers and industries has become in general one of strategic guidance coupled with commercial autonomy. This relationship is not always reflected in the institutional structure of control, and often leads to a confusion of purpose between ministries, the Treasury and the boards.

The dual responsibilities of the minister (*see* **17**) and their concentration in a single minister was considered by the Select Committee to be the principal cause of confusion.

31. A ministry for nationalised industries. The Committee considered that the new structure for control should be the creation of a single ministry responsible for the overseeing efficiency functions, with other functions remaining in the existing departments. The new ministry would deal with the following:

(*a*) appointment and dismissal of boards;

(*b*) pricing and investment policies, approval of capital structures and borrowing, reviewing investment programmes and agreeing financial objectives;

(*c*) furthering inter-industry co-ordination and co-operation;

(*d*) efficiency studies and general oversight of organisational efficiency;

(*e*) accounting to Parliament.

32. Advantages. These are as follows:

(*a*) optimum use of resources;

(*b*) increased specialisation and the development, through unity of experience and common purpose, of a more consistent relationship to the industries;

(*c*) effective co-ordination of commercial policies and promotion of common management and control techniques;

(*d*) inter-industry co-operation of pricing policies, demand forecasts and investment programmes;

(*e*) the possibility that the minister could act as a spokesman for all the industries.

33. Treasury objections. These were as follows:

(*a*) such separation as envisaged by the Committee was impracticable;

(*b*) ministers should continue to be responsible for sectors whether in public or private ownership, but the Committee considered sector control to be a policy responsibility;

(*c*) it would withdraw from policy-making departments the experience and overall view of the industries that they must have in order to have full regard for the sector of the economy for which they are responsible.

34. Consequences for other departments. These would be as follows.

(*a*) Other related departments would continue to be responsible for the initiation of policy towards the nationalised industries in so far as they were required to do so in the public interest.

(*b*) The sponsoring departments would be responsible primarily for preparation, negotiation and formulation of sector policies; e.g., transport would remain with the minister because of its wide outside ramifications.

35. The 1969 White Paper. The government expressed its views in the White Paper *Ministerial Control of the Nationalised Industries* (Cmnd. 4027). In particular the government did not accept the proposal for a Ministry of Nationalised Industries, its main thesis being that, although the responsibilities defined by the Committee could be conceptually separated, the disadvantages arising from the change in machinery outweighed the advantages, particularly as follows.

(*a*) Decisions previously involving one ministry would involve two.

(*b*) In practice, a distinction between sector and efficiency responsibilities would often be impossible, e.g. in power and transport.

(*c*) The position of chairmen of the boards would be made more difficult and equivocal through having to deal with two departments.

(*d*) Intervention in detailed management would not be reduced by the proposed change, and in fact might well be increased.

NOTE: The government did, however, concede that there might be advantages in establishing an organisation which would treat nationalised industries as a function of government in themselves.

36. Specific proposals accepted. The government did, however, welcome the following recommendations:

(*a*) that there should be discussions between the Treasury and the sponsoring departments with regard to control of investments;

(*b*) that the sponsoring departments should bring the industries together to discuss common problems, and that the industries should have opportunities to meet the economic departments;

(*c*) that the government would permit formal directions to be given in non-statutory defined areas, but as a whole would prefer ministerial relations to be worked out within the existing framework.

NOTE: With regard to the recommendations of the White Paper on economic and financial objectives, the government accepted the general approach to pricing policy, but not the recommendation that control over prices be given legislative sanction as this would involve both practical difficulties and undesirable interference in management.

37. White Paper: The Nationalised Industries (1978). The White Paper made two main sets of proposals:

(*a*) for improving the relations between the government and the nationalised industries;

(*b*) for reinforcing the commercial disciplines in the industries.

38. Relations with the industries. The statutory powers to give boards directions of a "general character" were regarded as being too blunt. The White Paper believed it to be wrong in principle that a minister could not statutorily intervene in matters of major importance, and consequently suggested that ministers should be given the power to compel the boards of nationalised industries, through the issue of specific directives, to take any action viewed as necessary in the national interest. This new power was seen as likely to improve accountability in that when such a direction was given it would "indicate formally and publicly when the Government had decided to overrule the Board's judgment".

39. Control of the power. The Chief Secretary to the Treasury indicated that the government only intended to use such a power sparingly, and in any case:

(*a*) specific directions would be subject to parliamentary procedures;

(*b*) compensation would be paid to the industries if the directions resulted in loss of money.

40. NEDC proposals. The National Economic Development Council proposals in this area made in 1976 suggesting the establishment of *policy councils* were rejected in the White Paper. These policy councils would have been established for each industry and would have been composed of representatives of the government, trade unions, management and consumers. The Government in the White Paper rejected the proposal on the grounds that:

(*a*) it would add an additional layer to the administrative structure of the industries without providing clear demarcation lines;

(*b*) industrial boards at present in existence can be widened to include the additional and wider representation suggested, and thus new policy councils would be superfluous;

(c) part of the functions of the policy councils are achieved by the implementation of the White Paper's recommendations on strengthening of consumer councils, and the extension of industrial democracy within the industries.

41. Commercial and financial proposals. The White Paper outlined the investment, pricing and efficiency policies to be followed to preserve the commercial soundness of the industries and to overcome the "mistakes of the early 1970s" when the prices of public sector goods were held down at the cost of mounting deficits, loss of management morale, etc. The government clearly intended that the industries would not be forced into deficits by a policy of restraints. To this end the White Paper returned to the philosophy of commercial discipline with regard to investment criteria, pricing policy, and financial targets as established in the 1967 White Paper. The main difference was the incorporation of the concept of required rate of return (RRR) on new investment projects as a whole which replaced the test rate of discount.

On the subject of pricing, the White Paper stated that the government must satisfy itself that the main elements of the industries' pricing structures were sensibly related to the costs of supply and to market conditions. Financial targets would be agreed with each individual enterprise, and tailored to allow for the circumstances of the particular industry.

42. Nature of the public sector. Although the 1978 White Paper returned in many respects to the White Paper of 1967, and in particular the concept of RRR developed within the 1967 principle of general financial objectives, some measure of capital costs which were more related to achieving performance and more even pricing, it must be questioned whether comparatively minor adjustments to the structure were still appropriate. The major factor was that the public sector had shown fundamental changes in the previous decade from the Morrisonian concept of socialised utilities. For example, the establishment of the National Enterprise Board (itself a public corporation) and its operation as a state holding company owning wholly or in part Companies Acts concerns such as British Leyland and Ferranti. Piecemeal change continues, however, with for example the creation of the Post Office Corporation in 1969 (from the Ministry of Posts and Telecommunications) and its subsequent division in the early 1980s into two separate corporations, with sections of the telecommunications side to be hived off or open to competition from private enterprise.

PROGRESS TEST 13

1. Outline the reasons for the state's involvement in economic activity. (2)

2. Outline, with examples of each type, the variety of organisational forms found within the public sector. (4, 5)

3. What are the advantages of having a public corporation rather than the direct provision of a service by a minister and departmental staff of civil servants? (7–9)

4. Give the advantages and disadvantages of ministerial intervention in the operation of a nationalised industry. (12–14)

5. Distinguish between the "commercial" and "departmental" views of nationalised industry operation. (16)

6. What basic principles did the Select Committee observe? (19, 20)

7. What ten principles of control did the Select Committee lay down? (22)

8. What did the Select Committee observe on the obligations of nationalised industries? (23–25)

9. What are the basic features of the economic and financial position of nationalised industry public corporations? (26)

10. What recommendations were made by the 1961 White Paper? How may these be criticised? (27, 28)

11. What recommendations were made by the 1967 White Paper? (29)

12. Comment on the Select Committee's recommendations for a Ministry of Nationalised Industries. (30–32)

13. Why was this suggestion rejected? (35)

14. Explain and comment on the proposals in the 1978 White Paper. (39–42)

CHAPTER XIV

Judicial Control of Public Administration

INTRODUCTION

The purpose of this chapter is not to present a detailed study of principles of administrative law, but to examine the broad judicial concepts within which the administration functions.

1. Fundamental issues. The overall context of judicial control in the administrative process has been aptly described by Professor S. De Smith (in his *Judicial Review of Administrative Action*, Stevens, 1973) as follows.

> "In the broad context of the administrative process the role of judicial institutions is inevitably sporadic and peripheral. The administrative process is not, and cannot be, a succession of justifiable controversies. Public authorities are set up to govern and administer, and if their every act or decision were to be reviewable on unrestricted grounds by an independent judicial body the business of administration could be brought to a standstill. The prospect of judicial relief cannot be held out to every person whose interests may be adversely affected by administrative action."

The following points will be dealt with.

(*a*) There must be established appropriate fields of action for the courts and for the administration.

(*b*) Administrative law must therefore be concerned with judicial aspects of administration and not with policy aspects, though this condition necessarily limits the effectiveness of judicial review.

(*c*) The courts are not concerned with maladministration (but see the role of the Parliamentary Commissioner, **17–18** below).

2. The need for a system of public law. In a completely authoritarian society public law has no application, as every decision by the state consists of the application of administrative discretion. Other opposition to the concept of a division between private and public law has come from legal philosophers such as Duguit and Dicey. The former insisted that complete equality before the law could not be obtained where different bodies of law applied to governors and governed. The latter, also concerned with equality before the law, misinterpreted the role of administrative courts, saying that they were not to provide equality, but to protect the government in its exercise of arbitrary power.

A system of public law is, however, necessary for the following reasons.

(a) Government has to govern, and thus complete equality on the basis of the private law system is not practicable.

(b) Interference with the activities of private citizens may be a necessary part of the governmental process, but would be prohibited by private law.

3. Public responsibility and private rights. Public law must be concerned with the balance between government responsibility and private rights. British administrative law, however, suffers from the following defects in this respect.

(a) Unlike continental systems of public law, which deal with the substance of administrative decisions, definition of the correct sphere of government, etc., British law concentrates almost exclusively on remedies and procedures against public authorities. It thus operates on the circumference of administration rather than becoming an integral checking force therein.

(b) The courts have imposed limits on their own province of intervention by their reliance on conceptualising in situations where they have been entitled to exercise discretion, and thus have effectively tied their own hands and made difficult the reversal of past judicial approaches.

(c) The absence of special administrative courts in Britain has had the following effects.

(i) It has prevented a more coherent and unified development of administrative law.

(ii) It has prevented the clear identification of the respective fields of judicial intervention and administrative authority.

(iii) It has resulted in a failure to indicate clearly the appropriate boundaries of public law and concepts it exclusively involves.

(iv) It has prevented a more adequate definition of the disparities between citizens and the administration.

(*d*) British public law has failed to establish basic principles upon which decisions on the limits of administrative discretion may be taken; i.e. "what is 'arbitrary' and where, consequently, the limits of discretion have to be drawn, depends on the scale of human values as it is enshrined in the contemporary legal system" (W. Friedman, *Law in a Changing Society*, Penguin, 1976). Although not providing a complete answer to all problems of administrative law, an attempt to rationalise the underlying concepts of liberty, etc., would provide a platform and establish a minimum jurisdictional approach.

4. General exemptions from judicial control. The following exemptions should be noted.

(*a*) *Policy areas.* Especially in the international sphere, it is accepted that certain major policy areas are exempt from court interference. Similarly, on a domestic scale, the underlying policy assumptions of administration are not subject to court challenge.

(*b*) *Administration.* "Planning" and "policy-making" decisions of government and other public authorities are not the subject of judicial intervention. In general, this means that the content of policy decisions made by public bodies is not to be the subject of judicial review on its inherent merits. English courts have, however, on occasions limited the effect of complete administrative discretion by construction of the "reasonableness" concept in administrative decisions.

NOTE: Distinction must be made between the exempt "planning" level and the judicially responsible "operational" level.

CROWN PROCEEDINGS

5. Background to the Crown Proceedings Act 1947. Prior to the Crown Proceedings Act 1947, actions against the Crown in contract or tort were severely limited. In both cases, proceedings could only be brought after obtaining a *fiat* by the cumbersome petition of right procedure, and then only on restricted grounds. In tort, petition of right only lay in respect of pure torts, i.e. torts connected with the taking of property; and in contract certain classes were exempt, namely contracts of service with members of the armed forces and Crown servants, contracts which fettered future executive action and contracts dependent on a grant of money from Parliament. In addition certain procedural defects existed in proceedings against the Crown (as typified by the

House of Lords decision in *Duncan* v. *Cammel Laird and Company* (1942); *see* **6** (*c*)).

The Crown was not vicariously liable for acts of its servants in tort nor was a servant individually liable in contract where the contract was entered into as part of his official duties.

NOTE: A few statutory exceptions existed which permitted actions against the Crown and in practice the Crown would often effectively defend actions by the practice of putting up nominated defendants or paying damages assessed against individual Crown servants. The practice of nominated defendants was, how however, subsequently judicially disapproved.

6. Crown Proceedings Act 1947. This dealt with the following matters.

(*a*) *Contract.* British common law has never distinguished between the government contract and the private non-government contract, and consequently has not recognised the inherent difficulties in the application of private law contractual principles to the often completely divorced governmental situation. With this may be compared the French approach which divided government contracts into *contrats administratifs* (public law contracts) and *gestions privées* (private law governed) and consequently provides special procedures for government contract administration and compensation of private parties in respect thereof. The British position as a result of s. 1 of the Crown Proceedings Act 1947 in general makes all government contracts judicially enforceable, but exempts those in situations where a petition of right would not have lain before the Act. However, the position is confused by the failure clearly to define the scope of these exemptions and the tendency of the courts in some cases to be guided by considerations of equity and fair play.

The exemptions from liability are as follows.

(*i*) Contracts fettering future executive action are not enforceable. This exemption, however, suffers from lack of clear judicial definition, and in particular from the fact that the two principal cases failed to establish beyond doubt the extent of the exemption In the *Amphitrite* case it was stated that "it cannot by contract hamper its freedom of action in matters concerning the state", whereas Denning's dictum in *Robertson* v. *Minister of Pensions* (1948), was that "it only avails the Crown where there is an implied term to that effect, etc", and thus the scope of the situation is left open.

(*ii*) Contracts dependent on a grant from Parliament are exempt from enforceability, and thus place long-term major capital works contracting in some uncertainty.

(*iii*) Contracts with Crown servants are legally exempt but in practice little difficulty of unofficial enforcement arises.

NOTE: Provision is not made for compensation in the above cases and represents the British courts' attitude that there is either a common law contract or no contract at all.

(*b*) *Tort.* English law has now recognised the equality of government and governed in this sphere (s. 2(1) Crown Proceedings Act 1947) and renders the Crown generally liable for torts committed by Crown servants in the course of their duties.

(*c*) *Procedural matters.* The proviso to s. 28(1) of the Crown Proceedings Act 1947, preserved the decision of the House of Lords in *Duncan* v. *Cammell Laird and Company* (1942) to the effect that the Crown may refuse to answer questions or produce documents on the ground that it would be contrary to the national interest to do so, and which left the determination of national interest to the appropriate minister. This rule has finally been breached by the subsequent decision of the House in *Conway* v. *Rimmer* (1968) in which it was held that *Duncan* v. *Cammell Laird* had been wrongly interpreted and that the determination of production or non-production on the grounds of national interest was a matter for the courts to decide.

REMEDIES AND PROCEDURES

7. British and continental systems compared. The recognition of a separate administrative law and jurisdiction has in France and Germany been accompanied by a clear and simple form of procedure and remedies. In France an aggrieved individual may file a petition stating his claim in the appropriate administrative court, the grounds upon which he seeks relief, and the relief sought. In Germany there is a similar position involving challenge by petition for nullification and declaration, or for performance. Although *locus standi* (*see* **8**) is required in both jurisdictions this is liberally construed; e.g. in France any consumer of a product affected by administrative action is entitled to petition for relief. On the other hand, the common law approaches have been criticised (by K. C. Davies, *Administrative Law*, 1951) for their unnecessary technicality and complexity: "for no practical reason the remedies are plural

... the lines are moved about through discussions of such concepts as judicial, non-judicial, discretionary and ministerial. These concepts are acutely unfortunate, not only because they defy definition but because of the complete folly of using any concepts whatever to divide one remedy from another."

8. *Locus standi.* Before consideration of the general nature of judicial remedies and proceedings may be undertaken, it is necessary to examine in outline the situations in which judicial relief may be invoked. In most systems of law judicial remedies may only be invoked by those whose personal interests or rights have been affected by administrative action. There is no equivalent in English law of the *actio popularis* of Roman law, which permitted individuals to bring actions in respect of certain public wrongs. In addition, the right in English law of challenging an act or decision varies in detail between the particular remedies sought. In general, however, two broad approaches may be discerned as follows.

(*a*) The Attorney General may act on his own or at the suit of an individual to enforce duties owed by public authorities. An individual, however, only has *locus standi* in such matters if he has suffered loss different in kind to that suffered by the public at large.

(*b*) Where statutory remedies are provided, it is usual to restrict these to "persons aggrieved". "Persons aggrieved" has never been absolutely defined, but in general has been restricted in meaning to persons who have been deprived of something to which they were legally entitled, or burdened with some obligation wrongfully. It does not cover mere dissatisfaction with a decision or being prejudiced by that decision. As Professor Davis has pointed out: "One whose interests are in fact subjected to or imminently threatened with substantial injury from government action satisfies the requirements of standing and ripeness to challenge the legality of that action unless for reasons of substantive policy the interests are undeserving of legal protection" (Standing, "Ripeness and Civil Liberties." *A.B.A.J.*, 1952).

9. Classification of grounds for review. The traditional areas of judicial review exercised through the media of the prerogative orders, injunctions, etc., may be classified as follows.

(*a*) *Excess of power.* Statutory bodies are subject to the doctrine of *ultra vires*, i.e. they may do only those things which they are expressly or impliedly permitted to do, and those things which are incidental to the performance of such powers. The courts have, however, extended this right to examine for "excess of power" by looking into the jurisdictional facts, i.e. had the inferior body reached its decision by wrongful interpretation of the facts which constitute its jurisdiction? Had discretionary powers been exercised for the purposes for which they were granted? Had the decision been exercised in good faith?

(b) *Procedural defects.* Courts will generally review the way in which a decision is reached, and in particular special emphasis is placed on the rules of natural justice which require that a person whose rights are subject to adjudication is afforded a hearing (though not necessarily oral), and that no man may be judge in his own cause (i.e. there must be no evidence of bias of the adjudicator, though this is construed fairly liberally in administrative matters).

(c) *Error of law.* Courts will intervene where there is evidence that a decision has been taken wrongly in law. Such error of law must, however, appear on the face of the record or documents contemporaneous therewith.

(d) *Reasonableness.* It was held in *Associated Provincial Picture Houses Ltd.* v. *Wednesbury Corporation* (1947) that the decision of a public authority can be upset if it is unreasonable in the sense that no reasonable body could have come to such a decision. This ruling, however, should not be construed too widely and in general some identifiable legal fault in the decision must be established.

10. Remedies. The principal judicial remedies consist of the prerogative orders of *mandamus, certiorari* and prohibition, injunctions, declarations and certain specific statutory remedies.

11. The prerogative orders. These are as follows.

(a) *Certiorari and prohibition.* These orders are conveniently dealt with together owing to the procedural similarities. The former lies to stop a wrongful action by a public body, whereas the latter lies to bring the decision of an inferior body up for review and to quash that decision if necessary. The basic defect in the remedies, however, is that they will only lie in respect of judicial acts, and not in those cases where the public authority is acting in a purely administrative or ministerial capacity. The concept of the judicial action is itself imprecise and varies according to the particular situation for which the definition is required—and often according to the court's particular designs. However, a decision may be said to be judicial in general terms where the body taking the decision had the trappings of a court, or the action resembled a *lites inter partes*, or where a pronouncement is made on the rights of an individual.

These remedies are principally invoked in cases of *ultra vires*, breach of the rules of natural justice and (in the case of *certiorari*) error of law on the face of the record.

(*b*) *Mandamus.* This lies to enforce a public duty. It cannot be used to enforce discretionary acts but will lie where a discretion is required to be exercised. Generally it only lies at the suit of the Attorney General, though in exceptional cases of interference with private rights an individual may maintain an action.

12. The declaration. The declaratory judgment is becoming the principal remedy of administrative law, owing to its flexibility, its absence of limitation to purely judicial matters, its ability to range widely across administrative matters and its non-coercive nature. It consists of asking the court to declare what the law is in a given case in the event of threatened illegality. It is in practice often coupled with a request for an injunction to restrain the proposed illegality. Owing to its non-coercive nature it is often used to decide disputes between public authorities, and to declare private rights.

NOTE: Statutory appeals are steadily gaining ground as legislative regulation of the administrative process increases.

ORGANISATION OF ADMINISTRATIVE JUSTICE

13. General. Where ordinary courts are not entrusted by the legislature with the settlement of disputes, one of three provisions has generally been adopted:

(*a*) special (or administrative) tribunals:

(*b*) ministerial decision following a statutory inquiry, e.g. planning and compulsory purchase appeals;

(*c*) ministerial decision which is discretionary without prescribed procedure, in which case generally only political redress is open to the citizen.

14. The Franks Report. The present system of administrative tribunals stems largely from the Report of the Committee on Administrative Tribunals and Inquiries (Franks Committee) which formed the basis of the Tribunals and Inquiries Acts of 1958 and 1966. The Committee considered that tribunals should only be resorted to in circumstances where the courts were obviously unsuitable, but that such tribunals should not be treated as mere appendages of government departments. They should be regarded as part of the machinery for adjudication, and not, as official evidence suggested, as part of the machinery for administration. Of particular importance was the rejection by the Committee of Professor Robson's proposal that a General Administrative Appeals Tribunal should be set up to hear appeals from tribunals, as opposed to appeal to the ordinary courts which was ultimately decided upon. The Committee rejected the proposal on the following grounds:

(*a*) it would not have the expertise of the individual tribunals (this would apply equally to the courts, however);

(*b*) it would involve departure from the principle that all tribunals should be subject to the supervisory jurisdiction of the High Court;

(*c*) it could lead to a dichotomy in administrative law decisions.

NOTE: An opportunity was thus lost to establish a body which could have had considerable unifying influence on the development of English public law.

15. Tribunals and Inquiries Acts 1958 and 1966. These are principally a matter for examination in a work on administrative law and it must suffice here to mention some of the more important points.

(*a*) A Council on Tribunals was set up with a general supervisory role over the administrative tribunals.

(*b*) Machinery for the appointment of members was vested in the Council and the Lord Chancellor and thus kept outside the administrative hierarchy.

(*c*) It was made possible to appeal to the High Court.

(*d*) Reasoned decisions, etc., were required.

16. Exclusion of judicial review. The courts have been reluctant to permit removal of the power of review, and such reluctance is manifested in the principle of statutory construction which prohibits exclusion of recourse to the courts only by the use of clear language. The following general points are worthy of notice.

(*a*) It is possible effectively to exclude review, however, and if effectively carried out there exists no principle by which the validity of a statutory provision itself can be called into question as, for example, by virtue of the "due process" clause of the 5th and 14th Amendments to the Constitution of the United States.

(b) The courts, in interpreting statutes purporting to exclude judicial review, construe them liberally in favour of the individual; e.g. the use of the word "final" in a statute does not preclude judicial review but generally only relates to the particular statutory proceedings in question. However, the expression "not to be questioned in any legal proceedings whatsoever" has been held effectively to exclude review (*Smith* v. *East Elloe Rural District Council* (1956)).

(c) Where a statute has made a specific remedy available to the person aggrieved by a decision taken under the statute by an administrative agency, the courts will decline jurisdiction to review that decision in other legal proceedings.

17. Ombudsmen. Although not strictly appropriate to a chapter on judicial review the various Commissioners for Administration that have been appointed since 1967 provide a further channel through which citizens may seek redress of grievances arising from administrative actions.

The Parliamentary Commissioner for Administration, the Ombudsman, was appointed in 1967 as a servant of Parliament, hence his title. The significance of this is that there is no direct access to him by the public, approaches must be made via MPs who thus retain their traditional role in redressing grievance. The national ombudsman's role in investigating maladministration is supplemented by others in the following areas: Northern Ireland (1969), the Health Service (1973), and Local Government (1974).

18. The impact of ombudsmen. By comparison with similar offices in other countries the UK ombudsmen perform a limited role, both in terms of the number of cases handled and the impact of their work on the public. This is due to several factors, primarily the relatively narrow definition of the term "maladministration" the office-holders have taken. Investigations are only concerned with the procedure by which decisions have been taken; in other countries ombudsmen have argued that "bad" decisions *must* represent maladministration even if procedures were formally followed.

It should be noted that the current holder of the office of Parliamentary Commissioner, Sir Cecil Montacute-Clothier, is a QC and may use his legal experience, supported by the Select Committee that examines his reports, to extend the role.

Usually ombudsmen simply produce a report of their findings and rely on adverse publicly to ensure that complainants' grievances are resolved. An exception is the Northern Ireland

Commissioner who may seek enforcement and compensation through the County Court.

PROGRESS TEST 14

1. Why is there a need for a system of public law? (**2**)

2. What are the main defects in the English system of public law? (**3**)

3. What general fields of administration are exempt from judicial control? (**4**)

4. Outline the provisions of the Crown Proceedings Act 1947. (**6**)

5. Compare the remedies and procedures in English and in continental law. (**7, 8**)

6. What are the basic grounds for judicial review? (**9**)

7. Describe the principal judicial remedies. (**10, 11, 12**)

8. What were the basic conclusions of the Franks Report on Administrative Tribunals? (**14**)

9. Comment on the "exclusion" of judicial review. (**16**)

10. Consider the role of the Parliamentary Commissioner for Administration and his relation to judicial control. (**17, 18**)

CHAPTER XV

Administration and the Public

PUBLIC OPINION

1. Introduction. Modern concepts of democracy imply that government should not only be representative of the views of the electorate at large but should also be influenced by public opinion between elections. That governments are susceptible to influence from the electorate is undoubted, but the extent of such influence is more difficult to assess. It is important to remember in this context that political power is not the monopoly of the government in any society. Political power must be seen as the ability to influence the decision-making process and will depend upon: *organisation* —structures designed to bring pressure to bear, though it may also be taken to include networks of "contacts" (characterised as the "old boy network", for example); *resources*—financial and human that may be used in the process of influencing and *support*—the numbers of people supporting the organisation or the ideas being promoted.

Any individuals, organisations or groups in society that possess a measure of the above qualities are at least potentially politically influential. Two groups of organisations—pressure groups (*see* **4**) and political parties (*see* **11**)—are established with the specific intent of influencing.

2. Problems of definition. The fact that in a democracy an election produces a government which is chosen by the majority of the people is in itself an inadequate safeguard of the public interest, even if it were always a correct assumption. In particular, note the degree of recognition of the interests of particular forms of public opinion, as follows.

(*a*) *Minority opinion.* British government is based at its most fundamental level on respect for the rights of minorities. This respect is both practical, in that governments must pay attention to the views of minorities when faced with fairly regular elections, and based on the principle which prevents the imposition of oppressive measures against minorities. It is thus manifested in the consensus approach of government. In addition, despite broad categories of social class support for the individual parties, each party relies to a considerable extent on a non-class-based vote; e.g. the Conservative party would be unlikely to be elected without a considerable working-class vote, and consequently this multi-class basis of government support in the country prevents the ready identification and oppression of minority interests.

(*b*) *Informed opinion.* The manifestation of public opinion, however, does not relate to numerical support. Informed and articulate opinion has a greater chance of exerting influence on the government. This process is clearly seen at work in relation to the work of university departments and research institutes in the field of economic policy. The London Business School and National Institute of Economic and Social Research, for example, will command considerable Treasury attention if there are significant deviations from their own diagnosis. Similarly their work will receive significant media attention and thus generate further pressures upon the administration by providing a focus and basis of criticism.

(*c*) *Group opinion* (*see* **4**).

3. Manifestation of public opinion. The limitations of the three methods by which it is often suggested that public opinion may make itself felt upon government may be considered as follows.

(*a*) *Doctrine of the mandate.* This basically involves the issue of whether a government is elected simply to govern or whether it is elected to govern according to particular electorally approved programmes. The issue is clouded in practice by political use made of the idea of the mandate as a justification for unpopular policies, as a means for self-congratulation after the achievement of policies, or as an opposition tool for castigating governments who fail to fulfil their election promises.

By definition, the doctrine implies that a government is bound to carry out those, and only those, policies approved by the electorate at the election which brought it to power. The doctrine is, however, subject to serious limitations as a practical constitutional doctrine.

(*i*) The multiple and diverse nature of election programmes must result in the impossibility of concluding that every part of the programme has received electoral scrutiny and approval.

(*ii*) The doctrine is unable to distinguish between ends and means, and thus, whilst theoretically approving broad general political policy, is unable to deal with the methods by which such policy is implemented, and which may well alter the end result of the policy.

(*iii*) It is impossible for precise directions to be given on technical or other complex matters. Without resorting to élitist philosophies it must be doubted whether an unwieldy and technically uneducated electorate as a whole could presume to dictate on certain matters.

(*iv*) Governments must have the power to deal with unforeseen circumstances and cannot therefore afford in the interests of good government to be tied to rigid programmes.

(*v*) Similarly, it is doubtful whether such a doctrine could be applied throughout the whole term of a government's office as policy must of necessity change in response to changing circumstances.

(*b*) *Referendum.* It is theoretically possible that a government could govern through public opinion by using the referendum. In practice, however, the administrative difficulties and the time-consuming factors involved would prevent effective decision-making by a government. In addition, it would necessitate, if taken to extremes, the reference of matters to a body not suited to deal with them.

The referendum has however now been employed in relation to Britain's entry into the EEC and was part of the Devolution Bills for Scotland and Wales. It would thus appear that there is a case for the use of referenda where the topic concerned is of fundamental political, constitutional, and social importance. The argument in these cases is that the matters involved go beyond the normal political decision, and consequently public opinion should be expressed on the matter.

(*c*) *Public opinion polls.* The political preoccupation with public opinion polls raises the question of whether they might be utilised effectively as manifestations of public opinion and as such influence governments. This, however, raises two basic questions, namely, whether the polls represent public opinion and, if so, to what extent they should be followed. In addition, the fundamental question as to their accuracy must be borne in mind, and in particular the following points.

(*i*) Persons are given purely hypothetical questions to answer.

(*ii*) Polls may be used (as are by-elections) for the recording of a purely "protest vote".

(*iii*) Although they represent mid-term unpopularity of governments it must be seriously questioned whether governments should be influenced by this or merely rely on long-term approval of their policies (or perhaps, more cynically, on the short memories and apathy of the electorate).

(*d*) *Direct action.* Overt action, such as marches and demonstrations often reflect political weakness in terms of the factors that we have analysed as being significant in influencing decision-making. However demonstrations may build support and provide evidence of the depth of feeling of at least some members of society. One of the "arts" required of effective politicians is to recognise the mood of the public in deciding which issues must be given priority and which will generate support personally.

PRESSURE GROUPS

4. Introduction. Nationally, 650 MPs represent the electorate on a territorial basis. This is not an effective way of representing the functional interests of the thousands of groups that "pervade every sphere of domestic policy, everyday, everyway at every nook and cranny of government" (S. E. Finer, "Anonymous Empire", *Political Studies*, 1958). In an open society groups thus compete for influence and much of the political energy of one group will countered by that of others in the competition for the ear of the decision-makers.

Professor R. McKenzie has commented that "pressure groups are more important than political parties for the transmission of political ideas from the mass of the citizenry to their rulers" ("Parties, Pressure Groups, and the British Political Process", *Political Quarterly*, Vol. XXIX, No. 1, 1958).

5. Definitions. Pressure-group politics has been defined as "the field of organised groups possessing both formal structure and real common interests, in so far as they influence the decisions of public bodies ... or in so far as they seek to influence the process of government" (McKenzie). Pressure groups in general may be categorised as "defensive" and "promotional" in the following way.

(*a*) *Defensive pressure groups.* These are basically concerned with the protection of their members' interests, and have a defined membership (though such membership in practice often exceeds that of promotional groups). Their membership is not based on any specific sections of the community but ranges from upper-middle-class membership of the Confederation of British Industries to the working-class membership of trade unions. They have been classified by Duverger as "partial", to the extent that they provide service functions for their members as well as undertaking "political" action.

(b) *Promotional pressure groups.* These are concerned with promoting some general public interest as opposed to their own self-interest. Although they are theoretically able to call upon a larger membership than the defensive groups, there being no formal limitation on their membership, they in fact tend to have smaller numbers with an essentially middle-class bias. Duverger has also classified them as "exclusive" as in general they offer no service functions to their members.

6. Focus of pressure groups. Although politically orientated, there is little formal affiliation within the pressure group structure, the principal example of affiliation being that of the trade union movement to the Labour party. The focal point of their lobbying tends to be upon the executive and the political parties rather than upon the legislature. This stems from the organisation of groups as promoters of specific interests which rarely neatly align with the generalised policy and positions of principle adopted by the parties. An even more important factor is that groups will want to exert influence on a continuous basis and not only when "their" party is in power.

In some countries groups representing significant sections of society may effectively become political parties. For example the Norwegian Senterparti is essentially a farmers' party.

7. Nature of the relationship between the executive and the pressure group. It is the nature of this relationship which explains the importance of pressure groups in the British system of government as exerters of influence on government and legislation. The expansion of government activity has resulted in a realisation that active co-operation of various groups is necessary in order to achieve effective policy-making and execution of policy. The two-way nature of the relationship may be illustrated as follows.

(a) Pressure groups have become institutionalised into the processes of government as a result of the government's need to obtain reliable information and opinion on matters which they are considering acting upon that fall within the area of interest of the groups concerned. Professor Kogan has described groups such as the British Medical Association, who are consulted as of right on matters affecting them as "legitimised" groups. Such a status enhances the ability of the group to influence and is much sought after.

(*b*) This recognition has received expression through the machinery of advisory committees, e.g. the Central Advisory Council for Education meets to consider papers prepared by civil servants and to represent the "consumer" view. This committee has in fact produced a series of important reports, viz. Crowther, Newsom, and Plowden, which have been major contributions to educational policy.

(*c*) The institutionalisation and importance of pressure groups may be regarded as both a duty and a necessity. Such duty may be statutorily recognised; e.g. the Agriculture Act 1947, makes consultation obligatory. Politically, this relationship has been expressed as follows: "It is our duty to consult with the Confederation of British Industries, the Trade Union Congress and others" (H. Wilson, House of Commons Speech, October 1966).

(*d*) The necessity of consultation has been expressed as follows: "Collectively, one of these organisations knows far more of government policy over a wide field than any individual can hope to attain to". "If firms and other interests were to starve the civil service of ... the information, the administration of the country would come to a halt" (J. Blondel, *Voters, Parties, and Leaders,* Pelican, 1969).

(*e*) In addition to formal machinery, considerable informal consultation exists with the group interests.

(*f*) The difficulty of making and implementing policies without pressure-group co-operation has been summed up by Blondel: "The intermixing between outsiders and the civil service has now reached a point where the distinction between 'administrative decisions' and 'decisions taken by private individuals' is more and more difficult and more useless to make".

8. Promotional and exclusive groups. The comments above apply to the defensive groups, the promotional groups not being anything near as institutionalised and having to rely on different access to government than that stemming from the two-way relationship of the defensive groups. In particular, their potentialities for success depend on such factors as the non-political nature of their aims, their ability to influence and win the support of individual MPs and the public, party adoption of their aims, etc. Their principal achievements thus lie in the extent they are able to publicise the moral issues with which they are usually concerned.

9. Criticism of group opinion politics. Criticisms levelled at the British system of pressure groups, particularly those of the institutionalised character, are as follows.

(*a*) They may result in unfair advantages being gained by well-organised groups or groups with large memberships and financial resources.

(*b*) There is a tendency within the groups for oligarchies to develop which may be remote from the ordinary membership, and also for the ordinary membership to be subordinated to the groups' paid bureaucracy which effectively controls the policy-making role.

(*c*) It is often suggested that the sheer power and importance accorded to group interests may operate to pervert the normal processes of democracy, However the formation of groups to express freely held opinions is a natural concomitant of democracy in an open society and the influence of the politically inactive is always going to be limited. Governments will ultimately heed their own interests and the expression of opinion through the ballot box, thus governments tend to take the *balance* of group opinions as *one* of their indicators of public and electoral feeling.

10. Conclusions on group influence. Although not being exhaustive of all interest affected by government activity, such groups do enable the vital process of consultation to be effectively carried out, and thus provide a major exercise in influencing the course of governments.

THE POLITICAL PARTIES

11. Channels of opinion. Political parties may act as channels of opinion from the rank and file to the political leadership in Parliament. However, the degree to which this occurs, and its effectiveness, are difficult to assess. Undoubtedly a government must pay heed to widespread discontent, e.g. the continued support given by the 1979 Conservative government to various nationalised industries despite original policy to the contrary.

12. Differences between Labour and Conservative parties. The Labour party was established at the turn of the century with a view to getting MPs into Parliament, and its constitution and structure were thus designed to achieve this. The parliamentary party has always been to some extent dependent upon the party machine outside Parliament which constitutionally remains superior. In practice the Labour MPs have been largely independent and free to determine their own policy on the grounds that they best know what attracts voters and that they command the support of the public via the ballot box.

Following the election of a Conservative government in 1979 the Labour party organisation outside Parliament reasserted its constitutional position *vis-à-vis* the Parliamentary party. Using constitutional processes the 1980 conference passed measures to enable constituency parties to reselect candidates for future elections as a means of eliminating those MPs who did not follow the agreed party line. Revised procedures for the election of party leader including voting by affiliated trade unions and members further emphasised the influence that the party outside parliament is able to exert over its MPs.

The Conservative party organisation developed, by contrast, largely as a response to that of the Labour party. Its origins lay inside Parliament and its constitution reflects this. The party structure is designed to be the servant of the leader and parliamentary party.

Thus a dramatic contrast is seen at the conferences of the two parties—Labour being characterised by acrimonious debate and overt manoeuvring of *blocs* of support; while the Tory conference is more of a setpiece with conspicuous demonstrations of support for the leadership. There is obviously internal politics in the Conservative party and the fact that more Tory than Labour leaders have been "obliged" to resign indicates that it can be rough.

PARTICIPATION IN THE GOVERNMENTAL PROCESS

13. Fulton Committee. In its report on the civil service, the Fulton Committee emphasised the need for less secrecy in the conduct of the administration, for increased consultation and for greater public participation in the policy-planning process. Of particular importance, it disagreed with the oft-quoted bureaucratic view that increased participation would lead to slowness and inefficiency in the decision-making process, believing, in fact, that less secrecy would result in more effective and acceptable decisions being made.

14. Participation. "Participation in the process of planning our inbuilt and natural environment, and the services which affect every individual and family, is the key to successful policy-making and implementation. At present the whole machinery of government is geared to a sequence which begins with the identification of a problem in a central government department, goes on through research conducted centrally or commissioned, and then evaluated behind closed doors, and ends in the announcement, from London, of a decision. The whole system is essentially paternalistic and centralist, with only the most exiguous scope for local variations from the central rules" (*People, Participation and Government, Fabian Research Series* 293, published by the Fabian Society).

The present process of decision-making is thus defective in the following respects.

(*a*) Its over-centralisation effectively prevents both public participation and recognition of local needs.

(*b*) Its conduct is invariably secret.

(*c*) Consultation is effectively limited to certain legitimised interest groups (*see* **4** and **7**)

(*d*) Government fails to communicate its policies to the people by virtue of its failure or reluctance to use the existing channels of communication, though ostensibly because of the technicality of much of the subject-matter.

(*e*) Ultimately this failure to involve the governed results in a decline in respect for government.

15. Problems of participation. Unrestricted participation in the process of government, however, raises the following problems.

(*a*) There are certain aspects of government policy which of necessity must be conducted in secret, e.g. in the field of economic and fiscal policy-making, participation in which would seriously hinder the process of government. However, it is necessary here to distinguish between participation which would effectively inhibit the government and that which would merely cause administrative inconvenience, and it is important that participation should not be prevented on the latter ground.

(*b*) The problem of the conflict between efficiency and democracy is raised by participation. The nature of governmental activities and the large sums of money involved place a duty on the government to exercise its functions with the greatest efficiency. However, undue extension of the participative process could lead to an extension of the time of administrative decision-making, tendencies to preserve the *status quo* and the down-playing of technical and administrative skills.

(*c*) Extension of participation could be undesirable in that it would favour the more articulate and politically organised sections of the community to the detriment of those in the positions of greatest social and economic need. Consequently, unless real safeguards were built into the system, the process of participation could result in a widening of social and economic disparities.

16. Possibilities of structural reforms. The possibility of offering participation through the existing machinery of government or through adaptations therein may be considered. The possibilities essentially involve placing decision-making powers closer to the governed in the following ways:

(*a*) administrative deconcentration involving the decentralisation of decision-making personnel of government departments and not those only exercising mere administration functions;

(*b*) regionalism of local government with a federalist approach adopted towards the type of powers devolved upon the regions;

(*c*) effective and accessible local government units within these regions.

Recent administrations have paid lip-service to the concept of "open government", though have failed to produce significant reforms of the Official Secrets Act which lies at the centre of the question of the accessibility of the administration to the public gaze. Proposals have been made for the introduction of a Freedom of Information Act along the lines of similar measures introduced in Sweden and the United States though as such a measure would represent a considerable step from the traditional practice it must be considered improbable.

A Bill of Rights has also been widely canvassed as desirable for the United Kingdom though again the implications for our unwritten flexible constitution are extensive, and again unless provoked by a crisis such a measure remains improbable.

17. Conclusion. This subject of participation is one which has been to a large extent ignored by political and public administration theorists, though it is one which goes to the root of effective and democratic public administration. In conclusion, the *Fabian Research Pamphlet* referred to above (*see* **14**) made certain valuable suggestions. It considered firstly a series of tests against which an effective participative system of government could be measured, as follows.

(*a*) Does the general array of authorities allow public services to be administered on a scale both efficient and amenable to local control?

(*b*) Are decision-making bodies so constituted as to be obliged both to need public approval for their policies and to evolve their policies in a process of continuous consultation?

(*c*) Are the rights of consumers guaranteed in the constitution of the bodies concerned?

(*d*) Does the machinery provide for the statutory representation of disadvantaged minorities within the decision-making process?

(*e*) Is machinery available for review and appeal which is so designed at the same time to prevent delay of implementation of plans and legislation?

(*f*) Is it so designed that no special interests can bypass or seriously delay the process of government?

In reply to these principles the pamphlet made the following general points:

(*a*) There is a need for fewer statutory levels of government but for more tiers for specialised purposes, e.g. regional councils.

(*b*) At the lower level there is a need for immediately accessible units.

(*c*) There must be institutionalisation at all levels of government of bodies set up to represent minority rights and interests.

PROGRESS TEST 15

1. What meanings may be given to "public opinion"? How may such opinion be manifested? (**2, 3**)

2. Consider the definition of pressure groups. (**4, 5**)

3. Where and why are pressure groups focused in Britain? (**6, 8**)

4. Consider the relationship of the executive and pressure groups. (**7**)

5. What comments may be made on group politics? (**9, 10**)

6. What effects do political parties have as channels of opinion? **(11, 12)**

7. Why is participation in the government process necessary? **(13, 14)**

8. What are the problems of participation?   **(15)**

9. How may participation be achieved?   **(16, 17)**

CHAPTER XVI

Management Aids and Public Administration

INTRODUCTION

1. Management problems. The Plowden Committee on the Control of Public Expenditure defined management as "the preparation of material on which decisions are taken; the technical efficiency with which large operations of administration are carried out; the cost-consciousness of staff at all levels; the provisions of special skills and services (scientific, statistical, accountancy, O and M, etc.,) for handling particular problems and the awareness and effectiveness with which they are used; and the training and selection of men and women for posts at each level of responsibility".

This statement may be analysed into distinctive but co-related management functions to which specific managements aids may be applied:

(*a*) planning and decision-making;
(*b*) control of operational efficiency;
(*c*) organisation for efficiency;
(*d*) manpower considerations;
(*e*) follow-up and feedback;
(*f*) information requirements.

2. Management services and techniques. Distinction is usually made between management services and management techniques. The difference generally turns on the fact that the former essentially involve aids to management in the wider sense, e.g. automatic data processing, computers, job evaluation, whereas the latter may be regarded as individual sciences and tools which offer specific solutions to individual problems, e.g. cost benefit analysis, work study, network analysis. This chapter will not, however, dwell on such distinctions but will collectively approach the subject as one of management aids, which will be dealt with according to their relevance to the particular management areas outlined above (*see* **1**).

3. Constraints in general on the use of management aids. The particular constraints involved in the use of specific aids will be dealt with as they arise in the text. However, certain general constraints should be observed as follows.

(*a*) *Objectives.* Unlike the business context, management aids cannot always be applied on a straightforward profit maximisation basis in public administration. The need to balance the often competing concepts of democracy and efficiency in itself constrains maximum use of techniques. There is thus an underlying necessity for careful definition of objectives and the operation of the aids within the social and political constraints involved.

NOTE: Given, however, the establishment of objectives, there is no reason why efficiency may not be maximised therein by the use of aids.

(*b*) *Social aspects.* Management aids which involve changing methods and procedures in order to improve efficiency cannot be applied in a vacuum. Such changes have effects on employees and there is a need to realise that ultimate efficiency as an organisational objective may conflict with individual objectives and values. In consequence, a purely mechanistic approach to organisational reform must be balanced against an organic approach which takes account of the social environment, both internal and external, of the organisation.

(*c*) *Personnel constraints.* The effective use of management aids depends on the education of specialised personnel, their appointment to positions of authority in the organisation, and their continued specialist training. The problems connected with the use of such specialists is dealt with in VI.

NOTE: In general, more effective use is made of such specialists in local government than in central government.

COMPUTERS

4. Basic uses. The operation of many management techniques depends on effective utilisation of computers in assistance. In addition, computers in themselves perform valuable functions in control and feedback systems and in information systems. Computers essentially provide better information for use in co-ordination techniques, and are capable of producing more comprehensive controlling and information retrieval systems.

The unique services provided by computer use may be classified as follows:

(a) speed of operation;
(b) ability to store and retrieve information;
(c) ability to handle large and complicated information;
(d) facility for calculation;
(e) use in modelling and planning exercises (see **23**).

They thus have particular value in complicated and repetitive situations, as centralised control points in organisations, as assistance to individual techniques, e.g. operational research, as central information systems and in the provision of more and reliable information upon which decisions may be made.

"Word processors" have a wide application in the public sector, for example in authorities corresponding with the public on a routine basis but with detailed variations in each case. Such correspondence is well-suited to the word processor which can be programmed with the "core" letter and operators will be able to generate individual letters by simply instructing the machine to insert the appropriate individual information.

5. Some effects of computer use. The following points should be noted.

(a) They reduce the need for some levels of middle and lower management owing to their speed in calculation and communication.

(b) They permit the changeover from scientific management based on functional specialisation to management based on integration of functions.

(c) They have both centralising and decentralising tendencies. They tend to cause a central movement in organisations in respect of repetitive and routine tasks, while providing opportunities for decentralisation of executive functions which may be controlled and co-ordinated by access to the central data bank.

DECISION-MAKING TECHNIQUES

6. Operational research (OR). This has been defined as "the application of scientific processes to operational problems arising within organisations, the objectives being to make more effective use of known facts, to enlarge the proportion of factual knowledge and to reduce the proportion of subjective judgment in making management decisions" (*Glossary of Management Techniques*, HMSO, 1967).

The object of OR is the establishment of optimum solutions to organisational problems; it involves the application of many tools founded in mathematical statistics. In practice, it operates as follows.

(*a*) A precise definition of problems in the context of the organisation's objectives is established.

(*b*) Measurement of relevant factors is undertaken. In the public administration context, the existence of unquantifiable factors is taken account of and in general sufficient statistics are collated in order to permit a gamble on these factors.

(*c*) A mathematical model is built.

(*d*) Information is established to describe the operation of the system and its divergence from the chosen system.

7. Uses of OR. In general terms, OR techniques have normally been used in the context of business profitability. However, they have also proved of value in the public administration context, where it is necessary to review multiple choices involving generally unquantifiable or unknown factors. Specific examples of the use of OR lie in work carried out by the Local Government Operational Research Unit and include such matters as population forecasting, design of financial planning models, planning urban growth, joint refuse disposal problems and research into purchasing methods.

8. Cost benefit analysis (CBA). This has been defined as "a systematic comparison between the cost of carrying out a service or activity and the value of that service or activity, quantified as far as possible, all costs and benefits (direct and indirect, financial and social) being taken into account" (*Glossary of Management Techniques*, HMSO, 1967).

It thus exceeds the normal accounting analysis involving inflows and outflows of cash and attempts to cover all the effects of a proposed project in quantified terms. The basic procedure of CBA is firstly to analyse the primary costs (or direct costs) of a project and the benefits thereof, and then to predict and quantify the indirect costs and benefits (including social factors). These are then evaluated on a common basis.

9. Uses of CBA. CBA is of particular value in the public context where administrative choices cannot be guided purely by economic factors, or where social factors predominate. Although certain difficulties arise in its application, e.g. the measurement of intangible costs and benefits, or where the reviewed projects contain different intangibles the process is of value in decision-making in that it involves detailed consideration and comparison of alternative courses of action. In particular, it is of value in reducing to statistical terms matters which would otherwise be the subject of unscientific value judgments.

Noted applications of CBA have been afforded by the Beeching and Buchanan Transportation Studies, the Victoria Line analysis, the M1 analysis and the Roskill Commission on the third London airport. Analyses on a local level have also been carried out and include such matters as alternative methods of staff training, low or high rise housing development and provision of longer runways for airports.

10. Discounted cash flow. Discounted cash flow is a form of investment appraisal of value where long-term investment decisions have to be made. It aims to provide a comparable rate of return against which the investment in various projects may be measured. In particular, it has the following aims:

(*a*) to ensure that investment takes place in those matters providing the highest rate of return;

(*b*) to ensure that investments are not made in projects that will provide a rate of return less than the cost of the capital employed in the business.

It thus provides a method of rationalising investment decisions which illustrates capital locked up in projects and the comparative cash flows therefrom. Although of great value in a business context, its value in public administration must be seen in the light of the various non-commercial factors motivating public investment, e.g. political and social considerations.

11. PPB. Formally the aims of "planning, programming and budgeting" have been described as follows:

(*a*) the identification of objectives of areas of government activity;

(*b*) the indentification of activities contributing to such objectives;

(*c*) the measurement of the costs of resources devoted to those activities;

(*d*) the assessment of the results of the various activities.
(*Memo on Output Budgeting by Treasury submitted to Select Committee on Procedure*).

The object of the approach is to increase rationality in government policy planning. The difference in accounting terms between this approach and traditional expenditure planning is that it relates expenditure to outputs and objectives, and not to inputs or the resources used by the organisation. If the costs of a department's programmes are known it is possible to evaluate the effectiveness of alternative policies leading to the same objectives, and to compare real demands on resources being made by different objectives (the concept of functional costs).

The procedure has been used by the Ministry of Defence to improve their evaluation of the resources used in individual programmes related to broad defence objectives, and by the Home Office in costing how individual policemen contribute to different programmes, and it has shown very different patterns of expenditure from those obtained by conventional accounting methods.

Its major problems are that it is often difficult to devise objective criteria of efficiency, it is difficult to identify costs relating to different parts of a programme, and there are problems of functional overlap where more than one department contributed to programmes in a particular area.

12. Management by objectives. Management by objectives involves the establishment of organisation objectives and the measurement of performance against such objectives. Its use in the public context may prove valuable in those situations where the profit objective is not appropriate. The advantages of formally setting out objectives are as follows:

(*a*) the risks of misunderstanding and of pursuing non-relevant ends are avoided;

(*b*) they are based on forecasting and consequently lessen the chances of future deviation from the overall objectives of the organisation.

(*c*) they provide criteria for assessing overall performance.

CONTROL

13. Network analysis. Network analysis is in fact a technique that could be included under either planning or control, though here it is treated as a control exercise to distinguish it from pure decision-making aids. It has been defined as "methods of planning the undertaking of a complex project in a logical way by analysing the project into component parts and recording them on a network model or diagram which is then used for planning and controlling

the inter-related activities in carrying the project to completion"
(*Glossary of Management Techniques*, HMSO, 1967).

The object of network analysis is to enable non-standardised
projects to be studied over the whole course of their operation,
and to estimate the impact of time on the varying factors involved
in the achievement of the final goal. In doing this, it highlights the
critical steps, the successful completion of which controls the whole
project, and provides controlling action thereby.

14. Critical path analysis. This is based on network analysis and
operates to distinguish the longest and therefore crucial parts of a
project which consequently control the overall completion time.
It thus establishes the matters upon which effort must be concentrated, as distinguished from parts which have floating time and
thus can be advanced or retarded without affecting the overall
programme.

15. Uses of critical path analysis and network analysis. These
techniques have valuable control functions both at the planning
stage of a project, in that they enable all departments involved to
establish clearly their respective functions and responsibilities
towards the overall objective, and in the operational stage, where
the overall project controller is able to survey the course of the
whole operation and pinpoint its weaknesses, establish points of
delay, speed up necessary activities, etc.

The techniques are of value in major complex undertakings and
are often employed in conjunction with a computer (this is essential in multi-dimensional projects). In the public sector they have
been used to great advantage by the UK Atomic Energy Authority
in reducing tooling time of uranium fuel plants, and consequently
improving the ability to meet production schedules and to utilise
plant fully. In local government they have principally been used on
the technical side of highways, school building, housing and
engineering projects. Their application is not limited, however, to
technical applications, e.g. they were used to establish new monthly
accounting procedures by Colgate-Palmolive Ltd.

16. Other control techniques. The following techniques should be
noted.

(*a*) *Management accounting.* This again represents a combined
planning and controlling exercise. It involves the application of
accounting knowledge and procedures to interpret the statistical
information necessary for promotion of maximum efficiency by

management in the form of future planning and co-ordination of policy.

(b) *Budgetary control.* This has been defined as "allocating financial limits to component parts of individual enterprises and accounting for outlays in such a way as to provide comparisons between actual and forecast results so that, if remedial action is necessary, it may be taken at an early stage or alternatively that overall objectives may be reviewed".

ORGANISATION FOR EFFICIENCY

17. Organisation and methods (O and M). O and M originated in public administration in the Treasury, though all major departments now have O and M sections. It has been defined by the O and M Society Constitution as follows:

"... an advisory service to management and its purpose is:

(a) to advise on the most effective organisation for controlling and co-ordinating the administrative elements of the various functions of the business or undertaking;

(b) to advise on the detailed methods and procedures to enable those functions to be operated with maximum effectiveness;

(c) to ensure that changes in organisation and/or methods which have been agreed are properly implemented."

The object is thus to examine both organisations and the methods employed therein and to eliminate inefficiency, duplication, waste, etc., arising as a result of an organisation failing to adapt to changing circumstances in such matters as the objectives of the organisation, its overall environment, etc.

18. Use of O and M. The utility of O and M is dependent on certain factors, the most important of which are adequate discussion with staff representatives, management support and independence of the O and M department from sections of the organisation reviewed.

It has been used in recent years to a considerable extent in local government, in particular to review the organisation and operational effectiveness of individual departments.

19. Work study. This involves detailed and systematic examination by use of a set of formal techniques and guides into an organisation's work procedures in order to maximise the efficiency of such procedures. In itself, work study is a generic concept embracing such techniques as method study, work measurement and job evaluation. Method study involves the determination of how work should be carried out in the light of current technology, work measurement involves measuring time/effort factors in performing a job within established working conditions and methods, and job evaluation involves determining how much work is worth in terms of its mental and physical demands.

20. Other organisational techniques. The following techniques should be noted.

(*a*) *Ergonomics.* ("The study of the effect of the working environment on the worker and his productive capacity, and the application of anatomical, physiological, and psychological knowledge to the problems arising thereunder" (*Glossary of Management Techniques*, HMSO, 1967).

(*b*) *Systems analysis.* This involves examination of the organisation with a view to reorganisation, in order to facilitate the carrying out of work by computer.

MANPOWER PLANNING

21. Introduction. Public administration is a labour-intensive activity and the techniques that have come to be described as "manpower planning" have a wide application.

Scientific manpower planning has developed as a response to economic need. Two factors are primarily responsible:

(*a*) Rising manpower costs have made it more important to ensure returns are maximised.

(*b*) Increased specialisation has made it more difficult to transfer labour units between jobs.

These basic factors have been supported by other developments in society including the development of *trade union power*, that has made it difficult for employers to adopt a casual attitude to hiring and firing. *Legislation* such as the Health and Safety at Work Act (1974) impose duties upon employers and guarantee workers' rights. *Technological developments* require longer-term planning and high expenditure and parallel planning of training and manpower needs.

22. Definition. Manpower planning represents a wider activity than simply "personnel management". It has been described as "a strategy for the acquisition, utilisation, improvement and retention of an enterprise's human resources" (Department of Employment, *Company Manpower Planning*, HMSO, 1974).

The trend towards an integrated manpower planning approach in the public sector can be seen in the creation of the Civil Service Department and in the local authority "manpower" departments that are replacing "personnel" sections and incorporating the work of Management Services teams.

23. The example of Civil Service manpower planning. The Civil Service Department created after Fulton (*see* VI, **13**) developed the use of computer models for central control of expenditure on Civil Service manpower and the development of standards applicable to the whole service.

The vast numbers of staff involved led to the creation of a computer database known as *Manplan*. The Personnel Record Information System for Management (*Prism*) became operational in 1975 and is used both by the Treasury in the preparation of its overall planning and by the Departments, some of which have satellite computers that use the central database.

Prism is more than a data store and is used as a basis for various computer models that may be used to forecast future needs, and the consequences of various policy strategies can be "tested" and compared.

INFORMATION REQUIREMENTS

24. Nature. An executive's range of competence is related directly to his available supply of information. "A good information system must furnish knowledge that is material to the manager's job, that can be weighed against the goals; it must be designed to determine how and where goals are being missed. It must furnish intelligible data" (H. Koontz and C. O'Donnell, *Principles of Management*, McGraw-Hill, 1976).

25. Particular aspects. In establishing information systems within an organisation the following points must be observed.

(*a*) The information system acts both as a planning technique and as a control technique during the operations.

(*b*) The use of the computer greatly facilitates the development of information systems but its use must be selective. The very ability of a computer to assimilate a large amount of information can place undue burdens upon individual managers and consequently there must be a selective approach and discrimination in that information which management requires.

(c) Information required by management covers financial, logistic and personnel matters.

26. The systems approach to organisation. The establishment of effective information systems depends not only on individual techniques of computer usage and new accounting procedures, but may be achieved through the design of the organisation itself. This latter approach is favoured by those advocating the systems approach to management (*see* III). It emphasises the necessity of a planned management information system that gives each level of management the appropriate information at the appropriate time.

PROGRESS TEST 16

1. What are the main areas involving management problems found in public administration? **(1)**

2. What are the principal constraints on the utilisation of management aids in public administration? **(3)**

3. Consider the basic uses of computers and some effects of computer usage. **(4, 5)**

4. What is operational research? Of what use is it in public administration? **(6, 7)**

5. Define cost benefit analysis and give examples of its use in public projects. **(8, 9)**

6. Define network analysis and critical path analysis and give examples of their uses in public administration. **(13–15)**

7. Of what value are organisation and methods and work study in public administration? **(18, 19)**

8. What factors have promoted a more rigorous approach to manpower planning recently? **(21)**

9. What factors must be considered in establishing information systems? **(24, 25)**

CHAPTER XVII

Management in Local Government

TRADITIONAL STRUCTURE AND PRINCIPLES

1. Introduction. The traditional management structure of local government is based on nineteenth-century concepts of democratic control and involves the interplay of councillors, committees and officers. In theory, the council is primarily responsible for policy and for holding the balance between individual departments and committees. The committees themselves are concerned with the detailed consideration of various aspects of local authority work, and formulate proposals for submission to the council. They also act as the link between elected members and paid officers and are engaged in the control and supervision of departments of the council. The officers are primarily concerned with execution of policy decisions, but owing to their position as operators they are also in the best position to give advice on questions of policy and practice.

NOTE: The fundamental concept of local authority management is based, therefore, on the theoretical distinction between policy and administration which is not realistic in the light of modern administration.

2. Co-ordination problems. The practice of dividing functions and the consequent functional specialisation leads to "departmentalism" and thus tends to result in a lack of unity in local authority administration. This has an attendant absence of corporate responsibility which develops isolationist attitudes. In addition, the position is worsened by the inadequacy of the present formal methods of co-ordination, i.e. by way of general purpose committees, finance committees, joint co-ordinative committees and formal definition of functions by the council. This results in the necessary development of informal machinery for co-ordination through committee chairmen, officers, committee clerks and political party machinery.

3. Delegation to officers. The traditional practice of delegation to officers in local authorities is based on the false dichotomy between policy and administration. Compared to the practice in many foreign systems, with general delegation of day-to-day administrative functions to officers and a reserve of major issues to the elected members, English local government is preoccupied with its attitude to democratic control. Democratic control in the English local government context, however, implies detailed control and, instead of permitting full delegation with checks and balances, the English approach misuses officers through its insistence on the reference of all but the most minor matters to committee or council authorisation.

4. Departmental organisation. The English practice of a functional department supported by a matching committee tends to lead to an excessive array of departments which often prove unwieldy or even superfluous and pose serious problems of co-ordination. In addition, co-ordination problems are increased both by the tendency to subdivide too for functions and the failure to establish any recognised hierarchy amongst principal officers.

5. Lack of head of administration and managing body. A further traditional defect of English local government was the absence of a recognised head of administration. Although this position was often accorded to the clerk of the council, his position was generally one of influence rather than control and it was rare for such a post to develop into that of recognised administrative leadership.

In addition, the creation of a central, unified managing body was generally prevented in local government by the practice of delegating management functions to individual committees, thus preventing the development of a focal point of management.

6. The requirements of management. T. G. Thomson (writing in the *Local Government Chronicle*) has suggested, amongst others, that the following principles of management organisation might be followed to considerable advantage in local government.

(*a*) The member structure within a policy committee should be concerned with setting objectives and allocating resources.

(*b*) Executive committees should be based on functional groupings to direct management of these functions.

(*c*) The officer structure should mirror the member structure, with a chief executive officer and functional groupings culminating in a chief executive officer's programming committee.

(*d*) The chief executive officer requires certain supporting machinery namely:

(*i*) to review objectives, test service effectiveness and to provide committees with relevant facts and courses of action open to them;

(*ii*) to deal with internal administration.

(*e*) Financial advisers should have two supporting wings, namely:

(*i*) to deal with financial appraisal and analysis;

(*ii*) to deal with exchequer and historical accounting.

At the conclusion of the chapter the degree to which these principles have been successfully applied will be evaluated (*see* **21**).

THE MAUD COMMITTEE ON MANAGEMENT AND THE REDCLIFFE-MAUD COMMISSION

7. The Maud Committee's conclusions. The Committee made the following general observations on the local government management pattern.

(*a*) It had its roots in nineteenth-century traditions of direct and detailed responsibility. This was necessary and relevant where the range of services provided was limited, where government involvement was minimal and where there were few professional staff. These factors had changed and had consequently removed the fundamental basis of the traditional approach to local government management.

(*b*) A distinction must be drawn between deliberative functions of committee and administrative functions. The then current tendency to exercise detailed administrative functions presents certain marked disadvantages, for the following reasons.

(*i*) Supervision is not practicable owing to constraints of time, technical complexity, etc.

(*ii*) It does not encourage discrimination between major objectives and consequential decisions and actions.

(*iii*) It discourages delegation to officers.

8. Proposals made for reform. The following proposals were made.

(*a*) *Members and officers.* A greater role should be given to officers in day-to-day administration, identification of problems and the provision of staff work necessary to enable members to decide objectives, etc. However, members should have the ultimate direction and control of the affairs of the authority, should take key decisions and should review periodically the programme and performance of services.

(*b*) *Central management*. Local authorities should establish a management board composed of five to nine council members with the following functions:

(*i*) formulation of objectives and means of attainment for presentation to the council;

(*ii*) review of programmes on council's behalf;

(*iii*) maintenance of overall supervision of authority's organisation, co-ordination and integration;

(*iv*) decision-making of certain kinds on behalf of the council;

(*v*) taking responsibility for presentation of business to the council.

(*c*) *Committees*. The following recommendations were made:

(*i*) committees should be deliberative not directive;

(*ii*) they should not exceed fifteen members;

(*iii*) their functions should consist of making recommendations to the management board, reviewing individual programmes, considering public reaction and conveying this to the council, etc., considering matters raised by their own members or by the management board;

(*iv*) there should be a drastic reduction in the number of committees.

NOTE: They should only take executive decisions when requested by the management board and under the board's strict supervision.

(*d*) *Central official*. The Committee considered that there should be a recognised head officer responsible to the management board, through whom other principal officers would be responsible to the council. He should be responsible for organisation and efficiency, implementing effective control systems, etc.

(*e*) *Principal officers*. They should work as a team, provide staff work, etc. and would be responsible, through the chief official, to the council for the running of their departments.

9. Note of dissent. Sir Oliver Wheatley dissented from the majority recommendations of the Maud Committee on the basic ground that they would vest too much authority in a small body of members. He consequently suggested that committees should continue to possess executive power and that there should be direct access of committees to the council.

10. The views of the Redcliffe-Maud Commission. The Redcliffe-Maud Commission basically accepted the recommendations of the Maud Committee in regard to the creation of a central committee, the delegation of executive functions to officers and the formation of a team of chief officers as a central management group. In particular, it made the following comments.

(*a*) *Central board.* The size of local organisational structure, even allowing for maximum use of management techniques, presented difficulties of co-ordination. A central committee or board would provide a focal centre which could transcend departmental interests. It should be concerned with advising the council on strategy and priorities, co-ordinating policies and the work of the service committees and ensuring the application of management techniques.

(*b*) *Committees.* The nature of local government work effectively limits the degree possible or desirable, and thus there must be a number of committees working with the central committee, such committees making recommendations to the council on general policy and on the specific services under their control.

(*c*) *Delegation.* This must be more extensive in regard to executive functions. If adequately implemented it would leave councillors more time to exercise their proper functions of control and scrutiny.

CHIEF EXECUTIVE OFFICERS AND THE CITY MANAGER CONCEPT

11. Chief executive officer. The evidence given to the Maud Committee by the Management Consultants Association recommended that there should be one officer in overall administrative authority and ultimately responsible to the council for anything entrusted to the officer body. Each principal officer would be responsible to him for the internal administration of his department. He in turn would be responsible to the council for implementation of council policy, establishment matters, etc., and for co-ordinating the work of departments.

12. The American city manager concept. In broad terms, the American city manager concept involves a small elected council (usually nine or less members), preferably elected on a non-party basis, which makes by-laws, decides the extent and pattern of activities, passes the budget and appoints the manager. The manager has all executive functions delegated to him. These will include appointment and dismissal of departmental heads, framing the budget and controlling the administration and the initiation of policy. He has thus been described as "the hedge between politics and administration, but he is not a politician himself" (Vol. 4 of Maud Committee on Management of Local Government, 1967). In general, managers attempt to operate on commercial management lines, and tend to co-ordinate and direct departments rather than to exercise departmental functions in their own right.

13. Advantages of the system. These are as follows.

(*a*) Professional skill and experience may increase interest in local affairs.

(*b*) The appointment encourages members to concentrate on policy, and thus goes at least part-way to the solution of the problem of marrying public control with efficiency.

(*c*) There are advantages if integrated management accrues namely:

(*i*) a sense of corporate responsibility is developed;

(*ii*) officers' views are brought into play at an early stage in policy formation;

(*iii*) business is more rapidly executed;

(*iv*) the manager provides a focal point for those dealing with the local authority;

(*v*) his position is well placed for checking unnecessary departmental growth and for the introduction of management techniques, etc.

14. Disadvantages of the system. These are as follows.

(*a*) In practice is has been found only to be workable in small to middle-sized, relatively homogeneous, communities.

(*b*) It tends markedly to underrate the political aspects of local government.

(*c*) Current management thinking has emphasised the disadvantages of concentrating authority in a single individual (*see* III).

(*d*) It greatly underestimates the possibility in practice of distinguishing between policy and administration functions.

(*e*) There is increased danger of domination being achieved by either the manager or the elected members.

(*f*) Too great a dependence is placed on personalities.

(*g*) In terms of economy in operation of services, it has proved a success. Its effect in communities where there are considerable differences as to the principles of what is to be provided, however, has not been effectively tested.

15. Inappropriateness to English local government. The system is not appropriate for incorporation into the English context of local government, for the following reasons.

(*a*) The political nature of English local government would not provide the proper basis for its adoption.

(*b*) The committee system which is at the basis of the English system would be destroyed.

(*c*) It would necessitate the interlocking of the administrative structure of local government with the political structure of society.

(*d*) In general, the much wider range of services administered by an English local authority would impose considerable strain on a single individual.

(*e*) The reorganisation in 1974 into larger authorities effectively places local authorities outside what has proved to be the appropriate size for the operation of the city manager approach in the United States.

16. Other North American systems. In addition to the city manager concept, the following North American approaches may be appropriately mentioned as being of comparative interest.

(*a*) *Commission government.* This consists of an elected mayor and full-time commissioners, each commissioner specially elected as head of a group of functions.

It has certain advantages:

(*i*) it is not so dependent on personalities as a "one-man" system;

(*ii*) it involves direction by full-time political executives;

(*iii*) it avoids delay in that it combines both political and executive authority;

(*iv*) it increases electoral interest.

Its disadvantages, however, are as follows:

(*v*) while it combines executive and legislative responsibility, it lacks the critical revision process of the English committee system;

(*vi*) its theoretical corporate responsibility is rarely matched in practice by harmony between the commissioners;

(*vii*) it tends to place little emphasis on forward planning;

(*viii*) in concentrating on a political and administrative approach, such matters as up-to-date personnel functions are neglected.

(*b*) *Strong mayor system.* The characteristics generally associated with this system are a politically elected council of five to fifteen members which acts as the legislative body, plus an elected mayor holding office for a two- to four-year term. The mayor prepares the budget and exercises full executive responsibility subject to the council's right to exercise delaying tactics or outright rejection of his policies. Committees are not a necessary part of the system but, where existing, function as sifters of material, etc. The mayor's powerful position rests both on his electoral mandate and his power as chief executive.

Legislative and executive co-ordination depend on various factors including the mayor's personality, party machinery and outside citizens' organisations.

Its advantages are as follows:

(*i*) it places at the head of administration a dynamic personality able to influence opinion, etc.;

(*ii*) it combines political and administrative authority;

(*iii*) according to American beliefs, it is closest to the people.

Against these merits must be set the following disadvantages:

(*iv*) that a political executive tends to lack technical expertise;

(*v*) political debts may be owed to sections of the electorate;

(*vi*) delays between policy formulation and implementation;

(*vii*) it is inadequate for the size of the job.

17. Problems of the chief executive officer. The principal functions of a chief executive officer may be regarded as co-ordination of the authority's activities and positive leadership, involving the bringing forward of new organisational ideas and policies. Problems which must be overcome in order to achieve these objectives include the following:

(*a*) the dangers and disadvantages of over-emphasis on individual powers and the centralising process;

(*b*) retention of the goodwill of members and other officers;

(*c*) establishment of effective relations with the authority's policy committee;

(*d*) the establishment of effective lines of communication;

(*e*) a clear definition of the respective roles of committees, chief officers and departments.

REFORM

18. Developments in the counties. Research carried out subsequent to the Maud Committee *Report* showed the following developments.

(*a*) *Management boards.* The concept of the management board was rejected by forty-three counties, for reasons including the feeling that it was undemocratic, that it deterred the attraction of suitable members and that members were incapable of absorbing the necessary amount of work related to membership of the board.

(*b*) *Central committees.* However, twenty-three authorities established a central committee with clear responsibility for co-ordination. In nine cases the central co-ordination committee was also the finance committee, and in fourteen cases separate policy and finance committees were established.

(*c*) *Committees.* In general, there was a reluctance to prune committees to the number recommended by Maud. Maud recommended six, but the county average was nineteen, plus in some cases thirty or more sub-committees. There was also reluctance to prune committee membership.

(*d*) *Chief executive officer.* Little interest was shown in the chief executive officer concept, but although delegation was not carried out to the extent recommended by Maud, there has been reappraisal and reallocation.

THE BAINS REPORT

19. Introduction. The Study Group on Local Authority Management Structures was set up in May 1971 to produce advice for the new local authorities on management structures at both member and officer level. In 1972 it produced its report *The New Local Authorities: Management and Structure*, generally referred to as the Bains Report (*see* also V, **20**).

The report is of particular significance in the development of management organisation in local authorities as most of its major recommendations have been adopted, though often with variations, by the new local authorities.

20. Nature of local authority management. The Bains Report considered that the basic problems existing in the management organisation of local government were:

(a) the dual nature of management consisting of elected members and officers both exercising "management function", and thus involving friction and competition, resulting in a loss of efficiency;

(b) the traditional departmental attitude.

Its fundamental observation was that the old structure needed to be replaced by one which fostered a "corporate management" approach to local authority organisation, viz. a structure which supported the achievement of overall local authority objectives and in which the member and officer structure was designed to contribute to the achievement of such goals.

21. The role of officers and elected members. The Bains Report made the following observations:

(a) neither members nor officers should regard any area of local authority administration as their exclusive preserve;

(b) the formulation of policy is not the exclusive preserve of a central policy committee, and, in many cases, it is appropriate for other committees to formulate policy;

(c) greater attention must be given to methods of assessing effectiveness against defined objectives resulting from the establishment of an overall plan of objectives;

(d) whilst recognising the desirability of the "professional" base of the officer structure dangers arose if this was carried to extreme.

22. Organisational implications of the members' role.

(a) The *council* is not to be a mere decision-taking body, but should be involved in policy formulation and as a debating chamber.

(b) A *policy and resources committee* should be established with the function of providing co-ordinated advice to the Council in setting plans, objectives and priorities. It should also exercise control over the major resources of the authority, and control and co-ordinate the implementation of the council's programmes.

(c) Control over resources should be exercised through the media of three sub-committees. These *resource sub-committees* should exercise day-to-day control over personnel, finance and land.

(d) A fourth sub-committee should be established charged with *performance review*.

(e) The committee structure should be rationalised and there should be a move from committees linked to individual services to links with areas of the council's overall objectives. These would be regarded as *programme committees*.

23. Organisation at officer level. The Bains Report gave little stress to the need to rationalise the departmental structure, placing emphasis on the need to achieve the corporate approach through more effective means of direction and co-ordination. To this end the following recommendations were made.

(*a*) *A chief executive officer* should be appointed to act as leader of the officer side of the authority and to act as principal adviser to the council on matters of general policy. The post would not be attached to any department.

(*b*) A *management team* should be established consisting of the principal chief officers of the authority, and should be formally recognised within the management structure. It would have responsibility under the chief executive officer for the preparation of plans and programmes in connection with the long-term objectives of the authority, and for the general co-ordination and implementation of these plans.

24. Response to the Bains Report. The response to the Bains Report has been as positive as that to the Maud Report was negative. The practical effect has been to apply the concept of corporate management through the great majority of local authorities. In particular there has been a move away from the traditional administration dichotomy of policy being reserved for the elected member and administration for the paid officer. The new organisation adopted recognises the role of officers in policy-making by institutionalising the management team and the chief executive officer as both co-ordinative and policy-making function functionaries, whilst at the same time strengthening the member structure by rationalising the committee structure in order to avoid unnecessary conflict, and placing formal power in the hands of the policy and resources committee and its attendant resource committees, and retaining the council as the ultimate policy arbiter.

25. Conclusions. In general, local government has now evolved a management structure which accepts the principles of the Bains Report as being basic to good management in local government. In particular the role of the chief executive officer is firmly established as is that of a central policy committee. It should be borne in mind however that local government is not amenable to a complete "management" approach for the following reasons.

(a) *Political reasons.* Theoretical management concepts which may be applicable to business organisations are subject to constraints in local government (*see* III). In particular British local government is as much a political as an administrative organisation, and any rationalisations implicit in management thinking must be applied against this background, e.g. the values of democratic control and administrative efficiency remain difficult to harmonise.

(b) *Participation.* Local government remains a field for participation by interested members of the community. Thus, increased efficiency is not accorded what theorists regard as its full due, as its implementation organisationally may reduce participation both by members and by outside organisations.

PROGRESS TEST 17

1. Outline the nature and problems of the traditional local government management structure. (**1–5**)

2. What are the basic requirements of management in local government? (**6**)

3. What comments did the Maud Committee on Management make on the existing local government management structure? (**7**)

4. What proposals did the Maud Committee make for reform? (**8, 9**)

5. What is meant by "city manager"? What are the advantages of the appointment? (**12, 13**)

6. What are the disadvantages of the use of the city manager system? Why is it considered inappropriate to English local government? (**14, 15**)

7. Outline other forms of North American management approach in local government. (**16**)

8. What problems face a chief executive officer? (**17**)

9. Examine the success of the application of the Maud recommendations. (**18**)

10. Explain the main provisions of the Bains Report, and comment why a "full management" approach is not appropriate to local administration. (**19–23**)

CHAPTER XVIII

Comparative Public Administration

FRANCE

1. Features. France has been referred to as a "civil service" or "administrative" state. Four dominant features may be identified in its system of public administration.

(*a*) The planning role of the government has been steadily increasing in regard to the national economy, and in this respect there is absence of clear demarcation between the public and private sectors.

(*b*) Freedom of executive action from the legislature's supervision and control was increased markedly under the Fifth Republic, and the executive is now firmly rooted in the Cabinet itself and in the President's staff.

(*c*) Policy is becoming increasingly the result of interaction between the administration and pressure groups, with a corresponding decline in the roles of the political parties and the legislature.

(*d*) Pressure-group activity is not filtered through the party machinery as in Britain, and consequently may work against the general public interest. In addition intra-administration groupings have developed, each seeking influence on administrative policy.

2. Organisation. The distinguishing features of French administrative organisation are as follows.

(*a*) The unity of the administrative machine.

(*b*) The dominance of the central machinery. This is not reduced by decentralisation of functions to local authorities and public corporations. These, though having a certain financial and administrative autonomy, do not have semi-independent status, as in the British system.

(*c*) The decentralisation of administrative functions. This results in the absence of a direct centre focus of administrative activity. French ministries operate through a complex system of regional and local branches, with many functional agencies concerned with keeping the minister in continuous contact with the localities.

(*d*) Co-ordination problems. These arise from this extensive decentralisation. Executive supervision is thus maintained through a network of personal secretariats, inspectorates, advisory committees, etc.

3. Central administration. This can be set out as follows.

(*a*) *The ministries.* Functional allocation tends to be much looser than that experienced in Britain. French ministries also vary from their British counterparts in the following ways.

(*i*) There is a greater emphasis on administrative deconcentration (only 55 per cent of ministry staffs are in Paris). They are thus more concerned with direct administration in the provinces, and do not rely on the British practice of semi-autonomous local agencies and officials.

(*ii*) Flexibility, manifested through reshuffling of functions and experimentation, is much greater than the comparatively rigid British practice.

(*iii*) There is greater use of technocracy (*see* VI). Specialist personnel are found to a much greater extent in advisory and policy-making roles. There is no general administrative class.

(*iv*) There is no figure comparable to a permanent secretary. The tendency to divisionalise departments (as in Britain) and to give each chief of "directions" direct responsibility to the minister is incompatible with the British practice of a co-ordinating head of department. This, however, gives rise to difficulties of co-ordination, and probably stems from the days of unstable parliamentary Cabinets.

(*b*) *Supervisory administration.* The French supervisory machinery has no comparison in Britain. It consists of the following bodies.

(*i*) A personal "Cabinet" (or secretariat) attached to each minister, inspectorate, and advisory council. These operate as the "eyes and ears" of the minister, as administrative co-ordinators and as ministerial supporters. They perform many of the functions of a permanent secretary, act as a form of "brains trust" and supervise the execution of ministerial policy.

(*ii*) Other supervisory and co-ordinating bodies include the inspectorate and advisory bodies. The inspectorate is composed entirely of civil servants and has wide investigatory powers in the field of the expenditure of public funds. In addition, it provides a pool of experience at the minister's disposal for special administrative or advisory functions.

The advisory bodies consist of two distinct groups: i.e. those of a representative character and those entirely composed of civil servants. At the apex of the latter is the Economic and Social Council which operates to give interest and pressure groups a focal point and a formal access point to the French administrative system.

4. Council of State. This operates as a body giving technical advice to ministers on the drafting of legislation, and acts as an aid in planning and preparing the legislative programme. Its chief functions are thus planning, advising administration and resolving administrative difficulties. It must be consulted by the Prime Minister on all public administration matters and, though having no formal co-ordinating or control powers, is a body of considerable influence.

5. Nationalised industries and organisation for economic planning. French nationalised industries (*établissements publics*) have two distinctive features:

(*a*) they are treated as a part of the unitary state machinery;
(*b*) wide use is made of specialised representatives on boards.

NOTE: Because of (*a*) problems of control and responsibility associated with the British nationalised industries seldom arise.

The organisation for economic planning is formally headed by a planning commissioner with a planning commissariat. These have relatively little formal power but exercise wide influence through a network of agencies. Influence is exercised partly through the widespread operation of the National Plan and through membership of key agencies.

6. Local government. The integrated, unified nature of French central government results in a relatively weak local government organisation. Effectively it does not have the semi-independent status of the British and German systems (*see* 7) but operates as part of the hierarchy of national planning, and thus tends to result in an intermixing of local and national responsibilities. Local services in fact are often administered through the field services of central ministries. Central power is highlighted by the weak financial circumstances of the French local government.

Local government is also denied independence by the role of the prefect who directs all state activities in his department and who exercises a powerful supervisory role (*tutelle administrative*) over local authorities.

NOTE: For a description of the French civil service *see* VI.

GERMANY

7. Introduction. Three major features of the German Federal Republic may be observed.

(*a*) Reliance is placed on executive leadership rather than on popular representation. This results in centralised and co-ordinated leadership, subject to the following two counterbalancing forces:

(*i*) the federal organisation of Germany;

(*ii*) the desire of social groups, etc., to have their interests represented in the executive.

(*b*) There is no genuine parliamentary system in the sense of enforceable executive responsibility to Parliament.

(*c*) The loose relationships between ministers and Parliament have strengthened the association of the political executive and the permanent bureaucracy. The absence of personal "Cabinets" or adequate parliamentary experience tends to place a minister greatly under the influence of the permanent bureaucracy, and gives the bureaucracy a large measure of control of government and administration.

8. The ministries. These are generally functionally organised. However, the federal structure of the state has given rise to problems of division of functions between federal and *Land* ministries. In many cases ministries have little administrative machinery or executive power, these being lodged with the different *Länder* and their ministries.

The authority of the state is diffused down to its local agencies and, whilst obviating confusion of authorities and jurisdiction, means that society is permeated by the bureaucracy.

Little inter-departmental co-ordination machinery exists, and difficult problems of co-ordination thus arise which are accentuated by the practice of German executive branches forming separate parallel hierarchies, each with their own pattern of organisation.

9. Public enterprises. Most of such public activity is handled at local level and comparatively few public enterprises exist at federal level. A general *laissez-faire* approach exists with an accompanying absence of central planning.

10. The German civil service. The German civil service is noteworthy in that it provides a working example of the basic difficulty in public administration of reconciling democracy and efficiency. Civil servants have a high public status and the following characteristics.

(*a*) They are accorded "well-established rights".

(*b*) They are employed on a basis of technical merit. However, this does not imply completely open entry to the service and a form of cast system based on family, education, etc., exists under which only a comparative few have access to the service, particularly to the higher ranks.

(*c*) In return for long and expensive training, the German official is provided with security and status.

11. How satisfactory is the German system? The German civil servant is established for life, his agency is unchallenged, he is protected from publicity and investigation and he treats the post as an honour. This might be compared to the democratic position of the American civil service, where the civil servant is generally temporary, he needs to justify his work to the public and various committees, he functions under publicity and investigation and treats the post as "just another job".

The advantages of the system are that it contributes to the acquisition of a sense of duty, industriousness, to probity and to expert knowledge. On the other hand the German civil servant tends to be "authoritarian when left alone; resistant when under democratic direction; and conformist when under the direction of a forceful though untraditional ruling group such as the Nazis" (Fleidenheimer, *The Governments of Germany*, Methuen, 1961).

More objectively, the German civil service tradition is probably more appropriate to a static than to a dynamic state, and results in too compartmentalised attitudes.

12. Rejection of reform. Suggestions for open competition, restricted need for legal training, promotion from the ranks by specialist examination and the use of more persons with outside experience has been rejected. There is, however, a growth in the use of "functionary" officials, and the distinction of the English civil service between policy and administrative roles is not made.

13. Federal and *Land* functions. The staff of most federal ministries is relatively small, and administration of federal programmes is often carried out by the *Länder*, either as a matter of traditional prerogative or as a service rendered at the specific request of the federal government. There are thus four different ways in which administration is executed, namely:

(*a*) execution of federal laws by the federal administration, e.g. railways and the post office;

(*b*) execution of *Land* laws by *Land* administrations, e.g. police and education;

(*c*) execution of federal laws by *Land* administration as a matter of right, e.g. labour and social welfare;

(*d*) execution of federal laws by the *Land* administration at the request of the federal government, e.g. *autobahnen* and waterways.

14. Federal control. The federal government has extensive control over the *Land* administration of federal laws. This is exercised through the giving of binding administrative regulations, demanding the rectification of inadequacies, and the use of investigatory agents. This tends to make the German federal system more unified than, say, the US system, and this is reinforced by the general practice of *Land* governments accepting federal administrative directions in order to further the general belief in the desirability of a relatively homogeneous system.

THE USSR

15. The Soviet constitution. Superficially, the Soviet government resembles a typical Western European democracy in that the constitution provides for a national two-chamber legislature (i.e. the Supreme Soviet) with executive and administrative power vested in a council of ministers technically responsible to the Supreme Soviet and the Presidium (i.e. the body representing the Supreme Soviet between its meetings). In practice, however, all these organs are controlled by the Communist party.

In addition, the federal system is designed to reflect the multi-racial character of the Soviet Union. In practice, however, it essentially represents a series of administrative units and not power divisions (compare the United States). This is the result of the existence of centrally directed, all-embracing economic plans, and of the complete control of every area of the Union by the highly integrated and disciplined Communist party.

NOTE: Both Western and East European political systems claim to be based on the concept of "freedom". However there is a fundamental difference in the interpretation of the concept. Western systems emphasise *legal and political* equality as pre-eminent, while communist systems emphasise *social and economic* equality and consider that the inequalities of wealth and social status found in the West undermine the "true" meaning of democracy. In the West, however, the abolition of private property and inevitable state control are seen as inimical to democratic principles.

16. The role and influence of the Communist party. The Communist party exists as a large pyramidal organisation, ranging from the base of over 300,000 primary party organisations to the apex of the Politburo, heading tightly integrated organs of power. The secretariat of the Central Committee is the supreme body for the preparation of plans and the making of policy. The central government is effectively an interlocking directorate, e.g. in 1978 Brezhnev became Premier of the Council of Ministers and Chairman of the Presidium as well as a member of the Politburo, as were the three first deputy Premiers.

The power of the political leaders is based on the following:

(*a*) control of party and administrative machines;
(*b*) the control of the propaganda machine;
(*c*) suppression of opposition.

17. Economic planning. Public administration is all-pervasive. The state, through its administrative agents, operates the whole economy. Economic planning has directed the growth of industry and now operates specific directions for the development of a state-owned and controlled economy. The status of economic planning was summed up by Stalin, who described economic plans as "instructions which are compulsory for all managements and which determine the future course of the economic development of the entire country" (G. M. Carter, *Government of the Soviet Union*, Harcourt, Brace & Wolff Inc., 1965).

18. Structure of administration. Whilst not being subject to the constraints upon public administration found in Western democracies, the administrative structure in the Soviet Union gives rise to problems of co-ordination and direction wider in scope and different in character. It is based on the following.

(a) *Ministries, state committees and regional economic councils.*
Ministries may take the form of "all Union" or "Union
Republic", the latter directing the work of corresponding ministries
at Union Republic level. All three organs carry out the basic work
of direction and supervision and the heads of the ministries com-
pose the Union Council of Ministers.

(b) *Administration of industry.* Features common to all organisation plans include the following:

(i) the breaking down of the industrial sector into segments
with plans for each industry determined and co-ordinated at
national level;

(ii) the use of "functional" bodies to deal with common needs;

(iii) territorial decentralisation of planning and operational
powers.

NOTE: The administration of industry involves interaction of
these three factors and considerable difficulty has been experienced in achieving machinery for smooth interaction.

19. The structure for planning. Planning in the Soviet Union involves three major tasks:

(a) the preparation of five-year plans;

(b) the preparation of the plans as detailed and unified entities
for the economy and related fields, e.g. education;

(c) the determining of the supervisory structure which is able
constantly to check the performance of all institutions involved
in the plan.

There is, however, no clear pattern of planning agencies; e.g.
the Gosplan's (state planning commission) functions have fluctuated in recent years. In 1955–56 it was responsible for long-range
planning; from 1960–63 it was responsible for current policy. Long-
term policy was returned to it in 1963 but at the same time a
Supreme Council for the National Economy was established which
is responsible for current policy.

20. Planning problems. The major planning difficulties have been
as follows:

(a) preparing the plan and interrelating the different sector
problems;

(b) putting the plan into operation and determining the authority
which the relevant agencies need to execute the plan and take on-
the-spot decisions.

In dealing with these tasks the planning machinery draws on the resources of a vast network of planning agencies.

(*a*) Territorially, each government area and subdivision has planning agencies.

(*b*) Functionally, there are planning agencies in every ministry and department, and also in every trust, factory and collective farm.

NOTE: The structure has an inbuilt inflexibility and change can only proceed slowly and within the framework of the overall plan.

21. Local level administration. The major local bodies are the local soviets. However, their position is more as agents of the central bureaucracy, owing to the pyramidal structure of the Soviet government. In addition, their functions may be usurped by large local industrial units. The purely local units of local government are administratively insignificant. The *oblasts* (regions) are no longer key economic units and *raions* (districts) are mainly used as organs for the retrieval of planning information.

Every administrative unit operates under a soviet and soviets are effectively controlled by the Communist party organisation.

22. Methods of administrative control. These are as follows.

(*a*) *Party controls.* The Communist party establishes a framework within which the administration must function. The party faction exists in each enterprise and branch of administration. The party thus provides the channels for securing detailed information on the workings of the economy, with counterchecking to ultimate levels.

(*b*) *The secret police.* This is a punitive as well as an investigatory body. It has been described as the ultimate symbol of "a system of power founded on the institutionalisation of mutual suspicion" (Merle Fainsod, quoted in G. M. Carter, *Government of the Soviet Union*, Harcourt, Brace & Wolff Inc., 1965).

(*c*) *Other controls.* Control is exercised also through the planning system, through centralised material supply and production and through agricultural procurement. This provides a centralised agency network, through which detailed administrative control on the working of the individual sectors of the economy is maintained.

23. The managers. No distinction is drawn between government officials and businessmen. The most important civil servants are the industrial managers who are chosen by the State Commission on the Civil Service. Training is technically and industrially orientated and no belief is placed in training in administrative techniques or cultural matters. Training, in practice, is effected through the training schools of the major administrative bodies.

THE UNITED STATES

24. The central administration. The federal government consists of a multiplicity of agencies. This conglomerate can, however, be narrowed down to four principal types of institution.

(a) *Departments.* These were generally created out of bureaux or agencies operating in certain general areas. In general they will be of Cabinet rank and may often take the form of "holding companies" encompassing what in effect are several disparate functions. Examples of departments include State, Treasury and Defence.

(b) *Agencies.* These are effectively indistinguishable from departments and may attain Cabinet rank, e.g. National Aeronautical and Space Administration, National Labour Relations Board.

(c) *Independent commissions.* These developed with the growth of the regulatory function of government and, while originally being concerned with quasi-judicial functions, may now exercise important administrative tasks in their own right. They are usually constituted of three to eleven members appointed by the President subject to Senate approval. The principal administrative feature of the agencies is that they have created serious problems of co-ordination as their positive powers have developed. Examples of such commissions include the Civil Service Commission, the Commission on Civil Rights, etc.

(d) *Government corporations.* These are generally created in the United States to undertake specific functions, e.g. the Tennessee Valley Authority, the Export–Import Bank, etc.

25. Common features in the administration. The following factors often exist in common between the various departments, agencies, etc.

(a) *Political heads.* Each generally has a politically appointed head, usually on a partisan basis. Political appointments normally reach down to under and assistant secretary levels and to some of the subsidiary bureaux chiefs. In general, the head is responsible for policy and public relations and is supported by professional assistants men. Also grouped with him will be the various staff services, e.g. budget, planning. Below this level will be a series of bureaux executing the practical work of the department.

As each head is an appointee of the President and has no power base of his own electorally the role of heads individually and in Cabinet is harder to characterise than in the United Kingdom and is dependent on personalities and presidential "style".

(b) *Field services.* These will generally be extensive and only a very small proportion of federal employees actually work in Washington. Such field services will be organised on a state basis or on regions of administrative convenience, though the state approach probably facilitates co-operation. Such deconcentration is not, however, unified and gives rise to problems of interdepartmental co-ordination and control problems, against which must be set the advantage of local differentiation and co-operation.

(c) *Consultation.* The departmental decision-making apparatus is supported by considerable consultation of interests. This machinery includes hearings, advisory committees and over 400 inter-agency committees. The structure for consultation is both statutory-based and also results from spontaneous development.

(d) *Contracting.* All the agencies exercise the power to contract for the performance of their functions with other departments and extra-governmental agencies, e.g. in defence.

26. Nature of administration. Ernest S. Griffith in *The American System of Government* (Methuen, 1976) has identified three features of bureaucratic development in the United States, as follows.

(a) The acknowledgement of the vital role of research.

(b) The bureaucracy has to some extent achieved the status of the fourth branch of government and is as autonomous as Congress or the executive. It is thus a subject of checks and balances and fully shares a mutually interacting role with both the legislature and the executive (i.e. President and Cabinet).

(c) Bureaucracy has come to be characterised by the agency–clientele relationship. This results from the dispersive nature of the American society and the realisation of the importance of government intervention. This, in turn, has resulted in a tendency to express group objectives in legislation and for agencies to be set up to facilitate the achievement of such objectives, and thus brings about a close relationship between the government and the groups concerned. "The bureaucracy is not an unfaithful mirror of a dispersive society, but is considerably modified by the assumptions and symbols and rituals of the public interest under which it operates" (Ernest S. Griffith).

27. The civil service: background. The present federal civil service stems from the Civil Service Act 1883 (Pendleton Act), and the percentage of civil servants under the "classified-merit" rules has grown from 44.8 per cent in 1889 to 85.6 per cent by 1963.

There is an open competitive selection system of recruitment. However, the idea of a closed career service has been rejected and preference has been expressed for practical job-orientated selection and the availability of lateral entry to the service. This lateral entry approach (i.e. provision for recruitment from industry rather than promotion through the ranks) has had two side-effects, namely:

(*a*) it refreshes the bureaucracy with industrial and business intake;

(*b*) it may, however, frustrate the career developments of "career civil servants".

28. The civil service: use of specialists. There is a generally established pattern of use of specialist skills, and comparatively little opportunity for the "generalist" administrator (*see* VI). Specialist competence is in fact regarded as a prerequisite to administrative efficiency. Sixty-three bureau chiefs were studied by Michael E. Smith (Bureau Chiefs of the Federal Government, 1958, *Public Policy*, Vol. 10, 1960, Harvard University) in 1958; it appeared in general that they were appointed to jobs for which their education and previous experience were particularly relevant. Similarly, studies of the educational background of higher civil servants by W. Lloyd Warner (*The American Federal Executive*, Yale University Press, 1963) and David T. Stanley (*The Higher Civil Service*, Brookings Institution, 1964) have shown that emphasis was placed on physical science and engineering backgrounds rather than on a humanities-based education (compare British Administrative Class intake, *see* VI).

The role of the scientist in high positions was described by Don K. Price as follows: "if administration is to serve as a useful layer in the pyramid of policy between peak of political power and the base of science and technology", there is a need for high-ranking scientists, etc.

29. The civil service: a summing up. In conclusion, the following general elements of the federal civil service may be noted:

(*a*) the use of specialists in specified and administrative positions;

(*b*) the widespread practice of departments having to write detailed job specifications;

(*c*) the loss of image of a federal civil service and emphasis more on particular posts and activities;

(*d*) disregard of the utility of the career generalist administration;

(*e*) regular interchange with industry;

(*f*) regular inter-departmental movements.

30. Planning and co-ordination. The greatest problem of American government is the bringing together the disparate and comparatively independent agencies of government. It is beyond the scope of this book to deal fully with these, but the principal instruments of co-ordination may be summarised as follows.

(*a*) *The presidency.* This will include the use of such agencies as the Bureau of the Budget (*see* (*c*)), and the Council of Economic Advisers, as well as Cabinet members.

(*b*) *The bureaucracy.* Through the use of inter-departmental planning and co-ordinating committees.

(*c*) *Congress.* Appropriations, committees, control of the executive, etc.

NOTE: The Bureau of the Budget is the central control and co-ordinating agency. It is responsible for estimates, clearance of legislation, surveys of administrative efficiency and some central statistical control.

31. Conclusions. In drawing comparisons between various systems of public administration and relating them to the British system, thought must be used in extracting points which might be favourably employed. So many political, social, cultural and economic considerations underlie any national system of public administration that great care must be taken to avoid hasty cross-applications. However, the following points which could be utilised profitably in the British system, and certain points which should be avoided, can be listed:

(*a*) the value of professionalism, as typified by the American federal civil service;

(*b*) the nature and value of the training and education systems underlying the French national administration;

(*c*) the difficulties of co-ordination in totally planned economies, as shown by the experience of the USSR;

(*d*) the dangers of inadequate political control, as expressed in the German system;

(*e*) the American use of consultation;

(*f*) the success of the French planning systems.

PROGRESS TEST 18

1. What are the principal features of French administration? (**1**)

2. Describe the major factors in the central administration of France. (**3**)

3. Consider the features of French administrative organisation for (*a*) the nationalised industries and (*b*) local government. (**5, 6**)

4. What are the principal administrative features of the German Federal Republic? (**7**)

5. Describe the general underlying features of the German civil service, and comment on its advantages. (**10–12**)

6. How are administrative functions divided up in Germany? How is federal control exercised over the *Land* authorities? (**13, 14**)

7. How does the Communist party's role affect the working of the constitution of the USSR? (**15, 16**)

8. Outline the structure of the administration in the USSR. (**18, 19**)

9. What are the principal methods of administrative control in the USSR? (**22**)

10. Distinguish between the various agencies which form the central administration of the United States. (**24**)

11. What common features in the central administration of the USA can be discerned? (**25**)

12. What basic features exist in the US administration? (**26**)

13. Outline the main features of the civil service of the United States. (**27–29**)

14. What conclusions may one draw from the study of foreign administrative systems? (**31**)

Bibliography

Public administration theory

Brown, R. G. S., *The Administration Process in Britain*. University Press, 1971

Chapman, R. A. and Dunsire, A., *Style in Administration*. Allen and Unwin, 1971

Greenwood, J., & Wilson, W., *Public Administration in Britain*. Allen and Unwin, 1984.

Self, P., *Administrative Theories and Politics*. Allen and Unwin, 1972

Parliament

Stacey, Frank, *British Government, 1966–75*. Oxford University Press, 1975.

Government

Stankiewicz, W. J. (Ed.), *British Government in an Era of Reform*. Collier Macmillan, 1976

Wilson, Harold, *The Governance of Britain*. Sphere, 1977

Civil service

Chapman, R. A., *The Higher Civil Service in Britain*. Constable, 1970

Fry, C. K., *Statesmen in Disguise: the Changing Role of the Administrative Class of the Home Civil Service*. London, 1969

Pollitt, C., *Manipulating the Machine—The Changing Pattern of Ministerial Departments 1960–83*. Allen and Unwin, 1984

Politics

Stacey, R. I. and Oliver, J. C., *Public Administration, the Political Environment*, Macdonald & Evans, 1980

Examination Technique

Before the examination. It must be emphasised that the key to success in any examination lies in adequate preparation supplemented by constant revision. In particular, it is important to prepare for an examination from the outset of the course, and not to rely on last-minute cramming. In a subject such as public administration the importance of wide reading cannot be over-emphasised. This does not mean that a wide variety of books should be studied in detail but that the basic texts should be supplemented by a sound knowledge of the viewpoints put forward in specialist works.

At the examination. It may confidently be stated that a good student can undo months of careful preparation by ignoring certain simple basic rules of examination technique. In particular:

(*a*) Read with care the instructions on the examination paper.

(*b*) Write legibly and use good English.

(*c*) Read with utmost care the actual examination questions, remembering that marks will be lost for irrelevancy and that valuable time will be wasted.

(*d*) Allow time to plan in outline each answer and to divide all relevant points into clearly defined paragraphs.

(*e*) Plan your allocation of time between questions in proportion to the marks that each question earns. It is useful to write down before you start the actual times you aim to start each new question in order to avoid wasting time making this calculation during the paper.

(*f*) Do not write for the sake of writing. Brevity with accuracy is absolutely preferable to a long and rambling discourse.

(*g*) In discussion questions be careful to give all points of view before settling on conclusions.

These notes are only intended as guidance, and it is appreciated that individuals may have developed their own personal examination techniques which suit them better.

Specimen Test Papers

Answer five questions. Time allowed: three hours.

PAPER 1

1. What, if anything, might be learnt from the selection and training of higher civil servants abroad which might improve the performance of the British civil service?

2. To what extent is it appropriate to apply principles of management organisation derived from the private sector to public administrative organisation?

3. To what extent and in what ways does the House of Commons exercise control over government expenditure? Do you consider such control could be improved? If so, how?

4. What is meant by the sovereignty of Parliament? How far does such sovereignty apply at the present day?

5. "Any Minister must inevitably be under the control of the civil servants in his department." Discuss.

6. "In a democracy it would be disastrous if all citizens were politically active." Comment.

7. Although the concept of the specialist committee is an important part of the investigative process in most democratic legislatures, it has been accorded little significance in the British system.

8. Comment on this view and consider the desirability of extending the process. "Governments not parliaments make law." Discuss this assertion with respect to the British system of government.

PAPER 2

1. In what ways and with what possibilities of effectiveness does Parliament control the nationalised industries?

2. "There is no longer a valid case for civil service anonymity." Discuss.

3. Explain the theory and practice of the decision-making process in British public administration.

4. Although central departments and local authorities may be considered as administrative bodies, their powers and organisation are very different. Examine this statement.

5. What main defects in the civil service did the Fulton Committee attempt to rectify? What evidence is there of its success or otherwise?

6. On what basis are functions allocated between central departments. Explain why there has been a reaction against the concept of the "super department."

7. How are central departments co-ordinated both between themselves and at government level?

8. "The Prime Minister is an administrator who has little time, or excuse, to administer." Comment on the truth of this statement.

PAPER 3

1. To what extent is it possible in public administration to distinguish between policy-making and administration? Is any useful purpose served by attempting to differentiate the location of these functions?

2. Explain the meaning of "bureaucracy". To what extent may bureaucracy be said to be dysfunctional?

3. Do you consider there to be a case for the subordination of specialists to generalist administrators in public and local administration?

4. What purpose do "policy units" serve within departments, how do they affect the relationship between Ministers and Civil Servants?

5. "The organisational structure of a body is less important than the interpersonal relationships within that body." "Without a scientifically derived structure discussion of human behaviour in organisations is irrelevant." Compare and discuss these comments.

6. "Inquiry into and the redress of citizens' grievances arising from maladministration is now so well developed that there need no longer be concern for the introduction of a new Bill of Rights." Discuss.

7. How may pressure groups in the United Kingdom be classified? Do you consider the existence of such groups to be beneficial or detrimental in a democracy?

8. Comment on the structure and effectiveness of economic planning in the United Kingdom.

Assignments

The following are examples of BTEC-style "situation-based" assignments.

1. In many public sector organisations younger members of staff have been consistently critical of the procedures for staff assessment and the resultant promotion selections. A group of younger staff at a training seminar has been asked to put positive proposals for improving the system.

TASK

Either as a member of this group, *or* by forming a small (3–4 person) working party devise an improved scheme. Present your results as a report.

NOTES

The report could usefully consider the following:

(*a*) a description of the existing system (for part-time employed students);

(*b*) proposals for report-forms—to be used as the basis of assessment;

(*c*) notes for the guidance of reporting officers.

There is considerable scope for group work in this assignment with each member contributing through a division of responsibility and for group discussion prior to final report preparation.

2. A newly formed local pressure group is anxious to use its resources effectively.

TASK

(*a*) Describe the situation in which the pressure group exists, real or imaginary.

(*b*) Outline the general principles and methods the group could adopt.

(*c*) Outline the tactics you feel the group could adopt.

NOTES

This work could be presented in a number of ways, e.g. as a report commissioned from the student by the pressure group; notes to be used as a basis for addressing the group's committee or a letter/report. Assessment would reflect knowledge of the general principles of political power and effectiveness together with knowledge of the institutions that the group would need to influence.

3. As a memer of a club or society contemplating the creation of a constitution you have been asked to help.

TASK

Draft in outline form an appropriate constitution for the club/society's committee to consider for adoption. In addition prepare some notes outlining the purpose of constitutions, for use in your presentation.

NOTES

It would be sensible to incorporate into your work some of the similarities between club and state constitutions. Assessment would reflect your appreciation of all of the functions of constitutions, as well as their application. The assignment could be adapted to deal with constitutions of clubs students are actually members of or imaginary ones.

Index

Wed 8 may Law
9 30a — 1230p

Thu 9 May Info Sys.
930a — 1230p

Monde — Euro Gov
20 May — 9 30 — 123p

fickle ade

Mond — 2pm — 5pm
13 May

---

22 Jun Results